wm

WITHDRAWN

BRITISH CHRISTIANS, INDIAN NATIONALISTS AND THE RAJ

BRITISH CHRISTIANS, INDIAN NATIONALISTS AND THE RAJ

GERALD STUDDERT-KENNEDY

DELHI
OXFORD UNIVERSITY PRESS
BOMBAY CALCUTTA MADRAS
1991

Oxford University Press, Walton Street, Oxford OX2 6DP

New York   Toronto

Delhi   Bombay   Calcutta   Madras   Karachi

Petaling Jaya   Singapore   Hong Kong   Tokyo

Nairobi   Dar es Salaam

Melbourne   Auckland

and associates in

Berlin   Ibadan

Typeset by Indraprastha Press (CBT), New Delhi 110002
Printed at Rekha Printers Pvt Ltd, New Delhi 110020
and published by S. K. Mookerjee, Oxford University Press
YMCA Library Building, Jai Singh Road, New Delhi 110001

Contents

Author's Note

This study is concerned with a specific 'public' in inter-war
British politics, the numerically small but attentive networks of
those who were concerned, for whatever reason and whether they
actually served there or not, with India as an imperial responsibility.
It will be referred to throughout as the 'Anglo-India public'. The
term 'Eurasian' will be used to refer to people of mixed descent.

Acknowledgements

Work on British sources for this project was supported by a Small Grant from the Nuffield Foundation, with supplementary assistance from the Faculty of Commerce and Social Science at the University of Birmingham. A British Academy Grant in the Humanities and the Social Sciences financed a visit to India in the cold weather of 1986. I am most grateful for all of this assistance. Friends and colleagues have been kind enough to read work in progress. I was encouraged by Dr B.R. Tomlinson, Professor Ron Amman, and Dr Eric Goldstein, who read early chapters. Dr Satish Saberwal and his colleagues at the Centre for Historical Studies, Jawaharlal Nehru University, commented helpfully on a general paper, and I owe much to an all too brief run of discussions in Birmingham with Dr Harish Trivedi of the Department of English at Delhi University. Dr John MacKenzie has improved more than one version of the entire script. I am particularly grateful to him, and to an anonymous reader for the Oxford University Press, for sympathetic and reassuring appraisals of my general approach to the material.

Every British scholar visiting India rapidly discovers his or her dependence on the sudden, unlooked for kindness that retrieves the inevitable moments of black catastrophe, when material suddenly becomes elusive or the exigencies of travel drive one to exhaustion. I was particularly grateful for academic and personal support from Dr David Baker at St Stephen's in Delhi, Diana Biswas in Calcutta, Dr Vincent Kumarados at Madras Christian College, and Susan Ram in Madras. Many others were generous with their time and resources, in Agra Dr Sharma of St John's, in Delhi Bishop Christopher Robinson and Father Hambye, in Calcutta Dr John of Bishop's College and Father Verstreetung of St Xavier's, in Bangalore Mr Manickam of the YMCA.

I am grateful to librarians at Churchill College, Cambridge, Lambeth Palace Library, the Scottish Record Office and the India Office Library, and to Dr Carter of the Cambridge South Asia

Archive. Mr R. B. H. Hall of the British-Israel World Federation allowed me an extended loan of many irreplaceable volumes. Bishop Leslie Newbiggin gave invaluable advice before my visit to India, and I would not have got far there without the guidance of Dr Eleanor Jackson.

My most extensive debts, and not for the first time, are to Dr Peter Cain and Dr T. V. Sathyamurthy. They have steered me clear of several kinds of failure. I am of course entirely accountable for those I have been unable to avoid.

Abbreviations

CMS	Church Missionary Society
CN	*Commonwealth of Nations*
CT	*Church Times*
D	*Dyarchy*
G	*Guardian*
ICF	Industrial Christian Fellowship
IER	*Indian Empire Review*
IOL	India Office Library
MR	*Methodist Recorder*
NM	*National Message*
SPG	Society for the Propagation of the Gospel
YMI	*Young Men of India*

CHAPTER 1

Introduction

A Christian Empire

This book is not about India itself, but about the British and their preoccupation with India in the period between the World Wars. There is no doubt another and very different sort of account to be written about the strength of that preoccupation today. The media certainly provide the material for a post-colonial orientalism. The prodigiously successful television serialization of Paul Scott's *Raj Quartet* whetted an appetite for contentious cinematic reworkings of political myth in David Attenborough's *Gandhi,* and of E. M. Forster's fiction in David Lean's *Passage to India.* Forster's novel, a significantly different judgment to that of the film on personal relations under the Raj, as critics were careful to point out, has itself been reissued, as has his ambivalent *The Hill of Devi* along with J. R. Ackerley's princely companion-piece *Hindoo Holiday.* A steady stream of contemporary work in every medium ranges in quality from the economies of Ruth Jhabvala's recovery of the past in *Heat and Dust,* to the workmanlike and the merely self-indulgent. The sounds and images of this celebration of the Raj interweave as one production succeeds another. Thus Dame Peggy Ashcroft fades out as Scott's missionary, Barbie, and in again as Forster's Mrs Moore; Tim Piggot-Smith moves from Merrick in the *Quartet* to a one-man stage version of Yates's *Bengal Lancer;* Forster's novel is read on tape by Ben Kingsley, fresh from his notable performance as Gandhi.

Less exacting coffee-table compilations evoke Curzon's viceregal splendours and the photographic record of a yet remoter and more glorious past, haunting images of the mined and battered Chutter Munzil palace at Lucknow Residency, canon balls stacked like melons inside the Red Fort at Agra after the Mutiny, maharajas, bristling and jaunty or flabby and sullen, and the naked fakirs. It was as a naked fakir, we might recall in passing, that Churchill saw M. K. Gandhi, in his celebrated diatribe on the threat posed by Indian nationalism to the Empire. His response to the Mahatma's reputation as a saint was less equivocal than some we will have to consider.[1] In seditious contrast, appropriate to the age of mole and supergrass, we have Michael Carritt's *A Mole in the Crown,* the refreshing memoir of an ICS man who worked covertly for the Communist Party from 1936 until his early retirement in 1938. The contact given Carritt by party comrades in London, with hilarious consequences for himself and intriguing implications for this account, was the Revd Guthrie Michael Scott, domestic chaplain to the Bishop of Bombay, R. D. Acland, and subsequently to the Metropolitan of Calcutta himself, Bishop Foss Westcott.[2]

Less obtrusive than the popular exploitation of Raj images and themes has been the intensification of scholarly interest in India. In the period immediately after Independence, India was not a field that attracted British students in large numbers, though it was invaded by the alumni of American graduate schools from every galaxy in the exploding universe of transatlantic social sciences. In the last couple of decades, however, British and Commonwealth scholars have made many important contributions to our understanding of the subcontinent and of Britain's relationship with it, and it is to this by now substantial literature that this study might make a modest contribution.

Scholarship is not concerned with nostalgia or with evocation for its own sake, but it is hard to believe that there are not at some level significant links between the vogue for 'India' as a source of recreation and entertainment and its importance as a source of problems that attract scholars from many fields. Certainly, in this account, purely personal elements of reconsideration and exorcism blend with the impulse to achieve a clearer understanding as a social scientist of the later years of the Raj. The nature of the reconsideration and the purpose of the exorcism can be read into a brief autobiographical note. The author was born in February 1933, (the month in which Churchill can be said to have launched in deadly earnest the 'diehard' attack on the Conservative establishment and the India Bill) in the bungalow of a missionary lady doctor, which lay, in the family phrase, 'under the shadow of the Residency' in Lucknow.

He was christened on 24 May, Empire Day,[3] amid much floral decoration in the Viceroy's chapel in Simla, and played out the better part of the Second World War in the security and the un-forgettable clarities of Kashmir. That christening of the son of the Assistant Chaplain of Simla was conducted by the Revd P. N. F. Young of the Cambridge Mission to Delhi, a cleric who had been thinking seriously about Indian nationalism since at least the period of the Great War. He appears in more important contexts later in this account. A few years later on, probably in 1943, the former Assistant Chaplain, now Senior Chaplain, and responsible for the large cantonment-gothic church with its indelibly memorable peal of tubular bells which is parked on the Ridge in Simla, ventured to suggest in a sermon that all the talk of post-war reconstruction could be given some practical Christian expression if members of the British community were to think twice about expecting poorly paid coolies to stagger up the foothills of the Himalayas carrying their pianos and other civilizing impedimenta. The bleak delegation that came round to the vestry afterwards to deal with this naivety was led by a famous English cricketer, one of the distinguished figures in the community who regularly collected the offertory for the morning service.

A consistency in recollections such as these raises questions about something that appears to be missing from recent scholarly accounts of that period. In seeming conjunction with many sharply defined images of power and authority, arrogance and paternalistic consi-deration, there are others, ubiquitous but diffuse, associated with 'religion', in a whole range of manifestations, from missionary evangelicalism to establishment observance. This is in no way to suggest that Anglo-India was a 'religious' society in a sense that would give much comfort to anyone seriously committed to the Christian faith. Indeed, as we shall see, such people were desperately anxious about the Christian witness of English men and women in India. The point, at this stage, can be made as a simple generalization with two sides to it: British Christianity had public importance as an institution integral to the Raj, and British Christianity had sub-stantive importance to many significantly placed individuals in the civil and military structures of the administration, as well as to others back home in England who had direct or indirect responsibilities or interests connected with India and the Empire.

The cantonments, for instance, meant parade grounds and barracks and the Club, but also church parade, attended by the more important elements in the local community, civil and military: though it must be said for those in the ranks whose attendance was enfored that there were often as many fly-buttons as coins of small denomination in the offertory bags.

The present writer's modest contribution to these official pieties involved helping to sort the tribute on the vestry table afterwards, when the orderly sergeants in their red sashes had marched away with the men, whose rifles had been racked neatly behind the pews during the service.

A final recollection is of the Senior Chaplain addressing a packed memorial meeting after an armed attack on the Kalka to Simla diesel train in 1942, an ambush which was allegedly perpetrated by 'dacoits', though the political implications of such 'criminal' acts communicated themselves clearly enough. The occasion was an official act of communal solidarity, at which were invoked both the providential expectations and the paternal solicitude of an Anglican God for his chosen followers. Uniforms, God , racial obligation, authority and social power and importance, keep reappearing as interlocked facets of the essential core of Anglo-Indian society.

It will be necessary to be more specific about what the term 'religion' is taken to cover, but in many excellent South Asian studies British established religion figures as a residual concept, with no significant analytical status. The respectably anthropological religions of the East have been given a very different kind of attention. Today, in retrospect, it seems so clear that imperial politics was essentially about power and material interest, that the evidence of Christian faith on the part of British imperialists, or of doctrinal acceptance, or of formal commitment, is almost inevitably treated as epiphenomenal, as mere ideological or rhetorical justification, humbug or a historical hang-up, with little substantive significance in itself. There is a specialist literature on Christianity *in* India, and on the Church of India (which underwent major organizational changes which have a great deal to do with the historical process of decolonization between the World Wars), but the question of Christianity, the British *and* India seems to invite judgments that are accepted as historically self-evident and uninteresting. The importance of religious beliefs to numbers of individuals in British

India and in the groups back at home most concerned with India is not seen as having any bearing on the crucial questions of imperial rule. Though there are doubtless survivors of the Raj who prefer to believe otherwise, this is surely true in the sense that the history of British rule in India was not directly determined by the religious beliefs of British imperialists. But that is not to say that such beliefs were insignificant. It will be argued here that a language of belief, interpretation and judgment, which can only be described in terms of the category of religion, had a pervasive and neglected importance in the impulse to retain imperial assets and, even more perhaps, in the associated impulse to control and direct the moments of concession and withdrawal which mark the imperial theme in this period. Imperialism is a global phenomenon and social scientists quite rightly struggle to identify its universal features, but there have also been substantial differences between one imperialism and another, and the Raj would have had a very different history if the British had appealed to a different vision of their place in the providential order of things.

Such a proposal, to penetrate a neglected network of imperialist assumptions, raises obvious questions which are difficult to answer. Discussion of religion and politics often treats these two categories rather as if they were chemical elements which in different circumstances might compound or mix with others, whilst themselves remaining in some empirical, molecular sense, discrete. But this can only be a manner of speaking. Christianity and being Christian meant a variety of things to varieties of people. We can at least indicate different versions of Christian belief and what held them together. For many, Christianity was no doubt a stock response, sustained well enough by the occasional public rituals. For a few, including a number who were politically very important, it provided a complete justification for the imperial mission. For many, though at different levels of self-conscious awareness, it was integral to a structure of assumptions about the western rationalism that gave Empire its coherence as an historical fact and a continuing obligation. Without being able to map the precise incidence of these varieties of assumption and belief onto the relatively small universe of public opinion concerned with India, we can go further than the analysis of that public opinion merely as a generalized predisposition, by considering a number of individuals who were demonstrably important in different ways, and we can look beyond them to the particular publics of admirers and supporters who endorsed both their judgments and their activities. The final section of this chapter will take up the question of how best to approach this theme, but it turns now to a contemporary historiography which appears to neglect it.

High Politics and Imperial Reform

The literature concerned with the British response to Indian Nationalism, and Britain's accelerated 'escape from Empire' under the pressure of two World Wars, has concentrated heavily on high politics and constitutional small print. The foreground of informed contemporary comment and debate, at least since the time of Morley's Indian Council's Act of 1909, has been mainly occupied by a succession of constitutional formulae. These raised hopes and alarms, pointed ahead, faded away and were overtaken by events, or, occasionally, found themselves winched laboriously into position to modify the operations of the 'steel frame' of the constitutional and administrative machinery of the Raj.

After the Great War, to take a salient example to which we must return at some length, a heavily disputed and structurally complex devolution of power was initiated by the Government of India Act of 1919, under the code word of 'dyarchy'.

I do not know whether they realize it, [declared Montagu in the course of introducing the Bill as Secretary of State for India] but if there is anyone in the House who has gone so far with me...they (sic) have swallowed the awful, terrible, much criticized principle of dyarchy. *An Hon Member.* Say duality. *Montagu.* Duality.[4]

Mostly people said dyarchy . This referred to the proposed transfer, in the provincial administrations, of certain areas, including agriculture, public works, education, local self-government and Indian education, to Indian ministers responsible to local legislatures, whilst other areas, irrigation, land revenue administration, police, administration of justice, prisons and control of newspapers, books and presses, would be handled directly by the provincial governors and their executive councils. Official majorities were to disappear in the newly enlarged legislatures at both levels and, of course topics like the army, foreign affairs, income tax and currency matters, communications and criminal law, would remain 'reserved' to the Viceroy. The arguments surrounding the birth, tormented infancy and demise of dyarchy appeal today only to a specialist interest. They appeared at the time in a full range of assessments, from the relatively specific and detailed commentary of distinguished old-India hands, in journals like the *Contemporary Review* and the *Fortnightly Review*, to regular coverage in the *Times* and the *Morning Post* and, in more attenuated form, in other organs of responsible public opinion with a particular interest in India, such as the *Methodist Recorder*, the *Church Times*, and the Church of England *Guardian*.

A decade or so later, a notable false hope was released by the pushing and heaving of the Round Table Conferences of 1930–2, the mouse of a 'Federal solution' to the problem of Indian constitutional progress briefly favoured by some of the Princes. Enshrined in the India Act of 1935, and a theoretical possibility till August 1940, it was effectively lost long before that in the hue and cry following its surprising appearance. Federalism was, in Churchill's view, a sham, and in that of Hailey, perhaps the outstanding Indian Civil Servant of the period, a red-herring. But Samuel Hoare, the Conservative architect of the India Act, with Sir John Simon (a former conservative), the Liberal Chairman of the 1927–9 Indian Statutory Commission, saw to it that it became a useful red-herring which pre-empted the attention of informed, or at least concerned, observers and provided a formula round which a consensus of British political opinion could be carefully engineered.[5] Did this or that proposal represent concession, expediency or constructive evolution? How to protect the electoral minorities, the Muslims, the caste Untouchables, the Christians? What formula would Gandhi agree to, or the Congress Party abide by? What did either deserve? Had the Viceroy gone too far too fast? What precise degree of 'self-government' was India ready for? Such questions constituted the refrain of informed British public opinion on India between the wars. They seemed at the time to be of consuming importance to the notoriously small proportion of the electorate, and indeed of their representatives, who appeared to take any sustained interest in the prospective fate of the jewel in the imperial crown. For the most part, they strike us now as having a peculiar irrelevance to what was happening and what was likely to happen in the subcontinent.

In the work of recent historians, these preoccupations with high politics and constitutional small print have been transformed into a sceptical analysis of the dynamics of a terminal colonialism. However, they have not really been displaced, because it is now easier to see through the disturbed topical surface of political and constitutional activity to the features of massive constraints and structural imperatives that were directing the current of events beneath the surface. Economic historians have thrown a powerful light into what Tomlinson refers to, in *The Political Economy of the Raj*, as the 'official mind of decolonization', by identifying the underlying and continuing economic expectations and realities on which the Raj was based in this period. Under this sharply focused illumination, old arguments about imperial trusteeship, for instance, and the rational evolutionary development of representative political institutions in India and of dominion status, feature as a screen of largely ideological justifications. They were important to the extent that they were sincerely believed in, or taken for granted by, the principal actors, but they are transparent against the back-lighting of British material interests and British financial crises. British politicians were not engaged in a planned withdrawal from India. There were, in any case, too many accidents and uncontrollable elements for that to be possible. They were, on the contrary, engaged in a tenacious defence of the material interests of Empire, a defence which was far from disinterested, and in important respects astutely managed and very successful. Dyarchy and federalism were only two of the weapons available from the imperialist armoury to politicians across the party spectrum. In this connection, the contempt with which Attenborough's *Gandhi* treated the British administrators was seriously misleading. British control of the subcontinent was threatened and from time to time compromised in some areas, but it was not lost, and for long periods at a time, during the 1920s and the mid-1930s and, more uncertainly, during the Second World War, a policy of intermittent constitutional 'reform' and more or less benevolent repression subdued the Congress Party and the Nationalists.[6] Specific manifestations of the Government of India's law and order policy were, of course, criticized in Parliament and elsewhere by MPs like George Lansbury, Ben Spoor and Colonel Wedgwood, and by the Indian Conciliation Group in the 1930s, for instance, but the policy itself was generally accepted, despite uneasiness in liberal circles. The British finally departed from India more on their own terms than not, to the tune of 'the logic of British economic forces,' which was 'working towards a developing independent India.' Subsequently, Britain followed the rationality of decolonization with some consistency, providing India with major economic assistance in the late 1950s, for instance, on 'hard-headed' and 'useful' terms—useful, primarily, to herself, in relation to the stabilization of the sterling area.[7]

British politicians implicated between the World Wars in this thoroughly materialist imperial strategy disagreed about India at many points. The Conservative Party, in particular, was deeply divided, and it was by no means unrealistic of Churchill and others to attempt to use India as an issue with which to bring down the Government in the savage disputes leading up to the India Act of 1935. But the more specifically political narratives of recent years, such as those of Low, Moore and Bridge, complement the analysis of the political economy of the Raj by showing just how narrow were the substantive disagreements between the major factions in British politics. The most serious arguments in the 1930s were not between left and right, or authentic liberals and die-hards , in the context of a principled conflict over imperial policy, though that is what a great deal of contemporary rhetoric suggested. They were between essentially conservative groups, under the colours of all three main parties, which were in substantial agreement over fundamentals but divided over considerations of timing and tactics. Some of these considerations had little directly to do with India, and were further complicated by personal and organizational ambitions and loyalties that had nothing to do with India at all.[8]

The continuing concentration of scholarly attention on cabinet, conference and department of state is appropriate, then, for several reasons. Much of the high political material was, of course, classified, and its accessibility now makes possible a far more detailed understanding than was then available even to well informed contemporaries. What they overheard was a censored fraction of what actually happened. But we can now see how the premises on which the principals were in fact acting did not necessarily or invariably correspond with the premises on which the policy was endorsed by whatever there was in the way of an attentive general public. Hoare and his Conservative Party colleagues emerge from Bridge's account as both pragmatic and cynical. That is not at all how they appeared to many of those who supported the national consensus on India. Furthermore, whilst even a willing reader of Moore's account of the Round Table Conference, or Bridge's of the 1935 Act, is likely to feel that he has learnt rather more than was strictly necessary about these episodes, any less obsessively detailed analysis would have missed significant gaps between what some of the leading figures actually did and how they were represented or how they represented themselves at that time or later. There was, notably, Hoare's successful attempt to mislead the Committee of Privileges, where he was challenged by Churchill in April 1934 over pressure that he had brought to bear on the Manchester Chamber of Commerce to suppress inconvenient evidence relating to cotton markets.[9] Bridge even sees 'deliberate deception'[10] in the subsequent memoirs of both Hoare and Lord Halifax, who, as the Viceroy Lord Irwin, had put forward 'the most imaginative and far-sighted solution to the Indian problem in the inter-war years.'[11] Both men blamed the opposition of Churchill and the inertia of the Viceroy Lord Linlithgow, apart from the onset of war, for the failure of the all-India federation scheme. But Bridge's conclusion, drawn from a story of devious complexity, gravely implicates them both:

The secret aims of the federal section of the 1935 Act, as the Conservatives in Cabinet saw them, were essentially negative . . . a classical Whiggish solution to the problem of how to accommodate nationalist demands for independence within a constitution which provided for the protection of Britain's imperial interests in India.

Not only has the record been straightened, but such sifting of the high politics of constitutional adjustment exposes the deep ambiguity of imperial postures and their maintenance in the context of British domestic politics.

Economic and political historians have complicated the story in the last three decades and, of course, the studies referred to so far are items from what amounts to a comprehensive transfiguration of South Asian studies in this period, as the most cursory inspection of the further reading indicated in Judith Brown's recent Oxford History, Modern India, makes abundantly clear. There has been a decisive shift of emphasis in this literature which has greatly enhanced the significance of the indigenous in all its diversity, at the expense of the initiatives of the dominant partner in the imperial relationship.[12] In this general historiographical context, to which we will return in the concluding chapter, the perceptions and implicit models which guided the judgments of British political élites now occupy a much less prominent and more contingent position than they have done in the past. A broader British public opinion, that saw the India problem primarily in terms of their activities might, therefore, seem hardly worth investigating. What an earlier generation of scholars reviewed as the judgments and misjudgments of British statesmen grappling with awkward but manageable difficulties, now seems to fall into place as a structure of rationalizations which justified accommodations to the deeper pressures and larger circumstances that were genuinely determinative. 'Public opinion' should perhaps be marginalized as a mere confused echo of the 'blatantly inapplicable'[13] explanations and constructions of those in power.

However, every perspective has its blind spots, and it is the argument of this study that this kind of judgment can be too easily made. Modern historians of South Asia have explained a great deal. The question is whether they are not also liable to explain away what appears to lie on the fringes of their field of vision. This possibility is in fact explicitly recognized by Bridge, who turns to the question of the 'classical Whiggish solution', referred to in his general conclusion, in an article which identifies the working of a 'pre-requisites model' in imperial constitution-making.

Here he takes the 'new model historiography' to task for pushing an argument that is too brutally reductionist. Scholars such as Seal,[14] Gallagher, Moore and Low (and this would apply also to Bridge's own study of the 1935 legislation) have adopted the position that Conservative policy consisted of nothing more than a series of 'blocking' positions, 'each more precarious than the last.' In this view, the question of the ideology of the British imperialist is, therefore, pretty uninteresting. As long as the main contest could be conducted in terms of the formalisms of constitutional adjustment, it was always possible for the imperial government to keep defensible negotiating positions in play. Whatever people outside the policy process might believe in, those on the inside would be acting 'realistically', that is to say dishonestly, but with a clear realization of what they were engaged in doing. Constitutional concepts such as dyarchy, devolution, reservation, federalism, and dominion status, would be developed by imperial élites in the light of expediency, in effect as symbolic inducements in order to buy time from a restless native population. But it is not plausible to suppose that British policy over this period consisted entirely of such a crude and unprincipled brand of party politics. It is psychologically unconvincing, and it contradicts what we know from many sources about some of those involved, such as Irwin himself, to name the most obvious, who was a prominent and widely respected Anglican manifestly committed to doing the best thing for India. Bridge's argument is that there was indeed high principle involved, irrelevant and inappropriate, to be sure, but with an independent vitality that impinged, for better or worse, on events. Irwin and those associated with him in a socially homogeneous political milieu, were not completely governed by pragmatism and expediency. Conveniently to hand, they had common models of historical change, national development and political evolution, and a received wisdom about the natural and rational structure of political organization in the modern world, which transcended any immediate predicament. These models structured their perceptions of events and therefore conditioned their responses. The essential features were so engrained as to be beyond question; a sophisticated common sense, which had been articulated and developed by figures such as Maine, Stubbs, and Burke, who, though historically more remote, was back in vogue in conjunction with Victorian versions of social Darwinism. Behind this Edwardian amalgam of evolutionary conservatisms lurked the German historicism associated with Ranke. The works of Stubbs and Maine, above all, were ingredients in the diet of social and historical wisdom provided by the history schools of Oxford, in particular, and of Cambridge. Very few of the politicians or senior British Indian administrators had not been to one university or the other. What they acquired there was more than a body of theory, in a speculative sense. Rather, it was a vision of the origins and development of England to which they could refer with untroubled assurance. Bridge quotes Stanley Baldwin's revealing and characteristically charming remark, made to an Anglo-American conference of historians, that he believed Stubbs to be quite unbiased as an historian. The meaning of history was, in its overall development, self-evident to those providentially placed so as to be able to review the past, and to contemplate their part in realizing the future immanent within it, without anxiety and short-sighted impetuosity.

It was self-evident to these products of the Edwardian upper classes that any political development worthy the name must be the natural outgrowth of organic continuities, of the rational consolidation over time of encapsulating social structures, evolving steadily towards a state of unitary nationhood, even perhaps, in the fullness of time, beyond it. The proof lay in a comparative reading of European history in which, anticipating much later American exponents of the academic construct of a 'civic culture',[15] they saw in one society, the British one, a paradigm of rational organic evolution. A unique combination of geographical and historical circumstances had allowed the British to evolve a socially coherent community which was capable of resolving its difficulties and of acting through the mechanisms of political balance, that is, through the established and competing political parties. The parties were nested firmly into the institutional structure of the law and administration, themselves the product of experience or purposive history. Whatever its shortcomings, this historical achievement must establish the only operational criteria available to politicians responding to pressures for change. Against the standard it provided, it was argued, other European states had fallen short. India was clearly not yet remotely in the running. Without the enforced administrative order provided by British rule it was inconceivable that she ever would be. Trusteeship, therefore, was to be defined as the obligation to provide the stability and the time and basic conditions for organic growth, to which there are, finally, no short cuts.

Behind the procedural obsessions of the inter-war constitution-makers lay a tension in their discussions, which derived from uncertainty about the subordinate, Indian social organism's capacity to seize upon and grow towards full maturity round the trellis-work of an extended or improved institutional structure. Whenever, in these debates, any particular proposal was deemed by its critics likely to fail, it was invariably because it was objected that Indians—civil servants, political representatives, lawyers, workers, voters, castes or just Indians in general—would abuse it or fail it at their present state of development or 'readiness'. Conversely, its proponents claimed that the hour had come to open the road to the practical experience through which mere readiness could alone grow into fitness and towards maturity.

Commonwealth historians have lamented the failure of the British government and Parliament to give the kind of leadership and guidance that the situation actually demanded, despite the available resources of moral earnestness and good will, knowledge and practical experience on which they could call.[16] Bridge's prerequisites model begins to suggest why such truly statesmanlike guidance was not forthcoming. The effective set of prerequisites was so deeply rooted in conservative ideology that any conceivable alternative would have presented an intolerable intellectual dilemma. In support of Bridge's argument, we can add that alternative structures were very weak *outside* Tory party circles, so the prerequisites model enjoyed a more or less unchallenged hegemony. Ramsay Macdonald was able to dominate those on the left of the Labour Party on India, and his own and the Party's response to Indian problems was a poverty-striken one that made few friends in India itself. Neither within the National Government, nor within the encounters of the Round Table Conferences, did Macdonald or those closely associated with him, such as the conservative trade unionist J. H. Thomas, present any kind of intellectual threat to the received wisdom which passed judgment on the Indian situation. A condescending Fabian imperialism was strong within the Party. Sidney Webb swallowed the 'Montford' dyarchy reforms whole, whilst the stylish radicalism of Bernard Shaw was hostile to jingoism and profit seeking, but accepted the right of higher civilizations to take over backward states. A few members of the ILP, like Lansbury, John Scurr and D. G. Pole, were in sympathetic contact with Annie Besant and there was some support in the Parliamentary Labour Party for her Home Rule League's version of Indian Nationalism, but there was, in Gupta's phrase, a 'curtain of incomprehension' between the Indian nationalists and British Labour by 1921. Lionel Curtis, the grey eminence of 'dyarchy', actually wrote the pamphlet on India commmissioned by the Labour Party for the use of candidates in the election.[17] Curtis's name was well known, and exceedingly un-popular, in Indian nationalist circles in connection with the Transvaal Asiatic Law Amendment Ordinance of 1906. He had then been Assistant Colonial Secretary in the Transvaal. The Ordinance required Indians to register with prints of all ten fingers. 'A deliberate attempt to harrass Asians,' it triggered Gandhian passive resistance in South Africa.[18] It is true that his constitutional proposals were misrepresented in India, but that hardly affected the nationalist judgments of the Montford reforms, that they were too late to be relevant and that they were designed to perpetuate imperial control.

Bridge's suggestion of a prerequisites model to qualify the reductionist treatment of ideology by the 'new model historiography' is constructive. There is no going back on the basic perception that what conditioned imperial policy were the perceived economic and political threats to British material interests. But it is acknowledged that the British response to these threats cannot be made sense of in terms of a strictly rationalistic calculus. The threats were registered, interpreted, and responded to within a complex structure of attitudes and beliefs. This combined, on the one hand, cool assessment of political costs and benefits, the shrewd appraisals of the resources and staying power of nationalist groups, an often adroit use of concessions to weaken provisional alliances between groups with very different objectives, with, on the other hand, a common perspective of the deeper significance of Britain's recurrent difficulties in her imperial role. The latter perspective cannot be treated as a residue, or as a mere habit of thought hung over from palmier days, merely providing the tone in which the British conducted their imperial business, a specific combination of self-righteous myopia and hypocrisy, which Gandhi understood well enough to attack on its best and weakest side. It was integral to the British response to the nationalists. There were, of course, plenty of hard-boiled and cynical defenders of the Raj, but for many others, and this is true of both Baldwin and Irwin, for example, strong assumptions about the moral coherence of human affairs and human history provided fundamental terms of reference for their involvement in politics. Recent scholarship on Irwin presents the 'holy fox', as he was known to his enemies, as more 'fox' than 'holy' in his pragmatic retreats from political confrontation with the nationalists.[19] But the appeal of Irwin to a wide spectrum of the public during his Viceroyalty was precisely that he appeared as a masterly and all too rare exponent of the art of combining the higher realism of an idealistic interpretation of history with the practical realism of the political market place. The combination was an authentic one.

But the restricted scope of Bridge's argument is, after all, unsatisfying. It refers to that small group of Oxbridge conservatives in the Cabinet who were active on India, the most important of whom were Baldwin, Irwin and Hoare, along with two conservative Liberals, Simon and Lothian.

Bridge establishes the pre-requisites themselves by reference to a very broadly sketched intellectual history, which derives its central propositions—organicism, a common law of political progress, functionally balanced political parties—from a handful of seminal but representative figures in late Victorian social thinking. He sees these central propositions as translating naturally into the federal principle in the Indian context: devolution and local participation would provide a school, as it were, for an incremental national evolution, whilst a federal organization under imperial jurisdiction would ensure both stability and the time necessary for organic development to take place. However, the conservative politicians were in no sense a socially or culturally isolated group, and their India policy enjoyed a broadly spread support. So what sort of scope might the prerequisites argument have at a more general level? There is, for example, the elective affinity of the British Labour leaders with the assumptions it recognizes. But on the left, one would expect rather different intellectual traditions to be operative. So what provides the common element and whom does it cover?

The question, then, is how best to approach the problem of analysing apparently pervasive, but manifestly elusive states of mind, beliefs and perceptions, which were integral to the imperial politics of the Raj, which had a variety of manifestations and affected different groups and individuals in different ways, and which appear to have had a bearing on the political process at a number of levels.

Public Opinion and Orientalist Discourse

The appeal by some leading Tory politicians to the inner meaning of history implies a belief in a fallen but essentially righteous world, remaining under Providential care, however conditional. There are of course other kinds of appeal to the inner meaning of history , which repudiate the idealism implicit in any such belief, insisting on an interpretation of change exclusively in terms of material sequences of cause and effect. It would be wildly inaccurate to suggest that the historiography of Stubbs and Maine is not also concerned with the material determination of structural change. Geographical accident, for example, is seen as making possible the privileged development of the British Commonwealth. But one can recognize a religious component in the prerequisites model to the extent that material description of that kind does not seem to exhaust the inner meaning of the historical process as these theorists think of it.

However, the general concept of religion cannot provide a point of departure for an historical analysis, because it begs too many questions and is intuitively relevant in such different ways in different contexts. For example, one might go on to point out that religion, religion in general and his Hinduism in particular, complicated responses to Gandhi throughout the period at every level of attention and involvement.

Whilst developing the approach which will be followed here, it will be useful to briefly review the evidence. It is both dispersed and fragmentary, a fact which may help to explain such novelty as the argument can claim to have. Each chapter is concerned with a different context of interaction between those who can be described as influential, and those in the broader Anglo-India public. The contexts, as will be seen, overlap and interlock, but each has also to be considered as a distinctive world of its own. Thus, the social and ideological networks within which Lionel Curtis operated as educator and constitutional expert impinged decisively but indirectly on those of the missionary, or of the Indian Christian, or of the evangelical ICS enthusiast of rural uplift. Many individuals in each of these imperial networks had access of one kind or another to centres of power. They were all taken seriously by one section or another of the public, of modest size, which concerned itself with the Raj. But the Raj was a ramshackle embodiment of the imperial idea, and this is reflected in some obvious discontinuities between the chapters. The idea of 'India' was formulated for the Anglo-India public in a variety of ways.

What they shared was a language structured around categories formulated within the British Christian tradition, in the terms of which they could describe and argue about the imperial relationship. The organizing concept of the analysis is, therefore, a British orientalism, a discourse shaped by a set of beliefs which defined imperial realities in a particular way.

The concept of orientalism has been extensively used, but variously defined. Its loosely descriptive use, which appears, for instance, in One form in Kopf's *British Orientalism and the Bengal Renaissance*, in conjunction with a dated confidence in the validity of orthodox modernization theory, is clearly not sufficient for present purposes.[20] What the concept draws attention to is a set of characteristics held in common by material that is in obvious respects highly diverse—in subject matter, focus, level of complexity, intention and even political orientation. In this perspective, the diversity of middle-brow and high-brow entertainment and enlightenment relating to the Raj, ranging from the *gravitas* of learned works on vedantic religion, to racy accounts of adventures on the North-West Frontier, instead of serving to fragment analysis of a public consciousness of the Indian Empire, can reveal, as it were down the tube of a kaleidoscope, interesting symmetries.

Edward Said's development of the concept of orientalism specifically in relation to Islam and the Middle East, is concerned to show that:

[A] field like Orientalism has a cumulative and corporate identity, one that is particularly strong given its associations with traditional learning (the classics, the Bible, philology), public institutions (governments, trading companies, geographical societies, universities), and generically determined writing (travel books, books of exploration, fantasy, exotic description). The result for Orientalism has been a sort of consensus: certain things, certain types of statement, certain types of work have seemed for the Orientalist correct. He has built his work and research upon them, and they in turn have pressed hard upon new writers and scholars. Orientalism can thus be regarded as a manner of regularized (or Orientalized) writing, vision, and study, dominated by imperatives, perspectives, and ideological biases ostensibly suited to the Orient. The Orient is taught, researched and pronounced upon in certain discrete ways.[21]

What are they, these discrete pronouncements which project themselves towards the reader through the complex or superficial constructions of scholarship and narrative and political analysis? If they have the importance which Said attributes to them, they must be persistent, recurrent, and dominated, as he says, by imperatives. The book is concerned with identifying them and demonstrating their regularized and pervasive presence. Said's use of the concept is shaped by the elaborate disquisitions on the concept of the 'discourse' or 'discursive formation' of Michel Foucault. Anyone approaching this extension of French structuralist thinking by way of Said's eminently readable analysis is likely to have second thoughts as he enters the minefield of abstract conceptualization that Foucault has prepared, for instance in *The Archaeology of Knowledge,* which he himself regards as both a reprise and an amplification of earlier arguments. It may be that Said himself has extracted from his source rather too simple a rendering of the idea, deliberately reducing the sustained intellectualism of abstract qualification and refinement. This discussion is certain to do so. However, the material being considered here does seem to invite exploration in these terms.

In fact, the material in these chapters does not require the one substantial modification of Foucault's argument which Said makes in order to establish the coherence of the full range of material with which he happens to be concerned. For Foucault is peremptory on the point that his category of 'discourse' transcends the individual author, book or *oeuvre.*

The frontiers of a book are never clear-cut: beyond the title, the first lines, and the last full stop, beyond its internal configuration and its autonomous form, it is caught up in a system of references to other books, other texts, other sentences: it is a node within a network.[22]

But it is important to Said's argument that the middle-eastern orientalism that concerns him *has been* critically influenced by the individual *oeuvre* and the individual author. Flaubert, for instance, creatively developed French orientalism. By such standards, however, the material for a South Asian orientalism to be discussed here is incontrovertibly mediocre. There is little in it to retain more than passing interest except, to use Foucault's image, as a node in a network.

What constitutes a network is a 'discursive formation', an entity that is elusive but not impossibly so. The component parts, Foucault identifies as 'sentences', statements, things that can be said. But here we are not to think of sentences in a paragraph related to each other by logic or by rhetorical connections. As in Foucault's account of the discursive formation, the 'sentence' is much more than an intellectual cliché or commonplace.

Discursive relations...are, in a sense, at the limit of discourse: they offer it subjects of which it can speak, or rather (for this image of offering presupposes that objects are formed independently of discourse), they determine the group of relations that discourse must establish in order to speak of this or that object, in order to deal with them, name them, analyse them, classify them, explain them, etc.[23]

The material considered in this study, various as it is, seems to belong to a coherent discursive formation in a straightforward way. It is remarkable for the frequency and regularity with which certain elements, statements of fact, interpretations of fact, associations between 'facts' recur from source to source. It is also remarkable for the consistent absence of perceptions we have come to take for granted in more recent South Asian studies that are rooted in a radically different response to the indigenous. The sources certainly seem to have Foucault's kind of anonymity. Individual writers or politicians or speakers respond to 'India' within a discursive formation of remarkable regularity, which makes available 'knowledge', includes the possibility of even extreme disagreement and conflict, but only within the limits set by the exclusion from awareness of alternative versions of the realities of South Asia, and indeed of British society itself.

So an exploration of the discourse of a Christian imperialism is not a study of the paths of intellectual influence, of the transmission of ideas from one individual or group to another. However, whilst seeking to demonstrate the pervasiveness and consistency of the elements in this network of ideas, one can recognize the contribution made by particular individuals, groups and episodes to consolidating and extending it. Thus Chapter 2 is concerned with two very different individuals, the flamboyant Lionel Curtis and the professionally unobtrusive Arthur Hirtzel, who were both, in contrasting ways, men who enjoyed political influence. Curtis will be considered in considerable detail, partly because of the extent and nature of his political activities, partly because of his comprehensive command of the span of 'sentences' of which the discourse is composed, and in part, finally, because of the selective and oddly misleading assessments of him in histories of the inter-war period.

No less firmly than Montagu, the Secretary of State in 1919, Curtis insisted that he was not the only begetter of dyarchy, but he certainly dedicated more thought and energy to this idea than anyone else. Above all, he developed at length in the three substantial volumes of his *Civitas Dei* and in his books on the evolution of the

Commonwealth, a philosophical justification for his intensive activities as a constitutional theorist.[24] It is remarkable that these disquisitions have been almost totally ignored in standard discussions and references. Curtis's entirely voluntary apotheosis as a constitutional theorist—he held no official brief—was warmly welcomed by many of those struggling to formulate constitutional policy, though it was deeply resented by others.[25] But he had the general support of well placed friends in the Round Table group of Milner's 'kindergarten', which had formed during Milner's period in South Africa.[26] This was a most remarkable event. Nothing can lighten the tedium, for the contemporary reader, of Curtis's relentless pursuit of constitutional detail, but that is mercifully irrelevant in its particularities to the present argument. Of interest, first of all, is the vision that drove him to it, and, secondly, the network of informed opinion that was responsive to it. For Curtis's premises were explicitly Christological. He was not unique in this respect among those comparable figures for whom India was of primary concern, as is clear from evidence which has also been ignored, relating to Sir Arthur Hirtzel, who was Secretary to the Political Department at the India Office between 1909 and 1917, and Permanent Under Secretary of State until 1930. Hirtzel was a powerful influence on Morley.

Curtis held the attention of an important public in England. The involvement of a Round Table group in the dyarchy debate implied various degrees of support for his projects, but for some, particularly Philip Kerr (Lord Lothian), who held minor office at the India Office in 1931–2, and his closest friend in the group, Lionel Hichens, Director of Cammell Laird, his premises and the arguments based around them were of central importance. Hichens had had important personal experience of India as the most active member of the Decentralization Commission sent out by the Liberal Government of 1906, and he participated in Round Table 'moots' on imperial and Commonwealth affairs.[27] Between the World Wars, however, he was also a leading figure in a highly organized and strongly supported attempt by churchmen of various denominations to shape public opinion about industrial relations in England. This movement has been analysed in detail in a previous publication, *Dog-Collar Democracy: The Industrial Christian Fellowship, 1919–1929.*[28] Curtis's social theology can be seen as an extrapolation to the imperial context of the ideology described in that study, which is how, in effect, it was recognized by other intellectual light-heavyweights who also addressed the imperial theme and helped fight the crusading battles of the ICF, such as William Temple, Bishop of Manchester and later successively Archbishop of York and of Canterbury.[29] Once again, it is a reflection of recent fashions in social and political history that a religious movement with political objectives, which succeeded in capturing the attention and support of large numbers of people for a decade and more, should have been largely ignored for so long.

Curtis appealed to theologians, who naturally welcomed the appearance of a public man who could make a central issue of his faith in a manner which they found sympathetic, which he did because, in turn, he responded to them. Chapter 3 is concerned with the more distinguished and influential theologians who concerned themselves directly with the Christian presence in India, notably J. N. Farquhar, Bernard Lucas, and A. G. Hogg who are placed in the context of the powerful, scholarly tradition of European orientalism.

Curtis had working relationships with Lucas and Hogg, at least, and also with other highly regarded figures in the church in India, such as the Revd P. N. F. Young. Such men stand out in the history of the church and mission world. But there were many more, some of them much better known at the time to the Anglo-India public in Britain, who maintained the Christian presence in India and justified it in terms that echoed those of the professional intellectuals. They reached a relatively wide British public through their books and articles and deputation work, and more indirectly through their reports home to the Society for the Propagation of the Gospel, the Church Missionary Society, and the Methodist and Presbyterian missions, which were used in the preparation of a variety of publications. By no means did they all speak with one voice. But their activities were dependent on public support, more effectively generated by some of their organizations than by others, and collectively they constitute a link of the greatest importance between India itself and British perceptions of the Raj. These connections are considered in the final section of Chapter 2 and in Chapter 4, which is followed by a discussion of two undeniably powerful evangelical influences on British understandings of imperial responsibility between the wars, the educational missionary C. E. Tyndale-Biscoe of Kashmir and F. L. Brayne of the Punjab, an ICS enthusiast and pioneer in the cause of rural uplift .

The two central Chapters, 6 and 7, draw on a wide variety of books, journals and letters, and turn to interpretations of the nationalist movement and of Gandhi's significance to it. They do so in the light of contrasting readings of the notion of Providence which distinguish the more liberal and the more conservative wings of opinion in the Anglo-India public. Responses to Gandhi as a politician polarized the Anglo-India public, and the complicating factor of judgments about his significance as a religious leader did so particularly sharply. There were Indian Christians, whose names were barely known in England, who saw him as a Christ-like figure and sought to assimilate an indigenous Christianity and a thoroughly independent Indian Church to the nationalist movement. A few Englishmen who moved onto the fringes of British Anglicanism saw him in much the same light, as an agent of the Divine Providence. Verrier Elwin of the *Christa Seva Sangha* was one, but there was also the more important figure of Gandhi's friend the Revd C. F. Andrews, (who appears in an unhistorically clean-cut role in Attenborough's film). Andrews, who was a vigorous and prolific writer, had a well-established platform as a publicist of Gandhian nationalism, though he was regarded warily by the church establishment. But there were nationalist Christians of another kind, associated particularly with the Indian YMCA, whose more qualified and ambiguous identification with Gandhi, together with their commitment to the British connection as the matrix for an emergent and authentic nationalism, earned them the support of British liberals. They were well represented at the Round Table Conferences. At that time, Gandhi himself used every opportunity open to him to win the support of British religious leaders, through the intermediary activities of Andrews and the Indian Conciliation Group and its Quaker activists, but also, as we will see in Chapter 7, through Bishop George Kennedy Bell of Chichester, who lobbied strongly for him in private correspondence as the religious leader of an authentic nationalism.

Grass-roots support for the Tory die-hards in the early 1930s is generally identified as a predictable reflex of unreconstructed imperialist sentiment which called for skilful management by a more enlightened leadership. 'India' is seen as an issue, like hanging and corporal punishment in later times, over which education and instinct were at odds within the Party. But the die-hard position was both more complex and more coherent than party managers could afford to admit. Its most popular spokesman at the Tory grass-roots, Brigadier-General Sir Henry Page Croft, articulated an imperialist providentialism with passionate conviction. Evidence, considered in Chapter 7, from the books and ephemera produced by the die-hards, suggests that he was not by any means talking to himself. The India public in the disputes surrounding the 1935 Act was much less interested in constitutional minutiae than in the appeal of broad positions that appealed to broad, ultimate sanctions within the terms set by a common discourse. By no means all the grass-roots die- hards, still less, spokesmen like Croft and Lord Lloyd, a former Governor of Bombay and a deeply committed Christian, were crass jingoes.

An explicitly imperialist form of Christianity did in fact flourish during this period, that of the British-Israel movement. The section on this extraordinary and now defunctive tendency, many of whose members contributed to the die-hard defence of the Raj, indicates the pervasiveness of religious sentiment among reactionaries, and identifies those elements in the discourse round which their reading of it was organized. British-Israel was a tendency *within* the Church of England (a considerable worry to Bishop G. K. Bell in the middle-class parishes of his diocese, in fact), and it could claim numbers of socially prominent adherents. It has not been a popular movement for scholarly investigation, but it produced a substantial body of persuasive literature in its heyday in the 1920s and 1930s, which will be drawn on here.

We can also observe the incorporation of this religious tendency in the career of an able and, in important respects, highly representative ICS man, Andrew Hume through letters home and other papers which are now in the India Office Library and the Cambridge South Asia Archive. The entire family was British-Israelite. His father, Colonel Hume had served in India as an army engineer, and the letters are detailed about work which brought Hume into direct and sometimes violent contact with nationalist activities. They are also abrasively candid about colleagues and superiors, and on the drift towards liberalism and the corruption of the state religion, which he associated particularly with Irwin. Hume supported the die-hard activism of his father by contributing anonymously, through the die-hard leadership, to propaganda in the national press against the India Act of 1935.

Constitutional historians, it was pointed out earlier, have shown that the conflicts in British politics over India in this period were much more those of orthodox versus heretic, rather than of orthodox versus infidel or non-believer. That is to say, they could be very fierce precisely because the protagonists shared so much common ground. The same is true at lower levels. Hume accepted a degree of social isolation as a consequence of his evangelical extremism, but his judgments and responses to India and the Indians were highly representative of his class and of officials like him. In Delhi in 1937, his Sabbatarian obligations sent him out to locate the least intolerable form of Christian worship he could find. It is entirely appropriate that he should have found himself at one point in this search subjected to the ministry of the Revd P. N. F. Young, whose liberal Anglicanism and political liberalism alike represented everything he abominated and, at the same time, in an important sense fully understood.[30]

So the relevance of what Hume represented on the side of a Tory imperialism, (in a minutely well-informed, practical and authoritative form) is not in the rather facile observation that both sides had, or could appeal to a 'religious' sanction or justification. The object is 'to show what the differences consisted of, how it was possible for men, with the same discursive practice, to speak of different objects, to have contrary opinions, and to make contradictory choices.'[31] An analysis of public opinion includes an understanding of what people and groups within the same frame of reference or discursive practice find it possible to disagree about, and of the terms in which they could do so. They were rooted in religious beliefs about the social order, the course of history, and the imperial connection. The strictly political analyses of British controversies over India referred to earlier arrive at the conclusion that the debates took place within a conservative consensus. The attempt to explore the structure of a broader context of public opinion strongly supports this conclusion. Neither Hume nor Young, for instance, could move outside a shared discourse which elaborated in all sorts of ways on the pre-requisites of historical change and the content of imperial obligations. What kept Hume fuming in his pew and barely under control as Young talked 'ill-informed nonsense about church and state' were primary convictions which they both shared about the realities of church and state.

CHAPTER 2

Jesus Christ and The Constitution

Dyarchy and Civitas Dei

Lionel Curtis is a convenient point of departure because his interventions in the constitutional debates were of considerable significance and because he is laboriously explicit about the premises on which his activities were based. He was in no sense an original thinker, but an expounder of commonplaces in which the social theology he had absorbed blended in familiar ways with political analysis and prescription.

The Christian historiography of our own times is the product of catastrophe over the central decades of the twentieth century. There has been a transition from an earlier Christian conception of the universe, which Curtis himself took for granted, to that of the most accessible and generally read modern exponents of a Christian history, Herbert Butterfield in England and Reinhold Niebuhr in America, though obviously it was not accomplished all at once or as an immediate response to the Great War. The transition hinged initially on the depression years of the 1930s, and then more decisively on the Second World War, notably in the work of V. A. Demant, N. Micklem and Maurice Reckitt.[1] Understandably, the eschatological premonitions of the First World War, mass death, mass destruction and the apocalyptic 'judgments' of defeat and disaster, were slower to affect British than German thought. Karl Barth was not even translated into English until 1933, and a symposium of Anglican essays, designed to perform the same synthesizing and inspirational function for Christians in the 1920s as had been performed for late Victorians by Bishop Gore's famous *Lux Mundi* volume of 1889, remained comfortably wedged in a traditional set of liberal Anglican preoccupations.[2]

The essay on 'The Spirit and the Church in History' by the Revd
E. Milner-White DSO, Dean of King's College, Cambridge makes,
in fact, the volume's unique direct reference to the First World War,
in connection with a thumb-nail orientalist sketch of the 'situation
in India'. The World War itself is seen as a sobering reminder of
the distinction between Christianity and civilization. In the same
breath, war provides a curious metaphor for the Church Militant
as an instrument of evolution.

Mohamedanism as a faith is static; Buddhism and Hinduism as certainly
retrograde, despite spasmodic efforts of moral and theological reform in
places where they are face to face with Christianity: the situation in India,
indeed, vividly resembles the conflict of religions in the later Roman
Empire. The Christian explosive shatters every civilization which it enters,
making way for one based on higher sanctions. Before the war of 1914 it
had become a popular article of faith that civilization itself was progressive.
If men are wiser now, they have not yet grasped the truth which gave rise
to that easy philosophy that in a Christian civilization the Christian motive
present is, regarded broadly, always progressive. Its swift motion, indeed,
creates more difficulties for Christianity than the attacks of its foes. The
army is frequently terrified at the far-marching of its pioneers, and would
cling to ancient bivouacs. Yet onward it goes...

Milner-White's press-on confidence in the future of Christianity
was not shared without reservations at the time. Niebuhr, writing
much later, in 1946, responded to a more resonant voice from the
1920s, that of another ex-army padre who had built up a considerable
popular following for the inter-denominational movement referred
to earlier in connection with Lionel Hichens, the Industrial Christian
Fellowship (ICF). As a public speaker and a highly successful writer
of popular verse and prose, the Revd G. A. Studdert Kennedy MC,
(a household name as 'Woodbine Willie'), had, unlike Milner-
White, confronted his audiences and readers with what Niebuhr
describes as a 'tragic sense of life,' suffused with the experience of
the trenches, and embodied in a sacramental theology that centred
on the continual presence of a suffering Christ in history, a Christ
who was bereft, however, of 'every form of the divine majesty and
power except the power of love.'[3] This popular theology was
emotional, unsystematic and questionable: Niebuhr describes it as
a very persuasive form of Christian faith drifting to the very edge
of heresy.[4] More important, however, it was quite incapable of

making the intellectual disengagements which came to seem so essential to later 'tragic' Christian versions of the human condition. However shaken by the experience of the war, the activists of the ICF continued to organize their commitment as Christian believers and their understanding of historical change round a political programme of popular persuasion which was designed to underwrite the climate of liberal consensualism in which MacDonald and Baldwin were competing 'to hog the crown of the road.'[5] Baldwin did so more successfully than MacDonald, in the face of weakly organized radical opposition and a General Strike in which the TUC leaders themselves hardly believed. MacBaldwinism was cautious, conservative and Whiggish in its confidence in a (British) history of constructive evolutionary change, the slow graduation of generations and classes into the maturity of citizenship under a responsible leadership and within the context of historically validated political institutions. Baldwin himself was a devout and observing Christian And MacDonald, as an undenominational Ethical Society man, relied on the 'indwelling impulse' of a religiose evolutionism which effectively protected him from more radical impulses in the Labour Movement.[6] They benefited from a social theology that enjoyed a popular platform at the time, less blandly complacent than much pre-First World War church teaching, but consensualist, cautious and evolutionary.

The Christian vision of history articulated in this milieu was in reality a painfully confused and ambivalent anticipation of the Christian visions of historical catastrophe which cooler intellects were yet to articulate. It is true that the popular speakers of the ICF came to see the First World War as a catastrophic judgment on collective pride, greed and anger, which was almost how Butterfield was to describe it more than twenty years later:

If Germany is under judgment, so are all of us—the whole of our existing order and the very fabric of our civilization. If once we admit that the moral factor operates in this way in history at all, then we today must feel ourselves to be living in one of those remarkable periods when judgement stalks generally through the world.[7]

But at the same time they were firmly committed to protecting the achieved rationality of the existing order, its economic basis in capitalism, its leadership, and its capacity to defend itself against a materialistic socialism, on the grounds of its natural, organic, historical tendency to institutionalise 'progress'. It was within the structure of this general perspective that many British Christians interpreted not only the problems of industrial conflict at home, but also the problems of Empire and particularly those of the 'Indian situation'. They shared with articulate public figures like Studdert Kennedy's friend, Bishop William Temple, and the layman Lionel Curtis (both of them Oxford men; Curtis was a Fellow of All Souls) a 'Christian' historiography which had complex intellectual roots, but a tap root in the British Hegelianism sustained at Oxford from before the turn of the century by the pervasive influence of T. H. Green, in particular.[8] The apparently self-evident strength of the assumptions behind this historiography for a great many churchmen of all denominations in the inter-war generation has been obscured from view behind Butterfield's subsequent conceptualization.

Butterfield's reconstruction takes off both from an epistemological, or what he describes as a technical premise, and from a philosophical assumption about the nature of man. The technical premise is the impossibility of an analysis of specific chains of causation in history. The search for origins, he argues, is an impossible one, because the historical process is far too complex to be treated like a logical unfolding. 'History is not the study of origins: rather it is the analysis of all the mediations by which the past was turned into our present,'[9] a process analogous, he suggests, on a number of occasions, to understanding the unfolding of a Beethoven symphony: what is happening at any given moment is understood as the product of all the preceding patterns.

The philosophical assumption attached to this premise is that it is 'essential not to have faith in human nature. Such faith is a recent heresy and a very disastrous one'.[10] It is not that the 'original sin' assumption is exclusive to Christianity, or dependent on the truth of any supernatural religion; rather it is an anthropological assumption. The point is that 'The difference between civilization and barbarism is a revelation of what is essentially the same human nature when it works under different conditions...modern barbarism...is a problem arising out of conditions.'[11]

In this view, social conditions decay and are corrupted by human inadequacy, but it is no less true that new and more tolerable conditions can emerge, even from the most extreme ruin. They can do so for a multiplicity of reasons at any time, among them on occasion, the Christian motive, so long as that is understood as a regenerative potential and not as some immanent idea unfolding within time, not as 'history encroaching like the Hegelian state'. For time and eternity cannot be related as route to goal. A past that seems to lead in any progressively evolutionary sense to the present is an optical illusion which completely misrepresents the human condition, and is, in any case, an idea that history as a form of knowledge cannot accommodate. 'The technique of historical study itself demands that we shall look upon each generation as, so to speak, an end in itself, a world of people existing in their own right.'[12] So the categories appropriate to historical analysis cannot be the scientific ones of cause and effect, still less of social Darwinist or liberal evolution. History requires categories of a very different kind, irony, for instance, as Dray suggests in his discussion of Niebuhr's philosophy of history.[13] In Niebuhr's words:

> The extension of human powers is the basis of the progressive character of human history. Every new conquest of nature and every new elaboration of human skills means that human actions and responsibilities are set in the context of a wider field. This is the creative side of human history. Yet every new mastery of nature and every enlargement of human powers is also the new occasion for pride and a fresh temptation to human arrogance.[14]

The main thrust of Butterfield's famous attack on the whig interpretation of history is presented in ostensibly technical terms:

> The theory that is behind the Whig interpretation—the theory that we study the past for the sake of the present—is one that is really introduced for the purpose of facilitating the abridgment of history.[15]

Worse still, many abridgments of history 'are in reality not abridgments at all—not the condensation of a full mind but mere compilations from other abridgments.'[16]

The alternative, of course, is not some unimaginably complete narrative, but abridgment of a different kind, a notation that represents complexity because it covers a past that has been studied for its own sake and not with immediate reference to the present day. The misguided Whig historian, however, takes short cuts from past to present, employing a principle of selection that gives dramatic salience to the 'progressive' transitions he is looking for. The supposed lessons of such history 'are really inferences from the particular organisation that we have given to our knowledge.'[17] Butterfield's attack on such Whig history is comprehensive, an analysis of a discursive formation at the most general level in which, apart from Acton, no individual rates a mention. Lionel Curtis, who brought out the first volume of *Civitas Dei* in 1934, three years after Butterfield's essay, moves without concern right into the centre of his target area.

He does so not on account of those specific components of Whig history which Butterfield identifies in *The Englishman and his History*,[18] namely, the ancient and free Teutonic constitution, Magna Carta and the antiquity of the House of Commons, all of which were intermittently important to nineteenth century historians concerned with the path of evolution,[19] but rather on account of the one thing which Burrow distinguishes as 'definitive in the sense of a Whig interpretation that we have all learnt from Butterfield,' namely, 'confidence in the possession of the past' and 'even more confidence, perhaps, in understanding the present.' Burrow quotes E. A. Freeman, an historian on whom Curtis regularly draws: 'Our ancient history is the possession of the liberal.'

But in the case of Curtis the confident liberal is also a deeply committed Christian. Discursive, repetitious, simple but comprehensive, Curtis's historiography informed his entire career in a direct and literal way which has barely been acknowledged in recent studies. It will be argued that it was shared, implicitly or explicitly, by the imperialists who will be discussed in this account.

It is not possible to tell from Nimocks's account of the Round Table Movement and India, or from Ellinwood's, that Curtis derived his guiding theory as a man of affairs from an understanding of his Christian commitment.[20] His contribution to the public opinion process has been regularly acknowledged, for example, in connection with the imperial federation movement and his opposition to the 'Unripe Time' doctrine for the transfer of power in Africa, which was supported by Margery Perham and others.[21] In the politics of Irish Home Rule, he figures 'as a major advocate of concessions in 1921' and then as the proponent, though, it has been said, on 'extremely questionable assumptions' of a tough line against the devil, in the person of de Valera, in 1932.[22] But the core of belief which justified all his activities has been marginalized. The urgency of his dyarchy campaign has been explained by Bowle simply in terms of the impact of the First World War in compelling England to recognize that the principles for which she was fighting must be extended to Asia and Africa, a point he certainly makes, though it cannot stand on its own.[23] McIntyre, who writes at some length on the Round Table movement, attributes its paradoxical impact to 'its most colorful personality, Lionel Curtis...something of a crank who tended to publicise his own highly idiosyncratic views' and who produced, after the failure of internationalism in the League of Nations, 'his apocalyptic book Civitas Dei, a somewhat inchoate survey of civilisation and religion.'[24] Inchoate in an editorial sense, the three volumes of *Civitas Dei* certainly are, and Curtis committed himself to the future organic world commonwealth with striking naïvety. But the evolution towards a stable world system is entailed by his general argument, and this is coherent enough, whatever else may be said of it, and nowhere near as peculiar, in context, as McIntyre implies.

Drawing on Deborah Lavin's useful article in his prolifically documented *Propaganda and Empire*, MacKenzie notes that Curtis eventually went beyond a racially bound imperial federationism to accomodate the 'dependent' empire, and he refers to the links Curtis and his sympathizers had with Exeter Hall and the Labour movement, but he does not comment on Lavin's reference to Curtis's Hegelian historicism, his deeply held faith in a 'constructive religion' located in the Empire itself, and what she describes as his tendency 'to transform the abstract speculations of the (Round Table) moot into a theology.' His colleagues, as she points out, were more cautious, but it was not only Curtis's own classicism and Anglicanism, nourished in his case by Haileybury and Oxford, that 'died hard'.[25] Many of his influential friends, like Hichens and the Christian Scientist, Lord Lothian, shared basic assumptions.[26] And Toynbee at least found Curtis disturbing:

The British Commonwealth Christ's Kingdom. That had been comic. But now, Shanghai the City of God. This was blasphemous.

These had been my pagan reactions to a Christian idealist's recipes for establishing the Kingdom of Heaven on Earth. But was it I, or was it Lionel, who had been right? Had Lionel's vision really been the comedy or the blasphemy that it had looked like, to me, at first sight.[27]

Throughout his career as a publicist and as an academic—he was Beit Lecturer in Colonial History at Oxford in 1912[28]—Curtis used compilation and abridgment and as he freely acknowledges, the compilation of abridgments, as a form of political theory and political persuasion. He makes no claims to be a professional historian, and indeed complains of the profession for failing to provide the 'statesmen who are trying to mould the future' with a service they greatly need, of showing how 'the past, as a whole, has produced the present.' The three volume *History of Europe* by H. A. L. Fisher, a statesman himself as author of the Education Act of 1918, has done us, he claims, a notable service, specialized though it is. But the man who is active in public service needs urgently to be able to follow the logic of change in a wider world, since his own practical involvement clarifies or obscures, accelerates or retards the articulation of that immanent impulse. Curtis discounts historical knowledge for its own sake with, so to speak, a liberal application of the Marxist concept of *praxis*.

There are striking features of Curtis's procedure as amateur historian and professional constitutional theorist, or, as he preferred to describe himself, as political journeyman (*Civitas Dei* vol. 3, p. 96), that give his work a representative quality. He was not an ordinary author in this respect and his peculiarities have a bearing on the kind of significance one can attach to him in a context such as this.

The books emerge from his management of a series of running discussions in an international network of groups. In a detailed analysis of the highly influential activities of the Round Tablers in Canada, Quigley points out that the collective authorship of articles in the *Round Table* journal itself was *more* representative even than Curtis and his colleagues liked to suggest, since articles were not generally passed for publication with less than unanimous agreement at the 'moot'. The Round Table presented itself as a study group, reporting diverse opinions, from a co-operative and Dominion-wide membership, but its prime concern was propaganda and influence; it insisted on unanimity, at least in the London group, and everything of real significance was controlled from London.[29] One must suppose, however, that the volumes appearing under Curtis's own name were modified rather than heavily conditioned by the process of 'co-operation' he employed.

So the craft of the compiler was never for him a solitary one. An early book, *The Problem of the Commonwealth*, like other material that was never published for sale, was based on reports stimulated by preliminary studies which had been distributed to all the participants in Round Table groups in Canada, Australia, New Zealand and South Africa, and in due course also in the United Kingdom, India and Newfoundland. These reports were consolidated, printed and circulated again for criticism and revision. Material accumulated in this way and relating to the origins of the British Commonwealth, was reproduced in *The Commonwealth of Nations* in 1916, a volume of some seven hundred pages, replete with unfolding maps. As editor, Curtis accepts responsibility for the content of all the material reproduced, but insists that 'on the other hand, it must be emphatically stated that the main report is the work of various brains and pens.' (*The Commonwealth of Nations*, p. ii)

Dyarchy is not abridged history, but a collection of discussion papers. Another stout volume of six hundred pages, it contains seventy-five pages of comments on his letter to Bhupendra Nath Basu, from twenty-three people, half of them senior members of the ICS, the rest European non-officials and Indian officials, lawyers and teachers, with one educated member of the depressed classes. The book also includes a joint address to the Viceroy and the Secretary of State, consisting of twelve points of agreement, which was published with the signatures, secured in Bengal , of sixty-four Europeans and ninety Indians. He claims that many others could have been added to this from other areas but for overstretched secretarial resources. Like his membership ten years earlier of the Transvaal Legislative Assembly, his work as town clerk of Johannesburg and head of the department responsible for Asian immigration, this was what he called his journeyman work. It concludes by reproducing in full the 1919 Government of India Act, and was intended as a comprehensive collection of reference papers for future Parliamentary commissions on India, 'ten, twenty, and thirty years hence' and to guide 'young civil servants and future governors who without previous knowledge are called on to work the new system'. (*Dyarchy*, p. xix) It is also an agenda for responding in the short term to the promptings of a Divine Purpose, the creative significance of which future rulers can recognize from their reading of history. Dyarchy specifies the remaining obligations they should meet as trustees of the Raj.

In South Africa he had entered close and long-lasting associations with those who acknowledged this challenge, with the original Milnerites and with (Lord) James Meston and (Sir) William Marris, both then on loan from the ICS to work on the development of municipal institutions and a National Government for South Africa. As an historian he seems to have striven towards an almost corporate authorial identity. The first and third volumes of *Civitas Dei* appeared in 1934. Volume two followed in 1937. There is a nervous intellectual history behind this irregular sequence. Volume one is dedicated to friends of the Round Table and at All Souls and Chatham House, The Royal Institute of International Affairs, which Curtis and James Meston had helped to establish. All of them had contributed criticisms to the manuscript. It is an abridgment that starts with the genesis of the state, takes in Hindu and Chinese society, Israel, the Greeks, Rome, Christ and the Church, Islam, Saxons and Norsemen, the Plantagenets and the emergence of the English Commonwealth. Volume three was written next, a much shorter book which 'attempted to show what I thought was the application to world affairs of the principle suggested in *Civitas Dei*'. Volume three was first printed interleaved with blank sheets for critical comments and submitted to friends, mostly connected with Chatham House, 'highly qualified critics', he calls them, so many in number that he could not even print their names without unduly expanding the preface to volume two. He redrafted the volume in the light of these contributions, and it was at this stage that he felt the need for an intervening volume, a further abridgement to pick up the narrative. 'In this breathless race from Plantaganet times to catch up with the present I found myself in December last dealing with news in the daily papers and closed the story at the end of the year 1936.'

It is not possible to tell how many of those involved in this curious production would have identified fully with the main argument of the three volumes. But the fact that the criticisms and the comments were forthcoming and that they are reflected in the final version indicates a substantial measure of agreement, which cannot simply have been limited to the 'Whig history', as distinct from the emphasis, Christological rather than ecclesiastical, which he gave it. Volume three, with the inescapable expectations of its blank pages in its circulated form, is commentary and application to present and to future, and not abridged history. Its sparse footnotes refer not to historians and specific events, but to such figures as Bishop Gore, Cosmo Gordon Lang, then Archbishop of Canterbury, and Scott Lidgett, the Wesleyan Moderator of the Federal Council of the Evangelical Free Churches (all three, incidentally, strong supporters of the Industrial Christian Fellowship). Curtis was highly gratified by Scott Lidgett's endorsement of *Civitas Dei* in the *Contemporary Review* of January 1938.

The passage of time has exposed the weakness of Curtis's disinterested premises, but there is a logical coherence in what he constructed out of them. To do him justice, we have to take his own starting point, a practical man's sacramental theology and confidence in history, which, however vaguely, was widely shared. This compound of theology and religious sentiment is representatively exposed in the final passage of *Civitas Dei*, where a poem by the Catholic writer Francis Thompson, 'The Kingdom of God' is printed in full to bring down the curtain on Curtis's *magnum opus*. It was a poem that had said a great deal to the ICF Messenger, who frequently quoted it on the platform and in his books, particularly the concluding stanzas affirming the presence of Christ in the urban banalities of the twentieth century.

> But (when so sad thou canst not sadder)
> Cry;—and upon thy so sore loss
> Shall shine the traffic of Jacob's ladder
> Pitched betwixt Heaven and Charing Cross.
>
> Yea, in the night, my Soul, my daughter,
> Cry,—clinging Heaven by the hems;
> And lo, Christ walking on the water,
> Not of Genesereth, but Thames.

Thompson's sacramental sentiment is reproduced in the imagery and the cadences of some of Studdert Kennedy's own immensely popular verse,[30] and Curtis, like a significant number of his contemporaries, responded strongly to a sense of Christ as a continuous presence in history, of which we should be aware, as we should of His neglected presence in ourselves. The *Times* review on 16 October 1937 quotes Thompson's last two lines in a portentous peroration.

This review, though unsigned, was surely written by the Milnerite Edward Grigg, MP, joint editor of the *Round Table* before the War, and responsible for most of the leaders on imperial affairs in the *Times* between 1910 and 1913. His admiration for Curtis as a thinker will be more fully documented below.

Over his career Curtis worked out the implications of his beliefs in a philosophy of history, a cruder version of which is to be found in the ICF Messenger's popular prose, and in a theology of 'Personality', which owes a good deal, as in fact does Studdert Kennedy's, to the more cerebral, but not less prolific reflections of William Temple:

If we think of God as goodness personified, as personality on the infinite scale, we are led to suppose that supreme reality would call into being further realities akin to himself....I cannot conceive a creative God not inspired by a purpose, with no plan in his mind...I think we can now begin to discern a purpose running through the history of man, which can help us to see how to fit in our work with that purpose. (*Civitas Dei*, Vol. 3, pp. 19–20).[31]

What the life and death of Christ demonstrated was the guiding principle which is to steer man through the flux of history, 'the infinite duty of each ...to all' (*Civitas Dei* vol. 3, p. 35). This principle is repeatedly obstructed by man's irrational craving for certainties, a craving which has been translated into systems of authority, autocracies, despotisms of one kind or another, military, political or religious (or both, like Hinduism), which claim to provide them, said Curtis.

It is only in a certain kind of society, effectively only in a Christian society, that individual Personality is capable of achieving a true sense of the interconnections and moral implications of 'fact' in a contingent and imperfect world. It is the Christian journeyman's task to work on facts in the light of that insight, for history has been diverted into strange loops and backwaters, which will only be linked to the main channel with difficulty. Those trapped in historically marginalized or aberrant types of social condition are incapable of recognizing for themselves a principle first acknowledged by the Greeks, transfigured by Christ and sustained through many failures by the churches. We, however, can light their way to a less limited rationality.

The painful growth of man towards a fully sacramental sense of reality, even in Christendom, is epitomized for Curtis in the fundamental error sanctioned by St Augustine's mistaken notion of the City of God (the deliberately ironic source of his own title). St Augustine gave authority to a dualism in which the Roman Empire was regarded as the city of *this* world, or even the city of the devil. His state is a temporary necessity, to be superseded in due course by Christ at his second coming. In this tradition, the structure of human society ceased to be a matter of primary importance, since the Kingdom of Heaven was not to be realized in this world but in the next. Europe lost contact with Christ's teaching on the perfection of human character as the end and purpose of moral life, an idea that had been remotely prefigured in the message of the Hebrew prophets.

The primary concern of the Church was not in the maintenance of order amongst men, or in the tasks inseparable therefrom, of which public finance is the most essential. It left such matters to princes. (*Civitas Dei*, vol. 2, p. 73)

A reality divided on these lines suspends the evolution of society. The doctrine of *maya* has been fundamental to Hinduism from its inception centuries ago.

The association of the British imperium with a distinctive ability to recognize 'the facts' and to interpret their interconnections and moral consequences is a central and stable feature of the orientalist discourse. Its reciprocal is the Indian's obtuse response to 'fact' and 'reality', despite his 'natural' talent for forensic agility and philosophical ingenuity. A capacity for disinterested, purposive social rationality, something inherent in the individual Britisher, is frequently and explicitly identified as the practical and unsentimental expression of what one means by Christian rule.

Careful, from painful experience, of giving offence, Curtis did not repeat in *Dyarchy*, a volume that was closely read in political India, the standard formulae about eastern religion. But they appear elsewhere:

Believing himself to be the slave of destiny (the oriental) does in fact become so. (*Commonwealth of Nations*, p. 9)
Hinduism is more than a religion. It is a whole system of life in which the purest remnant of white invaders are held by the darker strains to be the repository of knowledge and power...The religious belief of the Hindu

grew out of this social structure...behind the whole system lies the conception that the visible world and the life men lead in it are evil rather than good. Hence the idea of asceticism which permeates Hindu thought. In the Hindu mind pain, and especially self-inflicted pain, is the road to merit and spiritual power. (*Civitas Dei*, vol. 1, p. 14)

(The Buddhist reforms) served to emphasize the idea native to India that all things material are essentially maya or illusion. (*Civitas Dei*, vol. 1, p. 36)

Islam, on the other hand, escapes from mere negation, but only so far:

[In the Christian religion, the Greek idea] that human knowledge of realities must be found in the mind and conscience of man, as revealed and verified by experience, has always been dormant like seed, ready to germinate again in favourable conditions. The revelation of Mahomet as recorded in the Koran left little room for further development and has therefore sterilized thought wherever his creed had prevailed. The boasted science of the Moslems in Spain is no real exception to this rule, for its source was the science of the Greeks introduced by Christians whom these least intolerant of Moslems employed. (*Civitas Dei*, vol. 1, p. 226)

This kind of reductionism, needless to say, is not to be found in any well-informed introduction to the eastern religions for the general reader in the West. Curtis, as is clear, for instance, even from a cursory inspection of Nirad Chaudhuri's *Hinduism*, is making the standard mistakes of confusing philosophy and belief, text and practice, part and diversified whole to accomodate a banal idealist thesis.[32] It was, nonetheless, a thesis that had become an acknowledged 'fact'.

The urgency pervading all of Curtis's work on India derives from the parliamentary deadlines for new legislation, but also from the conviction that a momentous historical opportunity lies waiting to be taken up by an essentially Christian empire. The contemporary political science which he represents, therefore, 'is not merely a genuine science, but at this juncture in human affairs the most important of all the sciences,' so long as it is informed by a religious vision. It must represent a distinctive kind of positivism, a patient, intelligent and fearless study of fact by which the 'principles of life can be discerned'.(*Civitas Dei*, vol. 3, p. 99)

The public opinion which is needed to lift the course of human affairs to a higher plane must from its nature be religious in the truest sense of that word. It is for that reason that churches play an indispensable part in such movements.(*Civitas Dei*, vol. 3, p. 94)

So, having reached a juncture at which the principle of the *national* commonwealth has been carried to its highest expression in the British Empire and, in a different way, the United States, the real obstacles to further advance are now in our own minds and in the capabilities of national leaders. Our leaders may not necessarily be British. They could be Australian or New Zealander, depending on the evolution of the material demands of the Commonwealth. But at the end of the day 'the British Empire would have done its work and passed into history.' We will have repeated, at a much higher level of social evolution, the achievement encapsulated in Bacon's observation that:

It was not the *Romans* that spread upon the *World*: but it was the *World* that spread upon the *Romans*: and that was the sure way of Greatness. (*Civitas Dei*, vol. 3, p. 111. Also quoted *Commonwealth of Nations*, p. 58)

Should we fail, we face the calamity of centuries darker than those that followed the collapse of ancient civilization in Europe. If we succeed, we will have created a slip-stream within which the peoples of Africa and Asia, who are to their own advantage part of our imperial system, will accelerate their own evolutionary growth. Success is identified in terms of his four general themes: society's discovery of 'reality', the issue of force and authority, the nature of national maturity, and the idea of law and of the Commonwealth.

The discovery of the mundane significance of reality is itself a function of the legitimate use of force. Societies based merely on force can achieve a mechanical kind of stability. Legitimate state force, however, is an essential component of creative social evolution. There is a sacramental use of force open to political authority:

The function of force...is to give moral ideas time to take root. The habit of order could no more be acquired by all these jarring elements [in the Roman Empire] than it could by the numerous races of India, until they had been constrained for a period to the practice of it. (*Commonwealth of Nations*, p. 59)

The lesson is exemplary for the imperial response to Indian nationalism.

For the Asiatic provinces, steeped in oriental ideas and incapable of serious political understanding, Rome could never be more than an autocracy. The significance of her limited success as the first great imperium resurfaces in a subsequent western history which has been deeply interesting—for unfortunate reasons, Curtis delicately hints—to Indian nationalists.

Ireland was never freed from the habits of tribalism by Roman rule. She retained them to fester like an organ whose uses have long been outgrown,—an abscess torturing Ireland herself and sending its poison throughout the Commonwealth. (*Commonwealth of Nations*, p. 60)

Ireland's abscess, the long-term consequences of its incoherent social pluralism, raised the problem of responsible power in painful but clear terms in the demands for an Irish Republic in 1921.

At the root of the problem was a state of mind divorced from realities, which led the Irish to demand what the British in the plenitude of their strength were powerless to grant. This state of mind could only be cured, and that very slowly, by giving the Irish every power to manage their own affairs, which the British parliament could deliver as well as concede. (*Civitas Dei*, vol. 2, p. 404)

These arguments are to be taken as a blueprint for any understanding of the demission of power under the Raj. To surrender power before the achievement of moral realism and national maturity is by definition to abandon both the historical role of empire and the fulfilment of an international commonwealth.

Curtis can appear to be the prototypical paternalist that Indian nationalists generally took him to be, insisting on the eternally drawn out apprenticeship. However, in the light of his own vision, Curtis did not pursue the idea of dyarchy in a spirit of caution, but in a spirit of faith and daring. Ripeness is all. The greater danger comes from nerveless caution, rather than from calculated courage underwritten by the imperial power and authority. For it is not for Britain to grant responsible government to India.

The best she could do was to put India in the way of taking responsible government for herself. That she has done, and the rest remains for Indians to do... It is much that England should have found a way to her own freedom; but infinitely more that she has traced the path which other nations in Europe have trodden or will tread. And so it will be with India also. (*Dyarchy*, p. lxi)

The paternal relationship, an off-hand term of abuse for social scientists no less than for nationalists, appeals to a paradigm with complex and mysterious implications for serious Christians. It is a crude theology that does not identify the fulfilment of the divine purpose with the growth of the son, or fails to see the paternal relationship replicated in different forms and at different levels. Curtis is more concerned with an imperial failure which he would describe in terms of this analogy than he is about loss of empire on any other grounds. He is, therefore, always ready with the reminder that 'government is a condition precedent to self-government' (*Civitas Dei*, vol. 1, p. 87), 'the truth which a Liberal government forgot in ignoring measures taken in Ulster to resist the law.' (*Dyarchy*, p. lv)

Selective quotation can make him look crudely reactionary. But the ultimate function of government for him is to create the conditions in which the creative individual learns what self-government is, so that truly organic societies can come into their own in organic relations with others. British industrial civilization and the British Empire in India were both, he has no doubt, founded on greed and corruption. But rapacity has eventually been superceded by the rule of law and institution, which are in themselves nothing other than the crystallization of the experience, the experiments and actions of free and disinterested men. In industrial relations we have a system of legal agreements, and the challenge of securing for the organic commonwealth as a whole the willing and unselfish 'service' of the mass of workers (*Civitas Dei*, vol. 1, p. 165), a central preoccupation of the movement associated with the ICF in the 1920s in England.[33] In the imperial context, we must confront a longer haul, in his earlier work a very long haul indeed: '(The work) needs for fruition not years nor decades but centuries....' (*Commonwealth of Nations*, p. 177)

The three volumes of *Civitas Dei*, were heavily reviewed as they came out. There were intellectual clerics like Bishop Hensley Henson (writing in *Christian Realm*), who cavilled at the narrow space Curtis had left for divine intervention, but in the context of extensive appreciation this reads like a theologian's technicality. The tone of the reviews was set by a laudatory three column essay in the *Observer* of 1 April 1934, by Sir Edward Grigg. He was not simply obliging an old friend. In 1936 he published his own testament *The Faith of an Englishman*. In it he quotes from Curtis, 'one of our most radical political thinkers,' exclusively and at considerable length, on why peace alone cannot be the goal of constructive statesmanship, and adds:

Mr Lionel Curtis, from the first volume of whose still unfinished book, *Civitas Dei*, the above passage is taken, goes on to say that 'no political science will furnish guidance in practical politics unless it proceeds from a definite conception of ultimate values.' ...Most of us would also probably agree that the ultimate aim of political science must be 'to bring into being an order of society based on the duty of each to all, irrespective of national limits.' That is the democratic Greek and Christian ideal, which Britain has already carried further than any other country in the world.[34]

In this company, Harold Nicolson's put-down in the *Telegraph*, 'sentimentality dressed up as scholarship,' is out of line. The *Spectator* referred more kindly to the 'mixture of nobility and naivety in his philosophy,' and asked, rather inattentively, considering Curtis's complaints about St Augustine: 'What is the Commonwealth? Is it a Civitas Dei or is it a liberalised *Leviathan*? Perhaps, after all, there is more of Hobbes than of St Augustine in Mr Curtis's thought,' (*Spectator*, 6 April 1934). *The Morning Post*, predictably found the thesis hardly convincing, but approved the moving argument for more altruism in society and politics. But it was, overall, an enviable critical response, ranging from J. L. Hammond in the *Manchester Guardian*, G. M. Young in the *Sunday Times* and Lord Lothian in the *Listener*, to the other weeklies, a great many local papers, including Irish and Indian, and the entire church press. For scores of reviewers and for readers in numbers that surprised and gratified his publisher Harold Macmillan, Curtis had, by and large, said it right.[35]

Curtis has been described in his declining years living on in Oxford,

As the Ancient Mariner of All Souls, meandering from the organic union of the Empire to the organic union of the world in *Civitas Dei* (a book which few of his colleagues read but referred to as *Civitas Mei*), and buttonholing visitors in the quad to help him draft a constitution for the world.[36]

It is a diminishing high-table image, though no doubt Oxford between the wars was as bored by such matters as she was by the Indian Empire and by officially inspired teaching about it. Certainly, Curtis's attempts with A. D. Lindsay (the Vice-Chancellor), Lord Lothian and the former missionary and novelist Edward Thompson

and others, to rejuvenate Indian studies at Oxford through Rhodes
House, or an equivalent 'Irwin' or 'Asia House', got nowhere. But
his perspectives on the function of political science and the meaning
of history were not unique or unregarded in the wider Anglo-India
public.

Montagu had kept a detailed account of his cold weather visit to
India to work on the 1919 legislation, recording both the stresses
of the working week and the imperial week-end relaxations of
hob-nobbing with maharajas and shooting game. There are regular
references to Curtis, sometimes thoroughly irritable, but in general
deeply appreciative. In a furious erruption at Curtis's sudden wave
of anxiety about going too far too fast with the reforms, Montagu
refers to 'this extraordinary man', whose influence both with the
Milnerite circle and with Geoffrey Dawson, editor of the *Times,*
and Valentine Chirol its India correspondent, is 'much to be
dreaded'. He records that, 'at three o'clock there came the holy
man Curtis,' and glumly wished that 'he sometimes made a joke.'
But they did see eye to eye. 'At last here was a person unprejudiced,
keenly interested, properly equipped.' 'I have used Curtis's paper...It
is the best thing that the man has done, and I think the best scheme
I have seen yet, and is well written. Many of its conclusions are
those at which I have tentatively independently arrived...'[37]

After the developments of the first post-First World War decade,
the Round Table associate Sir William Marris, who also participated
with Curtis and Meston in Montagu's labours in Delhi, came to
think it 'possible that we overjudged the pace eleven years ago'.
But, like many others, he did not abandon his certainties about
Britain's historical mission in India.[38]

If nationalist India was a minority interest at Oxford, there was
nevertheless an academic mainstream of colonial and imperial history
to which Curtis belonged. The components of his historiography
are deeply embedded in the work of his successor as Beit Lecturer
(Sir) Reginald Coupland (who was Beit Professor of the History
of the British Empire from 1920 to 1948, a Fellow of All Souls, and
a late and highly active addition to the Round Table 'moots' on
India). Like Curtis, he believed that a 'political science', the capacity
to act as the effective midwife to history, emerges as the voice of
realism only in a society that has evolved a rational structure of
institutions and of social relations. Standard reading for even quite

recent generations of students, Coupland's usual idiom is a drab narrative, acknowledged by H. N. Brailsford as 'useful at the level of fact' though 'flagrantly biased',[39] but he takes off into solemn elevations whenever he touches on the historically critical transformation of the moral consciousness of Englishmen in relation to Empire which, he believed crystallized round the Clapham Sect evangelicals and was given political expression notably by Wilberforce and Pitt.

The dawn Pitt heralded may be broadening very slowly into day; but at least the civilization of Africa is now something more than a theme for peroration. ...[British rule] has tried to regard them as fellow members with Englishmen of a world-wide society, weak, ignorant, undisciplined as yet, their faculties for the most part cramped and stunted, but capable of a development to which only the centuries ahead can tell the end.[40]

Whilst the heroisms of Livingstone in the chaotic pre-history of Africa are 'consecrated ground',[41] the intricate impediments to progress in our relations with a highly developed Indian nationalism call now for the refinement of moral awareness on all sides, and for the dry auxiliary judgments of the constitutional expert, in another phase of the unfolding historical imperative.[42]

God's Purpose and the India Office: Arthur Hirtzel

In a complacent retrospective review of his years at the India Office, Samuel Hoare (Lord Templewood) celebrated the high quality of its permanent officials, notably Findlater Stewart's predecessor Arthur Hirtzel, Secretary to the Political Department for eight years till 1917 and then a Secretary of State until 1930 as, 'a notable scholar for whom the Greek and Latin classics were an inspiring guide through the forest of Indian problems.'[43] Hirtzel's immersion in the classics amounted to something more than urbane recreation, since he had edited the complete works of Vergil for the Clarendon Press in 1900.[44] The implications of Bacon's aphorism as a paradigm for the British imperium to which he was devoted must have registered in very concrete terms. Rome prefigured for him, as for Curtis, a more tremendous fulfilment of the 'imperial idea'.

Under the crude materialism in which it often manifests itself, there is a high idealism in the conception of Empire. For what really animates the Imperialist is the firm, even if mistaken, belief that the race to which he belongs is the noblest, and the civilization and ideals for which it stands are the highest—are, in fact, so high that all the world must needs accept them. Now, this is an outlook upon life that is at once familiar to the Christian.

The idea of kingship is bound up with the idea of Christ.[45] The kingship of Christ, he insists, is not primarily a promise of individual salvation, but, as St Paul in fact recognized, of 'the redemption of the whole human race.... The trend of modern thought—of the doctrine, or hypothesis of evolution, for example—is all in the same direction'.[46] The British Empire is an historical agent of this collective salvation:

> given to us as a means to that great end for which Christ came into the world, the redemption of the human race. That is to say, it has been given to us to make it Christian. This is to be Britain's contribution to the redemption of mankind.[47]

Hirtzel's contribution to Indian constitutional history, as an unobtrusive and seemingly indestructable grey eminence, strategically lodged in the governmental structure at Morley's right hand, is described without false modesty in his private diaries, and his claims are supported, as Wolpert points out, by a good deal of other documentary evidence, notably from Morley himself.[48] Wolpert's general assessment of Hirtzel is worth quoting at some length, for what it says and for what it passes by. He was:

> Efficient, unobtrusive, unemotional, and highly intelligent. Hirtzel won Morley's complete confidence thanks to his 'ability and character'... Morley's 'right hand man' (Morley's phrase), Hirtzel had more opportunities than Godley, Ritchie, or any member of the Council of India to affect policy at moments of critical decision. Like Godley, he served as Simla's advocate whenever Morley appeared to become short-tempered or irate at the Government of India's course of action. He, too, manipulated assiduously against Gokhale, supported Minto's position at every possible opportunity, letting Morley 'work off some of his feelings' (Hirtzel's phrase) on him if a particularly sharp conflict between Whitehall and Simla seemed about ready to explode, writing 'private letters' to 'J. M.' more fully stating his arguments if verbal appeals failed. Taken separately, none of Hirtzel's 'victories' was significant, but the incremental impact of his daily influence, exercised as it was over a period of more than four years, can hardly be over-estimated. His diaries show that he never missed an opportunity.[49]

Like the bracelet of a ball-and-chain, Hirtzel figures in Morley's career at the India Office as an unyielding reminder of the dead weight against which Morley's relatively expansive liberalism had to struggle, but he performed at the same time an acceptable office, pragmatic, 'realistic' and tactical, and committed, despite his subtle obstructiveness, in quite general terms to the liberal rhetoric of imperial trusteeship and national evolution. But what is missing in this assessment is any reference to other considerations that go a long way to explain his paradoxically conservative commitment to the evolution of Indian nationalism. The evidence for this is in his diaries, his publications, and in his activities as a leading layman for the missionary movement in general and as Treasurer of the Oxford Mission to Calcutta in particular. In Wolpert's account, Hirtzel appears as the archetypal bureaucrat and a covert agent of reactionary imperialism, a *retiarius* in the political arena, instinctively tossing the net of institutionally woven power over potentially lethal opponents. But, though he was clearly a master of the *bureau* and undeniably a conservative functionary, he can be described no less accurately as an ideological mole, utilizing the inertias of the governmental process for transcendent purposes but working on a time scale that would reduce Morley's fussing to irrelevance.

Temperamentally quite unlike Curtis, cautious and risk-averse where Curtis was tireless in his pursuit of institutional improvement, he complements him in ways that emerge from the *Diaries* for 1907 and 1908. As a professional civil servant, Hirtzel fell in with the priorities of the Liberal administration, but there is reason to suppose that his own attitude was ambivalent, or at least not without nuance. He succeeded in 'softening the challenge' to the Government of India, represented by the Commission, by keeping a watchful eye on its terms of reference, but he also accused Morley, in his diary, of funk over publicizing its composition. The threat of this investigation had considerably irritated Minto, Simla and the ICS, but Hirtzel, revolving the possibility of 'forcing Gokhale to show his colours,'[50] and disown the 'extremists', had during the summer months of 1907 helped to negotiate the membership of the Commission, to which Hichens, despite a reported 'stiffness of mind' was to make his particularly industrious contribution. The Commission's eventual proposals, which included Gokhale's for working elective majorities on municipal councils, and for the constitution and development of village *panchayats,* were to come too late for the

1910 legislation, but 'were in good measure incorporated in the Government of India Act of 1919.'[51] Its nine volumes of evidence were a point of departure for Curtis.

A year later, the question of the vacant Bishopric of Bombay seems to occupy a more fundamental position in Hirtzel's frame of reference. On 4 March, 'J. M. allowed me to write to Gore' and, on 9 March, was,

> as amazed—moved, in fact—as I was at Gore's offering himself for Bombay. I told him I thought church and country could ill spare Gore, and gave his sermon on 'Church and the Poor' to show why: but it would be so splendid for India that I felt *hic est digitus Dei.*

This was no commonplace piece of ecclesiastical patronage. Gore, who identified himself closely with the Oxford Mission to Calcutta, had gone out in 1884 and again in 1890 to help the Mission at a time of crisis. He agonized over Bombay for some weeks before withdrawing.

He was to make a final visit in 1930, when he returned the orientalist commonplace that the trouble with Mahatma Gandhi, as with all Indians, 'is that he is entirely uninterested in facts.' But as the representatives of mammon in Birmingham were discovering at the time of the Bombay vacancy, Gore himself was very much interested in 'facts', and his 'realistic' liberalism, the spirituality of his theological scholarship and his personal saintliness seemed to both Hirtzel and Morley exactly what was required to 'stir' India at the time.[52]

Hirtzel was much less inclined than Curtis to see 'progressive' political and institutional arrangements either as a measure of spiritual development in themselves or as providing the essential structural precondition for it. In terms of the timing of constitutional development this difference places him to the right of Curtis, but there is really very little that separates them as Christian imperialists. They disagreed about the truly effective agencies of a history informed by the divine purpose. Both assumed an evolution towards inter-nationalism. But the political theorist looked to an administrative rationality sensitive to diffuse social developments, whilst the administrator looked to the only agency to his mind capable of advancing the full imperial idea, namely the missionary arm of the church. Curtis valued Gore's spiritual and intellectual authority, but for Hirtzel Gore was also an active pastoral figure, his feet firmly on the ground, just the man to lead the church in India into a delicate process of reorganization that was fundamental to its long mission of collective salvation and a precondition for India's authentic national maturity. He was the man also to remind the English in India of their individual obligations as the servants of a Christian monarchy and Empire.

On the first score Hirtzel was a radical, an enthusiast for the reunion of the churches in India and quite ready to accept changes in doctrine and liturgy that would accompany the growth of a truly self-governing Indian church. This was less true of Gore, who, at a number of points in the earlier stages of the controversy expressed his anxieties over reunion, and with whom Hirtzel openly disagreed on doctrinal aspects of this ecumenical development. No less advanced than E. J. Palmer (who was in the end installed at Bombay and worked for reunion over many years[53]), Hirtzel was scathing about evangelization through 'Anglican churches built in the suburban gothic style', where missionaries expounded the Bible in the light of the Thirty-Nine Articles, 'while clean little black choir boys in clean little white surplices sing their various versions of Hymns Ancient and Modern, or, it may be, the Hymnal Companion.'[54]

The concept of evangelization with which he identified will be discussed more fully in the following chapter, but it had its own urgency, and he was by no means complacent about the outcome.

The nationalist spirit is growing—and properly growing, the Indianization of the Government will proceed more rapidly as time goes on; India is steadily drawing nearer to the goal which Great Britain has set before her. There is no true liberty but Christian liberty, and the Church has no time to lose if, when Indians come to govern themselves in accordance with Indian ideas, Indian ideas are to be Christian ideas.[55]

What he means by 'Christian ideas' is conveyed in terms of a distinction between evangelizing and proselytizing, for which he found support in the work of the missionary Bernard Lucas, and in terms of: 'the conception of Personality, and above all, of course, in the Personality of the historical Christ. We lay increasing stress upon that point of view nowadays...'[56] Gore was as fine an instance of the developed Christian personality as could be found, and such an example:

Is of the very greatest importance in dealing with India, because what India needs is personality. The great defect of the character which Hinduism engenders is lack of personality. Not only does all pantheism tend to weaken the sense of individuality, but the particular form of pantheism which the Hindu religion takes annihilates it altogether, regarding it simply as an illusion, to be finally dispelled only by the complete suppression of the will to live and lead a separate existence.[57]

Gore's example would work, as the Oxford Mission had always worked, on the educated classes of India. It would also work, where it was badly needed, on the British representatives of the Raj, providentially heirs to a spirit of individual enterprise that 'is the glory of the Anglo-Saxon race,' but at risk of running to seed if it is not 'taken up into and controlled by, a wider whole,' within the 'organic parts of a living Empire.'[58]

The British as Christians in India

It is very easy to find comment on the importance of the behaviour of the individual Englishman and woman in India. The implicit terms of reference are provided by moments in the folklore of the Raj, the authoritarian 'service' of the Punjab school of administrators, for instance, but also Curzon's infliction of collective disgrace and severe sanctions on the 9th Lancers, after a notorious incident involving the beating and subsequent death of a native cook. There were other incidents, more trivial but contentious and symbolically important, such as the two affairs involving Sir William Lee-Warner, vice-chairman of the Council of India in 1906, in allegations of verbal and physical violence involving Indians in England. He was cited as an assailant in one case and claimed to be a victim in another.[59] Serious imperialists of every kind saw larger purposes being defeated by the accumulating episodes of arrogance and discourtesy, minor detonations gradually loosening the avalanche of a Himalayan catastrophe. Keir Hardie lamented the 'growing estrangement between native and European.'[60] Edwyn Bevan set the 'seamy side', the 'very ugly fact' of the frequent rudeness of the Englishman against the moral justification for British dominance, its utilitarian defence of the good of the greatest number under the guidance of 'British character' and the 'spiritual influence of tradition.'[61] A doctor with experience of India entered his own examples of British arrogance against Katherine Mayo's itemization of oriental depravities in *Mother India* and derided the hypocrisy of British preaching of Christian gentleness, self-control and humility to a subject population.[62] The wickedness of British race feeling was a recurrent theme in the journalism and the popular books of the Revd C. F. Andrews.

This note of guilty apology is not sounded by Hirtzel. Indeed, when Morley received a missionary's letter, forwarded by the Archbishop, complaining about the overbearing arrogance of Kitchener and blaming unrest on a 'wicked race domination', he promptly reminded Morley of Kitchener's circular to British officers:

And he agreed that this was not the language of wicked race domination. The letter did not make much impression; in fact, writing to Lord Minto immediately after, though he sent an extract from it...he actually suggested Kitchener for Punjab.[63]

Morley's letter to Minto had omitted an invidious allusion to Kitchener's influence at Simla. Shortly afterwards Hirtzel complained that Valentine Chirol of the *Times* was 'poisoning J. M's mind against Kitchener.'

But Hirtzel also believed that Christianity would 'find its way' in India if every Englishman there recommended it by his example and his influence, or at least did nothing to check it by his conduct.[64] By the end of the Second World War concern among influential figures at the failure of many of their compatriots to do anything of the kind was pervasive.

There are two interesting indications of this concern, and neither can be described as the product of a merely expedient view of the undesirable consequences of individual bad behaviour for an orderly management of the Raj. Both were expressions of the Christian imperial frame of reference. The first is in *Dyarchy*. *Dyarchy* was one of Curtis's most 'collective' publications, and it does individualize at least part of the constituency he drew into the porous structure of his India inquiry. Ellinwood points out that on the British side he contacted journalists, educators, businessmen and officials in India, and that 'although many conservative Englishmen opposed his ideas, in Bengal he found a group of British businessmen and Indian leaders who were sympathetic.'[65] He lists the sixty-four English and ninety Indian signatories to a Joint Address justifying the twelve points on which they agreed, a version of the dyarchy proposal to all intents and purposes the same as that contained in the letter to Bhupendra Nath Basu. But Ellinwood's description of the English is somewhat misleading. Curtis claims that the list was limited only by the physical problem of collecting signatures and would, under less hectic circumstances, have been considerably longer. Furthermore, of the sixty-four Englishmen, while twenty-seven are listed in the directories as businessmen, with at least another eight falling in all probability into the same category, with four journalists (working for *Capital,* and the *Civil and Military Gazette*), a lawyer, a soldier and a couple of professional educators, no less than eighteen were directly involved in mission work of one kind or another. K. T. Paul, an Indian Christian, active for nationalism and increasingly well known in England, appears on the other list. There are no chaplains, as is hardly surprising, from the Indian Ecclesiastical Establishment, but the missionaries were, of course directly in contact with Indian Christians, and in particular with non-Christian groups of students. They came from a good range of organizations and denominations and included most of those who were well known to and highly regarded by church-people back in England. The best known were W. E. S. Holland, the author of widely read books about India as well as a distinguished teacher, P. N. F. Young of the Cambridge Mission to Delhi, A. G. Hogg, the theologian from Madras Christian College, and Bernard Lucas of the London Missionary Society, with whose evangelical theology Hirtzel had identified.

It would be foolish to suppose that all of these different groups, from businessmen to missionaries, converged on such a set of proposals for quite the same reasons. But there were broad arguments about the empire which were accepted on much the same terms, and it was to those arguments that the twelve points of agreement are logically related. They agree on the potential evolution of a Christianized Empire, and on the fallible instruments for its realization, on the 'witness' of individuals (often unconscious, embedded in British behaviour) to the saving and exemplary reality of Christ in Indian society, the quickening reality of what the theologians described as personality, developed but also wilfully denied by Englishmen and women of the Raj.

Eleven of the numbered paragraphs in the introduction to *Dyarchy* are addressed directly to Morley's exclamation, which Curtis quotes, that 'India is a country where bad manners are a crime.'

They give a particular emphasis to a running discussion about the effective exercise of political authority.

My point is that government must have legal powers to maintain order wherever it is threatened. But I want to add that it will fail utterly, and deserves to fail, unless it deals with the ultimate causes of disorder...Amongst educated Indians with whom I am acquainted there are some who are, as I feel, definitely and finally embittered against the British connection. In every instance this bitterness had its roots in some rankling memory of insult at the hands of a European. (*Dyarchy*, p. xlix).

He goes on to provide illustrations, and to argue that the class of Englishmen who consider it their duty to insult Indians whenever the occasion arises,

constitute an incomparably greater danger than anarchists. And in offering this opinion I am not echoing the views of people like Mrs Besant, Mr Andrews, or Mr Ramsay MacDonald. I am saying what was said to me insistently by experienced senior officers who honestly regarded my own political views as dangerous.(*Dyarchy*, p. il)

Curtis suggests that those guilty of such behaviour have accepted the principle of mutual exclusion embodied in the caste system. They misrepresent Christianity as a white man's religion and open the field to a proselytizing Islam. The threat of 'bad manners' is unequivocally a threat to political authority itself. We should, therefore, revive the old power to 'deport Europeans whose conduct is a danger to the peace of India to the country of their origin...a far milder measure than to exile Indians for a like reason.' A footnote observes, with satisfaction, that Lord Cromer had given a European guilty of improper behaviour to an Egyptian forty-eight hours to quit Egypt.

The suggestion was not taken up, but in 1922 another response, reflecting perhaps Hirtzel's angle of vision rather more than Curtis's, materialized from inside the upper levels of the Church of England establishment. Hirtzel was a member of the committee, chaired by the Bishop of Stepney, which launched a Mission of Help to the English in India in the cold weather of 1922–3. A letter of support in the *Church Times* of 24 January 1922 was signed by Lord Crewe (Morley's successor as Secretary of State for India), Lord Curzon (Viceroy till 1905), Lord Chelmsford (Viceroy till 1921), General Claud Jacob, and others. This was not in fact a venture such figures could afford to support lightly. As the final report was to point out: 'the national flag might have been waved, or an India for the Indians proclaimed, by well meaning and injudicious speakers.'[66] The thirty-five missioners were in fact recruited from the same pool of dependable and enthusiastic clerics as sustained the crusading activities of the ICF:[67] they were upwardly mobile in terms of the church hierarchy, the incumbents of well endowed and important 'livings'. An unrepresentatively high proportion were former army padres, with a VC, two MCs, a DSO and other honours among them. A substantial proportion, including the best known, like Theodore Woods, Bishop of Peterborough and later of Winchester, J. C. Pringle of the Charity Organization Society and Canon Spencer Elliott of Sheffield, were themselves ICF Executive or Council members, or active supporters. For most of them India was a new experience, and they had no intention of venturing to offer patronizing 'political' advice. The language of mutual service, duty and goodwill within the established order covered both the domestic social conflicts of the post-First World War period, moralized by 'Woodbine Willie' and others in the powerful imagery of wartime sacrifice and unity, and also the alien complexities of India within the historical evolution of the imperial order.[68]

It was a notable decade in Britain for religious crusades, missions and movements. Translated for a few weeks to a scattering of the suburban-gothic churches of the Raj, the Mission of Help was an attenuated echo of the extensively reported meetings and overflowing churches of the ICF crusades. But traces of its passage survive in the Indian Diocesan magazines, the press and published reminiscences.[69] There is no reason to question the references to crowded congregations (particularly in Bombay and Colombo), the keen support given by leading figures, commanding officers and civil servants in the communities visited by the dispersed missioners, earnest discussions in the clubs among groups of businessmen and lawyers, and the like. These references may or may not be evidence of 'success'. They are remarkably consistent evidence of the pervasiveness of the field of discourse more elaborately deployed by figures such as Hirtzel and Curtis.

Bishop Foss Westcott, the Metropolitan, ran out the Personality argument in the *Calcutta Diocesan Record*, registering the 'conviction that the development of the Indian personality, both individual and national, required the increase of liberty and responsibility which the transfer (of power) would bestow,' applying the argument also to the Indian Church Measure.[70] A letter in the *Bombay Diocesan Magazine* pointed out that the Mission was not for the heathen, though 'indirectly of course it will be for the evangelisation of the heathen, as the greatest power for drawing them to Christ is by seeing Him in us.'[71] References to the new stresses on the British in India were frequent; as they also were to the exemplary standards many of them already set. In Madras Lord Willingdon emphasized on behalf of the Mission the 'need of a spiritual anchor in these years of doubt and unrest.' The Bishop of Peterborough twice addressed the Législature in Calcutta. In Lahore the Mission enjoyed the support of the Governor and his wife, and was joined by American Presbyterians and by Non-conformists. In New Delhi the Commander in Chief and Lady Rawlinson were at home to four hundred guests, who were addressed by the Dean of Manchester.[72] The establishment was behind the mission, and despite faltering moments, the missioners met with a receptive and well organized response. The *Bombay Diocesan Magazine* gave a couple of pages to William Law's *Serious Call* (1728), pointedly quoting it as a 'book for the present time here in India:'

It is not left to any women in the world to trifle away their time in the follies and impertinencies of fashionable life, nor to any men to resign themselves up to worldly cares and concerns: it is not left to the rich to gratify their passions...[73]

The Editor also took up the Bishop of Peterborough, who had ventured to suggest that the 'A' Class servants of the Raj were being shepherded by 'B' and 'C' class chaplains, by pointing out that 1200 communions had been made the previous Easter in Bombay out of a possible 6000 Church of England adherents, a fair trawl for 'B' and 'C' Class chaplains responsible for 'A' Class congregations. Could any town in the Diocese of Peterborough do as well?[74]

It is pointless to speculate on the consequences of such an enterprise. Among others, the Chaplain of Deolali spoke bravely of the 'great and permanent good' done by the mission, but recalled the parable of the sower, a warning against 'slipping back into the slack, careless, materialistic habits of pre- Mission days.'[75] But the Mission of Help exposed a facet of the official mind that has been neglected, partly perhaps because of the British reticence of those, like Lord Lloyd, Governor of Bombay at the time, who were not themselves its ordained spokesmen. Lloyd, as his biographers make clear, had an unadvertized but intense personal conviction as a Christian, in the light of which he saw his own compulsively arduous service for the Empire.[76] His accepted place on the political right, as one of the ablest of the Tory die-hards, distracts attention from an aspect of the public significance of his position, by insulating that private commitment from his commitment to the Raj. His sternly authoritative support for the missionary enterprise[77] expressed convictions shared with Hirtzel, but also with the 'liberal' Lord Meston, who had shocked many of his ICS colleagues by officially attending the opening session of the Congress meetings in Lucknow in 1916 and, in Curtis's company, a Muslim League session.[78] Back in England since 1918 on account of poor health, Meston had inspired the 1921 Annual General Meeting of the Cambridge Mission to Delhi.[79] Like Coupland, he shared Curtis's urge to push his faith in what he took to be a Christian universe as far as reason would let it go.[80] The impulse places both of them to the left of Lloyd and Hirtzel on the continuum of political judgments on the evolution of the Raj. But the distance between them on that dimension was not as wide as appeared to many at the time and, more important, this kind of political geometry is an impoverished model of the discursive space in which they all moved. For they were all Christian imperialists in more than form. The following chapter examines in greater detail the stable structure of what they and others believed and disbelieved about the 'eternal things', the beliefs which, according to Gore, determine what a society is in the long run to become. It does so by concentrating on those who were most seriously concerned with the nature of religious belief and the varieties of religious experience, specifically the theologians and intellectuals who gave their attention to the confrontation of faiths, Christian, Hindu and Muslim, in South Asia. But behind them one must first acknowledge a European preoccupation with the East and its religions which had already been flourishing for many years before the first stirrings of modern Indian nationalism.

CHAPTER 3

Nationalism and Theology

The Oriental Renaissance and British Orientalism

The British response to its Indian Empire in the nationalist period, it need hardly be said, is only one episode in encounters of immense practical and ideological complexity involving the whole range of European civilizations and an orient of vast extent and diversity over many centuries. These encounters have included every kind of response, from the eagerly receptive to the obtusely contemptuous, and on this panoramic canvas the debts of West to East, even more than diffusions and borrowings in the opposite direction, have hitherto been inadequately exposed and even, in sometimes rather obvious instances, neglected, as Raymond Schwab has argued in an erudite and richly allusive study of what he calls the Oriental Renaissance.[1] Gandhi's western admirers, for instance, often pointed to the 'Christian' influence that reached him, during his period in South Africa, through his correspondence with Tolstoy on non-violence. But Tolstoy's Christianity was itself 'underpinned by the great Hindu doctrines, confirmed by the Buddha,' and he had immersed himself in the Indic scholarship of such European students of oriental religions as Burnouf and Schopenhauer, as well as the Vedanta of Shankara, the Upanishads and Swami Vivekananda.[2]

This extensive but still somewhat obscure flowering of an Oriental Renaissance provides a broad historical background to this study. It was sustained by scholars who travelled less frequently to India than between England, Germany and France, successively the leading centres of Indian studies, and was overwhelmingly a process of discovery based in the first instance on the philological penetration of texts and the recovery of lost languages. It was the work of scholars and literary thinkers bound to Europe and looking for fresh resources with which to enter, more or less indirectly, into an extended process of renegotiation with their own cultural inheritance.[3] But it needs to be distinguished from the much narrower theme of British orientalism itself.

'It is unfair to paint a West peopled exclusively by contemptuous missionaries and stiff philologists through whom together India had supposedly been entirely misunderstood,'[4] for the European scholarship that started to emerge after 1830 was truly formidable, and even much earlier there were remarkable achievements. The French missionary Father Pons, who led English linguistic scholarship by four decades, is described by Schwab as 'accurate and broadminded' in a remarkable letter of 1740. The letter contained some 'dubious parallels' but nevertheless, 'one is amazed at the perspicacity with which Pons analysed the authentic essence of Hindu systems and applied fundamental distinctions.'[5] He was, notably, the first to distinguish the two theologies of the 'Brahmanic' and the 'popular', a distinction with dialectical implications for the connections between religion and the social order which have been illuminated in modern Indian scholarship.[6]

Finer distinctions, between Vedism and commentary, between practical and mystical religion and between different sects and schools of Hinduism were pursued with great clarity by Pastor Jean Jaques Bochinger of Strasbourg (d. 1831), who was primarily concerned with the importance *for the Christian* of Indian contemplation and mysticism. The title of his last work, 'On the connections between the Contemplative Life among the Indic and Buddhist Peoples and the similar Phenomena in the History of Islam and Christianity', suggests an equivalence, inconceivable in an earlier age, between the different forms of spirituality. He even opened up the possibility that western Platonism and Neoplatonism are outer ramifications of an originally Indian mysticism. The scholars of the Oriental Renaissance commenced a serious dialogue between creeds and systems of belief, by the analytical comparison of terms used in the different traditions, in effect developing a lexicon of religous categories, and exploring the more or less misleading matching of concepts, (for example: Trinity and Trimurti, Incarnation and Avatara, Duty and Dharma), and the significance of gaps and untranslatable elements. And, of course, their data was not exclusively textual. The Abbé Dubois left France before the end of the eighteenth century to spend many years in Mysore 'trying to understand the society and its religion and finally giving an excellent description of it.'[7] Commenting critically on Dubois's 'voluntaristic explanation' of the development of the caste system, (it attaches a doubtful importance to the ancient legislators), Dumont acknowledges him as 'this father of anthropologists.'

This was real scholarship, the beginnings of a 'long and exacting task.' It had to contend, however, against a looser kind of general interest, a 'prolonged rush to know somehow, after a fashion...the use of partial knowledge...'[8] and, of critical importance in the context of the British Raj, there was the decline of England as a centre of scholarly activity. For:

The civil servants imbued with the Victorian spirit, to whom Macaulay must have seemed a dazzling precursor, no longer went to India to gain knowledge of a new world or its mode of existence but to maintain British prestige or complete a useful phase in their careers. The literature written by company employees or their relatives prior to Rudyard Kipling created a new view of India. This phenomenon occurred precisely at the time that the fashion for orientalism which invaded European salons and intellectual reviews was taking shape: this explains why Great Britain was not the home of the Oriental Renaissance. One would have expected to find it there, since India was under British dominion, but that was precisely why it was not.[9]

There was perhaps a local contributory factor to this decline. The German Max Müller, a brilliant popularizer of Indian studies who went to Oxford to publish his edition of the *Rig Veda* in 1848 and stayed till his death in 1900, (without, however, ever visiting India) was defeated in 1860 for the Boden Chair of Sanskrit by Monier-Williams (d. 1899), allegedly because the Tory country clergy powerful among the fourteen hundred or so electors suspected the Prince Consort of a plot to stiffen Oxford with a German professoriate. Müller continued to produce important work on philology and comparative religion but his bitter and not entirely unjustified hatred of the colourless Monier-Williams was to cramp the development of the Indian Institute at Oxford. Latterly, Monier-Williams developed a sour evangelical hostility to the non-Christian religions, and to Müller's Oxford University Press series of the Sacred Books of the East in particular.[10]

The scholars and semi-scholars of the European Oriental

Renaissance identified the civilizations of India centrally in terms of religion and of societies organized round religious systems. Racial themes were of great importance, particularly the idea of a common Aryan root linking East and West, an idea that was put to various uses by Englishmen in relation to the Raj. But race was seen as expressing itself in the variants of a pervasive religious idiom, of ultimate categories and their correlates in social orders and forms, and this was true whether the observers' impulses were charitable or critical.

The British themselves, after Macaulay, continued to respond to India as a complex religious civilization. But the British imperial connection as it developed introduced a decisive difference. It built antagonism and subordination into the confrontation, and restricted the terms in which change, assimilation and development could be conceived. There is no mystery about the structural process through which this took place. Francis Hutchins has sketched the transmutation of the domestic British class structure that inevitably ensued in British India. This decomposed J. S. Mill's optimistic compound of professional middle-class and liberal sentiment, which had accounted for his attempt to protect the East India Company from Parliamentary control, and from corruption by an illiberal system of party patronage.

The later nineteenth century saw just the reverse of Mill's expectations emerge, with a conservative official class, dedicated to preserving the *status quo* as a way of insuring their own privileges and position, indignant at the intervention of liberal parliamentarians.[11]

The British official class, which had fought self-consciously at home for individual rights against the English aristocracy, itself became in India a middle-class aristocracy, invoking duty and loyalty to underwrite a highly rewarding *status quo*. In the process a subtle and effective blend of utilitarian political theory and evangelical religion emerged, increasingly preoccupied with the problem of order and authority, and now interested in Indian principles of government and the Indian religions only in terms of their compatibility with British purposes and as a benign supplement to the exercise of force.[12]

But Hutchins is sweeping about the secularization of the British ruling class in India itself, its substitution in the vacuum created by the Victorian loss of faith of a vague norm of good conduct, industry and integrity, for any authentic religious commitment to the transformation of a benighted East. It is no doubt true that for many the code of 'good conduct' was indeed 'the only thing remaining and was adhered to with a vehemence proportional to the anguished doubt about the loss of that faith.'[13] Sir Malcolm Darling, the Etonian son of a clergyman, lost his faith in 'the all questioning atmosphere' of King's College Cambridge, but was sustained by the advice of Bishop Creighton, that 'every life has to be built upon something...do that duty which lies nearest to hand.' But there were many others, like Sir George Cunningham, Fettes College, and Magdalen College, Oxford, Private Secretary to Lord Irwin from 1926 to 1931 and a formidable Governor of the North West Frontier province in the decade before independence, who committed themselves to imperial service in the tradition of the Lawrences, Nicholson and Edwards: 'sound British training, sound character, profound religious conviction.'[14]

In any event, anguished doubt about loss of faith has seldom been a universal condition while habitual, unreflective commitment was sustained, at least in the English public schools which furnished the official class, until relatively recently. It was not the well-bottomed faith urged by clergy and missionaries,[15] but it survived to provide ultimate sanction for the imperial connection for at least a significant proportion of British imperialists in India and their supporters at home. Behind the utilitarian preoccupation of the Raj with the operation of a system of law and administration, lay an evangelical reforming impulse, and it was from the rational operation of this system that both India's moral and her material well-being were now assumed to derive.[16]

In general, any indigenous challenge to this system was seen by the official class in India as morally outrageous as well as politically foolish. However, our concern here is only in part with the middle-class aristocracy of the British in India and their clear perceptions of material self-interest, because:

[The] regrettable fact...was that the English public did listen to the Indian nationalists and their English supporters, and the Government of India found itself increasingly ham-strung by a self-conscious, conscience-striken government at home, the result being a disastrously equivocal policy towards the nationalist movement.[17]

The conscience was, politically, a liberal one, but the language of equivocation was expressed in a discourse with distant roots in the Oriental Renaissance. The 'utilitarian' voice of the official 'man on the spot' commanded respectful attention back home, but never as much as it demanded, because there were other voices, reaching the public at one or more removes, particularly from those most directly and professionally concerned with the religions of India. They did not speak in unison and some carried further than others, though these were not necessarily the most acute, and in general what was picked up from the missionary theologians by a wider India public was a degraded version of the original message. However, though they cannot always be described as supporters of the Indian nationalists as a political species, these theological interpreters of the imperial connection did provide arguments for endorsing 'Indian Nationalism' as an historical process.

An adequate historical examination of the influence of theological and missionary thinking between the wars remains to be undertaken,[18] but we can at least identify what appear to be the major components of a 'Christian' response to the imperial predicament. It was structured round a comparison and evaluation of religious categories and constituted a stable and recurring element in debate over the Raj.

British Theologians and the Problem of Hinduism

In the early months of 1931 some comments from Gandhi on the future of foreign missions under Swaraj caused considerable turbulence in Christian circles, both in India and at home. Closing down correspondence on the subject in his newspaper *Young India* on 4 June, he blamed the 'incautious zeal of reporters who trusted too much to memory' for promoting a discussion he would 'fain have avoided'. A month earlier he had pointed out that his views had not in fact changed since 1916 and that he had repeated them often enough on Christian platforms. No doubt under Swaraj foreign missionaries would be permitted to continue their proselytizing as before, in his view in the wrong way, but the facts remained that there is no one true religion, that India's religions are adequate for her peoples, and that the Christian's task in India is service to its peoples and not the promotion of culturally irrelevant doctrine. Some, but not all, missionary opinion was outraged, and the missionaries were not left unsupported.[19] At the SPG Anniversary in London, the Hon. Edward Cadogan, who had accompanied the Simon Commission of 1928 to India, took Gandhi to task for ill-informed resentment, as did A. I. Mayhew, formerly Director of Education for the Government of India in the Central Provinces and the Rt. Hon. L. S. Amery, who was a close friend of both Curtis and Coupland in the Milnerite circle, Colonial Secretary 1924–9 and subsequently Secretary of State for India, from 1940–5. Amery, an imperialist who had been born in India, observed that a 'pioneer Empire and a stay at home church went ill together.'[20]

The church newspaper *The Guardian* for 7 August printed a lengthy assault by the Rt. Revd Henry Whitehead, formerly Bishop of Madras, on the 'perverted and exaggerated patriotism' of Gandhi's view that 'religion is essentially a national product and that to hold fast to the national religion is a part of true patriotism.' Such reactions expressed not just anxiety about the future of the missionary enterprise itself, but also about the quality of the nationalism lying behind Gandhi's attack, the threat, errupting like a boil beneath a dangerously taut surface and promising catastrophic historical consequences, of a comprehensive rejection of Britain's contribution to the evolution of the subcontinent.

As a theologian Gandhi was eclectic and unsystematic, but he has, for the time being at least, been left with the last word in a major theological debate. In the mainline Christian tradition, 'exclusivism', the claim to the possession of *the* truth about the ultimate reality with which religion is concerned has, in the words of the distinguished contemporary theologian John Hick, 'largely faded away'.[21] Gandhi's position on the valid diversity of religious languages is very generally accepted.

Hick, in fact, makes a number of basic distinctions for his own purposes in the process of justifying this gradual 'revolution' or trend away from theological exclusivism which may help to clarify a discussion of the confused and selective British response to Hinduism and, indeed, to Islam.

His own position seems to correspond very closely to the one adopted with far less intellectual labour by Gandhi, and this he describes as 'religious pluralism'. Hinduism as a religious tradition is notoriously receptive to variation, inclusivism and alternatives, so such a position was quite natural to Gandhi. It must, however, represent a serious problem for the Christian. For there is an apparent contradiction between faith in the truth of Christian revelation, most crucially in the doctrine of the Incarnation and God's unique intervention in history through the historical person of Jesus Christ, and, on the other hand, the recognition that though all forms of access through religion to the ultimate reality are highly imperfect, all, or several, can provide access to *different aspects* of that reality. This is clearly a far stronger position than the familiar and patronizing concession that non-Christian religions are informed by a religious impulse or craving which, though fatally misshapen, is at least in itself authentic, a concession for which even an exclusive theology can find room.

The Oriental Renaissance furnishes examples of relatively thorough-going religious pluralism, but there are only slight gestures in that direction in British thinking about South Asian religion between the wars. *Ex*clusivist dismissals certainly recur, but far more common, indeed almost standard, is one version or another of what Hick decribes as *in*clusivism, an intermediate position which he also rejects. The inclusivist asserts that a transformative salvation *through Christ* takes place not only in what acknowledges itself as Christian history but in the other great religious traditions as well, so that we can reasonably speak, (even more positively, it seems, than the Middle Ages spoke of those who had lived without sin '*dinanzi al Cristianesmo*' existing in sadness but without torment in Dante's first circle of Hell)[22] of 'honorary Christians', or of the 'anonymous Christian' described by Karl Rahner, or even of the 'unknown Christ of Hinduism.'[23] Christ may be present in individual or society, unannounced and unacknowledged.

The *theological* problems with this view are generalized by Hick, but as far as this discussion is concerned they will emerge with more pertinence in the context of later comments on Hogg's contribution to missionary theology. The theological argument may in itself be of no great concern to the incorrigibly secular social scientist, for whom such categories are, in Hobbes's term, of unusually 'inconstant signification', names of things which 'please and displease us' rather than names for verifiable entities,[24] but they do throw an oblique light on the non-theological, ultimately political implications of what can be broadly identified as the *inclusivist response* to 'Hinduism' in the period between the World Wars.

The belief that non-Christian religions could, and indeed must grow towards and eventually into Christianity was earnestly articulated by Christian thinkers. It permeated the missionary world and percolated through to those lay people who took their churchmanship reasonably seriously. The corollary, of course, was that the emerging spirit could be stifled and perverted. The staple judgment that such distortion or perversion was taking place was promptly and emphatically invoked when events in India took an unacceptable turn. The flurry following Gandhi's reported statement on missions was just one example. A brief comparison of reactions to Gandhi with those provoked by less Christian but no less self-consciously religious figures in the nationalist movement establishes the general pattern.

British Christians conducted a prolonged and uneven courtship with Gandhi which will be considered in greater detail in a later chapter. The view was that he offered much to the inclusivist paradigm: his Christlike gentleness, conciliatory impulses and gestures, his acknowledgement of the ethical teachings of Jesus. In his personal conduct so evidently a better Christian than most British Christians themselves, he nevertheless persisted in dismissing as inconsequential the most fundamental elements of Christian belief, and endorsing practices and commitments on the far side of the critical divide between a rational society and one caught in the trap of its own historical failures. The Christian vision of Lord Irwin was the only one to indicate the path for an authentic and transformative nationalism. Therefore, it was seen as a tragedy that Gandhi as India's leader should stall on the antagonism to 'reality' built into Hinduism's flawed repertoire of fundamental insights.

Far less ambivalent than the reaction to Gandhi was the response to the Hindu nationalism of B. G. Tilak, who died at the opening of the inter-war period. As the Marxist Bipan Chandra points out, in a period when the socialist alternative was not yet available as an option to Indian nationalists, 'neither Tilak nor Gandhi transcended the Moderate economic political programme or social vision.'[25] The theory behind Tilak's nationalism was anti-imperialist but, in Chandra's terminology, bourgeois, congruent with the interests of the emerging industrial bourgeoisie. Tilak's extremism was none the less thoroughly alarming to the British. This was in part because it was uncompromisingly anti-imperialist, but also because, unlike Gokhale, who was immensely attractive to British liberals as a representative of Indian nationalism,[26] Tilak's political programme struck at the tap root of imperialist assumptions about leaders and masses.

In sacrifice and courage G. K. Gokhale was no whit a lesser man than Tilak. But the former had no faith in the people; he was afraid that any mass movement would incur the wrath of the British Government which would result in the total destruction of the existing political movement.[27]

The founding of Tilak's Home Rule League in Karnataka, Maharashtra and Bombay in 1916 (in parallel with Annie Besant's, with its strength in Madras, but with extensions in Gujarat and Sind), confronted the authorities with unprecedented popular involvement from outside the 'brahman' category, and even from the supposedly politically backward.[28] Furthermore, Tilak attempted to develop his mass appeal in a religious idiom deriving from his Maharashtrian home base, though, to be sure, with only limited success where the brahmanical idiom of his revivalism could not carry.

Standard British responses to Tilak's extremism focus not on his popular appeal but on the unreason of which this evidently regressive and theologically reactionary Hinduism was taken to be both symptom and agent. A representative response is summarized in a standard public school textbook which was reprinted seven times between 1930 and 1948, D. C. Somervell's *The British Empire*. Somervell taught first at Repton public school, where, incidentally, he used Curtis's *Commonwealth of Nations*, to which William Temple (himself Headmaster of Repton from 1910 to 1913) had introduced him, and then at Tonbridge. His paragraph on Tilak refers to the gradual abandonment of the pursuit of social reforms 'which alone could provide a healthy foundation for Indian self-government' in favour of 'barren agitation' and the 'senseless glorification of Hindu *culture*.' Sommervell specifies, in particular the revealing, even incriminating defence by Congress of a legal age for marriage at ten rather than twelve years.[29] There is no place, quite clearly, for Christ in this nationalist perversion of Hinduism. Elsewhere, Somervell notes, however, that the other side of the movement 'is now once again bearing fruit, reinforced by the influence of the Christian missions, an influence far wider, as has been said, than the statistics of actual conversion to Christianity would suggest.'[30]

Tilak's attempt as a politician to reach out to form alliances on a continental scale, using whatever cultural weapons lay to hand, is reduced here to the congenital unreason of a 'religion' which offers nothing in response to the inclusivist invitation of a liberal theology, and is in itself a sufficient measure of the pathological infirmity of the extremist politics associated with it.

For the British, however confusedly, what Hinduism was taken to represent as a system of belief was of continuing concern. We should now turn to those for whom it was a particularly serious preoccupation, the 'professional' Christians, many of whom were greatly disturbed by Gandhi's attitude to the corporate expression of British faith in the Gospel.

For the theologian, religious doctrine and religious practice can only be allowed a limited justification on merely anthropological or sociological grounds. This must be true whether he chooses to concentrate on the intransigent and adversary in his consideration of encounters between Faiths, or on dialogue, outreach, interface and meeting point. At one level or another, he is bound to ask fundamental comparative questions about the adequacy of the approach afforded by any given religious tradition to an ultimate Reality. Such comparative problems present themselves differently to the 'exclusivist', 'inclusivist' and the 'pluralist'. Hick's three broad categories, in fact, seem to an outsider to represent ascending levels of theoretical difficulty, a series of steps from relatively easy dogmatic and doctrinal solutions, which label other religions as 'wrong', towards an active and exploratory theoretical relativism. But whatever position the thoughtful Christian may take on this continuum, he will presumably need to be able to see his own faith in comparison with others and to make discriminations and qualititative judgments.

Gandhi's reaction to the missionary presence in general was dismissive and had its origins in bad experiences early in his life. It was barely modified by subsequent friendships with people like C. F. Andrews and the American, Stanley Jones. But it has been shown, in defence of the missionaries, in the detailed studies of Eric Sharpe and others, that 'the libel of missionary obscurantism is not supported by advances in understanding through the 1920s and 1930s.'[31] A number of influential thinkers explored the encounter of faiths with clarity and rigour in a situation that was greatly complicated by rapidly fermenting changes in both European and

Indian Christianity itself and, over a long period of time, in Hinduism. None of these developments, however, whether in Hinduism, in Indian Christianity, or in the work of non-Indian missionary theologians, can profitably be considered apart from the development of the Indian nationalist movement.

As far as the theological debates themselves are concerned, there was much emphasis on sympathetic understanding of the oriental religions, and Gandhi's criticisms seemed particularly wounding on that account. However, it must be added that there was no simple correspondence between political liberalism, on the one hand, and theological liberalism, on the other, for it was perfectly possible to sympathize with the nationalist movement and still to believe that Hinduism and Islam stood in the way of the development of God's purpose. Such a position would call for a fundamental and inescapable confrontation of beliefs, to be pursued, of course, in terms of its 'challenging relevance',[32] rather than through crass attempts to convert the heathen.

The possibility of productive rather than abrasive confrontation seemed to be enhanced by the appeal to a distinction which was frequently invoked between Christ and Christianity, between the indwelling spirit and the historically contingent western institution. The distinction could be construed in different ways. It was made by Gandhi himself. It could also be made in a radical, even subversive spirit by 'eccentric' British clergymen like C. F. Andrews and Verrier Elwin. Both, in different ways, tried to get closer to Christ by distancing themselves from their church as an institution, (Andrews finally in 1914, when he went at Gokhale's insistence to join Gandhi in South Africa, and Elwin in 1935). It could be made by Indians, both Christian and non-Christian, and by others who felt less guilty about British imperialism, or less hostile to it, and who optimistically anticipated a new and indigenous Indian witness to a common faith.[33]

However, the project of disconnecting the universal Christ from the merely western institution of the church was not always thought through. Did it, on reflection, open the way to a fulfilment of Hinduism in Christ? A. G. Hogg was a missionary theologian who sympathized with nationalist aspirations and who also pursued a fresh appeal to the Hindu not in terms of doctrine, but of the revelation of a personal God through the person of Christ. However, he also attempted a rigorous appraisal of doctrinal differences, between a Christian theology which assumed a moral universe, and a Hindu theology which assumed a judicial one. On this basis he arrived at a comparative judgment on Hinduism which found it fatally flawed as a religious tradition.

Hogg reached India in 1903, was ordained in 1915, and was Principal of the Madras Christian College from 1928. His book *Karma and Redemption* (1909) is described by Sharpe as having a great impact on missionary thought of the day, before falling into an undeserved limbo, but his *Redemption from this World* (1922) was the only one of his books fairly widely read in the West.[34] At the risk of stumbling over issues familiar to the professional theologian, a brief attempt will be made here to set Hogg against what could be called the theological mainstream of his period in relation to the subcontinent. This is partly in order to convey the relative complexity and unqualified seriousness of the 'professional' Christian response to rapid change in India, and partly in the interest of an account of the mainstream itself, since it was from the mainstream, rather than from critics like Hogg, that less arduously achieved judgments on the Indian religions were derived. More or less clumsy versions of mainstream comparative theology became the staple for the ordinary and more liberal Christians in the Anglo-India public. They were self-consciously aware of this orientation as an advance on the narrower evangelical exclusivism widely associated with the missionary spirit. But Hogg himself is not so easily categorized, for in this contrast he emerges as, in Hick's terms, an *ex*clusivist, albeit a sympathetic and careful one, and a critic of the vague but well established *in*clusivism, whose best known exponent was J. N. Farquhar.

Farquhar, to whom we must return, went to India originally for the London Missionary Society, and was then with the very active Indian YMCA from 1902 till 1929 as a writer and as head of the Literature Department, a commanding position for an energetic propagandist.[35]

If Hogg's conclusions are exclusivist in comparison with the inclusivism of Farquhar, one must also, to complicate the comparison, acknowledge Hogg's pluralist impulses in his sensitivity to Hinduism, which is expressed in the belief that somewhere, though only at some innermost level, all religions worth consideration must converge on a radical, inexpressible faith which they share. But the problem for Hogg is to demonstrate sympathy with the Indian cultural and national heritage,—because 'there is in Hinduism a finding of God as well as a seeking after God,'—whilst at the same time preserving the unique and essential character of Christianity. Intellectual and doctrinal differences remain for him of immense importance. Old beliefs can create new perplexities which have to be faced and not set aside. His sympathetic, but at the same time rigorous and uncompromising exploration of differences between Hinduism and Christianity reflects an unusual degree of detachment from the temptations to relativize and to conciliate the educated Indians with whom he and the other influential missionaries were continuously in contact.

Somehow, Hogg argues, the theologian must bypass the doctrinal rigidity of the missionary's message. He must transcend differences of culture and national background to secure assent, not to a doctrine in the first instance, but to a sense of God's presence in the world through the historical person of Jesus. The missionary's primary message must be a witness to a faith in the *uniqueness* of Jesus in history. Such a conviction, however, implies a theology, which stands, as it were, as Copernicus to Ptolemy in the encounter between religious traditions. There can be no accommodation of central categories in the two systems of thought, any more than there can be between the rival cosmologies of the Middle Ages and the Renaissance. Thus, to summarize some basic contradictions, it is, in the first place, fundamental to the Hindu world view that the mundane world (*maya*) is something to be transcended and denied; to do that is the purpose of religious endeavour. Hogg's response, like that of the socially concerned Christians of the ICF movement, reflects an increasing emphasis in church teaching in this period on divine immanence, and he presents this doctrine as wholly antithetical to the Hindu notion of *maya*. Hindu thought is of course more richly faceted than these summary abreviations can suggest, and Anglican theologians who stressed the sense of divine Immanence had already turned on occasion to Hinduism to recover an awareness of it which they felt materialism had parched away in western man.

The feel of God in all things, the sense sympathetic to his touch, as it thrills through the universe around us, the consciousness that all that exists is impregnated with Him and with his influence, that 'He is not far from each one of us,' 'that in Him we live and move and have our being'—these animating characteristics which pervade the mind of India, which constitute its spiritual atmosphere, which are categories in all its speculations—it is by these, as a gift from on high, that Christianity may look to be helped.[36]

But in opposition to the standard interpretation of *maya* as a rejection of reality, Hogg asserts a unique world that is to be lived in as the medium of man's encounter with the divine.

The Hindu category of *dharma*, in a second fundamental contradiction between the two religions, translates loosely as 'service', but signifies something very different in the context of Hindu thought. In the Hindu tradition, service to another is given as a step in the development of one's own religious growth; it is service to oneself through the form of another. By contrast, Christian 'service' is given in the manner of Christ, to *another person* without reflexive reward. The contextual difference is between a universe that is conceived of as judicial, in which performance is rewarded and punished, as in Hindu theology, and a universe conceived of as moral. This distinction is of critical importance to the categories of *Karma* and *Redemption*. *Karma* is the cycle of bondage to performance in previous lives, from which the observance of rules offers the prospect of a kind of redemption, an escape from bondage, liberation from a penal sentence. The doctrine of *karma* provides a plausible explanation of evil, as the consequence of lapses against the rules, in the main rules of pollution, in this life but also in previous lives. It is, as an explanation of evil, neither more nor less verifiable than any other, but it is a chill doctrine from the Christian perspective. For the concept of redemption in Christian theology is an expression or aspect of the concept of faith, and it is faith that dissolves *real* evil, by taking the Christian beyond it, to rest in confidence on the divine purpose, which is love rather than judgement.

Finally, in a severely truncated summary, the divine purpose is itself meaningful only in relation to a concept of human history, which is not a dimension that exists in the abstract cycles and recurrences of Hindu philosophy. This again raises the question of what kind of a Christian 'history'. Hogg is concerned to insist on Hinduism's misconception of the nature and significance of the dimension of time, but also to distance himself from the theological Whiggism encouraged by Farquhar.

Hogg's *Karma and Redemption* was distributed to delegates at the World Missionary Conference at Edinburgh in 1910. But Sharpe observes that it was Farquhar whom the Conference tended to accept, without particularly close examination. His very different hypothesis of 'fulfilment' dominated Protestant missionary debate until the Tambaram Conference at Madras Christian College in 1938, when a book by the Dutch scholar from Java, Hendrick Kraemer, *The Christian Message in a Nonchristian World*, refocused discussion. The inclusivism of Annie Besant, who argued or at least was taken by churchmen to argue, during her leadership of the Theosophical Society in India, that the Hindu tradition could contain and do no wrong, was relatively easy game.[37] But Farquhar, though conceptually vague, was not. He and those, like Andrews, who shared his vision, were responding to what they saw as a potent and valid nationalist impulse. It was expressing itself through the revival of a Hinduism already in reality in an advanced state of decomposition and transformation by intellectual and spiritual energies that were derived from Christianity. The possibility therefore lay open for the educated Hindu to choose to recognize the evolutionary moment. Andrews, indeed, claimed to discern the providential guidance of the Great Artificer making all things new even in the anti-Christian Arya Samaj of northern India, based as it was on the purified 'Vedic faith' of Dyananda Saraswati (d. 1883), though this does seem to be an expansive development from his teacher Bishop Foss Westcott of Durham. A contemporary student of Andrews's career observes that 'here, surely, in such perceptions, liberal orthodoxy provides a profound and meaningful dimension to the *theology of national renaissance*.'[38] After another half century of nationalisms, this is impressive evidence of the appeal to a committed scholar of Andrews's assimilation of the nationalist impulse to the divine unfolding of history. The contemporary political theorist is more likely to see national renaissances as leading to ambiguous and threatening modernities.[39]

As a relatively broad-based movement, Indian nationalism in the first instance took an expressive religious form that had nothing to do with the mild and decorous reformism of the Congress Party of Gokhale, Naoroji, Mehta and Malaviya. The sense of that early excitement for nationalist India, simultaneously political and revivalist, is conveyed in Amrit Rai's biography of his father, the novelist Premchand:

When Vivekananda scored a triumph over all others at the Congress of

World Religions in the United States in 1893 and in the process gave utterance to the radiant soul of India, Indian breasts swelled with pride, blood coursed faster in Indian veins, and there was a new gleam in Indian eyes. The transformation was magical. In no time the lectures and speeches of Vivekananda were adopted as their new Bible by the patriotic youth of the country. The sagging spirit of the nation revived. The inferiority complex was got rid of. A feeling of self-respect ran high.[40]

In the teaching of both Bankim Chandra Chatterji and Vivekananda, as Nirad Chaudhuri points out in the first of his two remarkable retrospective volumes, a nationalism that was in the first instance religious and conservative 'wrestled for the soul of modern India' against the secular liberalism of the Brahmo Samaj.[41]

Such effervescence turned to the obvious available rhetoric: nationalism itself was identified as an avatar, an incarnation, born with the purpose to save India from the western instrument of illusion, of *maya*. A new and wider form of patriotism overtook the well established tradition of respectable reformism within Hinduism, dating from the placid unitarianism of Rammohun Roy's (d. 1833) Brahmo Samaj.[42] The new nationalism had disquieting features, but many Christians were prepared to see in this whole development a powerfully positive response to the Christian presence in India, and to think in terms of an analogy with Christ's fulfilment of Judaism: 'Think not that I am come to destroy the law, or the prophets; I am come not to destroy, but to fulfil.'[43] In the work of Farquhar himself there is an imagery of fulfilment, as the discovery and refinement of riches already owned, in imperfect form. 'Christ passes everything through His refiner's fire, in order that the dross, which Hindus know so well, may pass away—but the gold will then shine all the brighter.'[44] He associates the idea with other familiar, but untheological images of evolutionary development:

The education and the science of England or of Germany are not perfect— yet India, China, and Japan are adopting Western education and Western science as fast as they possibly can. The Government of Britain is by no means perfect, yet every awakened nation of the East, Muslim, Hindu, Buddhist, or Confucian, is panting after British freedom. Spiritual religion can be absorbed without loss of nationality, as truly as these other activities of the human mind.[45]

The evidence for apparently inevitable evolutionary growth in science, education and politics seemed obvious at the time. It was by no means obviously absent in the case of 'spiritual religion' in India, since it appeared to be the case that theistic ideas had been absorbed into Hinduism from Christianity, that the distinctively Christian propositions about individual personality had been acknowledged as problems by Hindu thinkers, and that an emulative commitment to social action informed a significant number of Hindu organizations, particularly the Arya Samaj. The irritation of many local missionaries with whom they came into competition is well documented.

Vivekananda himself, far from hostile to the redeeming figure of Christ and familiar with western thought, was a theological inclusivist with a vengeance, boldly assimilating Jesus as one, but only one manifestation of the principle of Christhood within the endless cycle of worlds such as ours. All are held within the manifestation of the power of *maya*, from which man is to be liberated only through the knowledge of his own identity with God.[46] Hinduism in Vivekananda's view thus itself crowns Christianity with the discovery of Christ, not as the unique person of Jesus, however, but as eternal, re-manifested principle.

Such theological confusions seemed to many Christians such as Andrews to matter less than other signs of progress, such as,

A really important contribution...on the moral side in the interpretation given to the Upanishad doctrine of the identity of the self with Brahma. This is called by the name of practical Vedanta. According to the school of Vivekananda, the identity of the soul with the Supreme is to be attained not only by passive contemplation, but also by absorption in active selfless service.[47]

Farquhar, like Andrews and others, was in no doubt about the stumbling nature of such religious 'growth', and they were quick to point out that despite all the words of socially conscious Hindus, the oppressions of caste and outcasteism, the monstrous deprivations inflicted on widows, and the rest, were all still fully in evidence. But they could see heartening signs elsewhere.

Farquhar's references to social change are strongly coloured by general evolutionary assumptions:

The three outstanding features of the modern social movement—the demands for complete social equality, for full social freedom, and for real social justice in our social relations—are simply the culmination of what we found to be the characteristics of all social progress in the ancient world, *viz*. a wider society, greater freedom and fuller moralization.[48]

But in his own work the concept of fulfilment has anxious overtones which were not always attended to by his readers. He insisted that the actual acknowledgment by Indians of the 'Christian' substance, latent in the spiritually dynamic tradition of Hinduism, required choice on their part and was not inevitable. As to whether that choice would be fully made, theology could have nothing to say. The answer would lie, for instance, in the practical life of social service to which the Indian YMCA moved during his time, seeing religion, in the first instance, as what is done rather than what is believed. What was at issue was not conversion in the traditional sense, but a grateful and spreading recognition of the person and presence of Christ in their practical lives by, above all, educated Indians. But many of Farquhar's readers anticipated this nondoctrinal Christianity with confidence, as a necessary prelude and a virtually inevitable outcome.

So Hogg was an effectual but not an effective critic of Farquhar in his own time. His writing does not make much reference outwards to the contemporary political context. His contacts with young Indians were largely confined to the context of College life. Farquhar on the other hand, from the time he joined the YMCA in Calcutta in 1895, was at a much more exposed interface between Hinduism and Christianity. The Indian YMCA was outside the missionary structure, an American initiative dedicated to aggressive evangelistic work, and over the years under close scrutiny for its 'political' activities.[49] Bengal, too, was the most active centre of Hindu revivalism, of the religion of loving devotion (*bhakti*), proclaimed by Ramakrishna Paramahamsa and K. C. Sen, of the neo-Krishnaism focusing on the *Bhagavad Gita*.[50]

But of the two men, Hogg was much more the theologian, more aware of his theoretical concepts, and the constraints they imposed on the impulse to shift and modify an intellectual position. What in reality was it, he asked, that the notion of fulfilment contained? Farquhar uses it to signify three broadly different things, the 're-placement' of Hinduism, the reappearance of the truths of Hinduism in higher form in Christianity, and Hinduism's discovery in Christianity of a resolution to its own religious quest.[51] But what was the practical substance of all this? Sharpe sums up Hogg's objections:

The claim that Christ is the crown of Hinduism is little more than a debating point.' (Hogg in *International Review of Missions*, 1914, p. 172) For if the theory be pressed, then it must be admitted, first, that in practice Christ leaves out a great deal of the content of Hinduism, and, secondly, that he 'fulfils' a great deal that was never in Hinduism...what Christ directly fulfils is *not* Hinduism, but a sense of need; and once that need has begun to be felt, India is no longer altogether Hindu.

In Hogg's own words, 'we think that the message "You need Christ now" is really more telling than "Christ fulfils your old religion". The latter message can hardly be freed of condescension.'[52]

However, Hogg's sympathetic exclusivism was not acceptable currency in popular theology at the time. He had the more coherent theoretical position, and one can see that its further development could be within the macro-theory of Hick's theological pluralism. Be that as it may, the *political* implications of his position are not the same as those of the position he criticizes. Missionaries often had mixed feelings about the historical church because they were embarrassed by its western ways. But for Hogg the church as an historical, corporate body, notwithstanding its departures from the spirit of Christ, was a surer hope than any national community, however 'purified' its patriotism. The fulfilment writers regularly appear to confuse the two, the spirit of Christ and the spirit of national renaissance. Though he was one of the signatories of Curtis's letter, Hogg is not prepared to elide the polity and the City of God, and he does not encourage a loose equation between political, or even moral and religious development. But it was, nevertheless, the vaguely evolutionary and inclusive connotations of 'fulfilment' that expressed a preferred state of mind. In the case of articulate 'professional' Christians like Andrews and Lucas, this actually retreated from theology, in order to bring together an assortment of generous aspirations and assumptions. It was less a theory than a network of self-confirming notions that one could enter from any angle.

Andrews himself was not greatly attracted by Vivekananda, but he wrote with reverence in *The Renaissance in India* about the Bombay social reformer Justice Ranade (d. 1901), founder of the Prarthana Samaj on the model of the Brahmo Samaj. He stressed the central pillars of Ranade's thinking, his belief in 'the overruling Providence

guiding his country and his race,' his confidence in 'Christian civilisation from the West...the greatest of all the factors which were to
change and discipline Indian life, and make it more worthy.' He
follows Ranade's development of the concept of *karma* as a law
'that can be controlled and set back by a properly trained will made
subservient to a higher Will than ours.' He endorses Ranade's belief
in social reform directed to the whole man in a political system
based on reason and justice.[53] Ranade's reformism and faith in the
providential outcome of the Raj is taken to be further evidence of
the gradual organic penetration of Hinduism by Christianity, which
'will lead to a deeper understanding of the great words of Christ,
"I come not to destroy, but to fulfil".'

What is to be fulfilled had already, Andrews claims, been part
of Hinduism from well before the appearance of Christianity in
India:

We may surely believe that the eternal Word was the Light of the Buddha
and Tulsi Das in their measure, even as He was, in so much greater a
degree, the Light of the Hebrew Prophets; that Hinduism in its higher
religious history was a true *praeparatio evangelica*, even though in its lower
forms it has sometimes proved unspeakably degrading.[54]

This was written for a lay readership. More academic readers of
the church newspapers in the early 1920s would shortly be directed
to the Hibbert Lectures of S. C. Carpenter, the climax of which is
an extended discussion of Tulsi Das (d. 1623) as a voice preparing
the way and attended to over the centuries by vast numbers. Carpenter
concludes his lectures by emphasizing the importance to his listeners
as members of the Empire of a sympathetic though critical awareness
of the flawed history of Hinduism.[55]

It is worth stressing that Andrews was to move away from the
positions taken up in *The Renaissance in India*. This vigorous and
attractively produced volume had been commissioned for CMS study
circles, but caused offence among some mission supporters because
of its criticisms of missionary foot-dragging over the opportunities
to be discovered in India by the 'fulfilment' theory. These objections
were mild beside the abuse that came his way after his resignation
from the Cambridge Mission to Delhi, and the development of his
association with Gandhi. The seeds of his disillusionment with
empire had already been planted. It was Andrews who had written

the letter about 'wicked race domination' that had reached the Archbishop, Morley and Hirtzel, through Bishop Montgomery in 1907.[56]

In his period as a lecturer at St Stephen's College in Delhi, however, Andrews made very explicit links between British imperial Christianity, whatever its failings, and Indian nationalism, in enthusiastic articles in the College Magazine, which he edited for six years till 1913. Christianity itself raises the level of civilization and evokes the self-conscious manhood of the younger nation. The seed maturing in China, for instance, 'after many years of depressing and fruitless work' is to deliver a 'harvest which will soon be reaped.'[57] Christianity makes possible the development of individual character which is 'the first principle of a national movement.'[58] What remains in India is to strip Christianity of its foreign dress, to release its extraordinary power...to reach down to the masses inspiring new life.' (Andrews retained his hopes for China. In 1937 he wrote to Curtis, complimenting him on the immense range and outlook of *Civitas Dei*, vol. 2, which Lord Lothian had given him, but observing that: 'I think your view of China, if I may say so, is rather of the surface than of the depth. What you say is true but there is a far deeper truth. China and India are both going very far in the interior life of the spirit, because their essential mind does not rank force and violence high as Japan does...')[59]

Andrews dedicated himself at St Stephen's to presenting the Christian life to educated middle-class Indian students not only through his ministry as a priest, but also through the social life, the competitive games and the exercises in 'practical Vedanta' of students at the College, and by introducing into his teaching of history what was in effect a proposal to bring the methodological approach of the Christian Whig historian into the study of the subcontinent.[60] In a lecture entitled 'Indian history, its lessons for today', in May 1908, he takes history, as Curtis does, as 'the last cordial for drooping spirits,' because of its revelation that Indian freedom is no second-hand western idea, but a natural growth struggling to find expression and actually achieving its essential conditions in the Buddhist period in India. The country in this period was relatively free of caste restrictions, with a *Pax Indica* under Kshatriya or warrior rule, but with a religious leadership, ethical rather than economic priorities and a devout religious spirit among the people. But the growth points of Buddhism were cauterized by subsequent invasions and clogged by the accretions of a rigid system of castes. They are still there, however, to be rediscovered as a source for the new patriotism, which is to be based not only on politics but on a purification of religion and on divinely implanted love of one's country.[61]

A devout idealization of Buddhism as the high point of a temporarily aborted religious evolution is not unusual in commentary on Indian history, and is repeated by people as far apart politically as the Labour MP Ben Spoor and an uncompromizing propagandist for die-hard toryism, Captain J. Ellam, (a figure who will re-emerge in a later chapter).[62]

Another theologian signatory of the Curtis letter was Bernard Lucas (d. 1920), one of the founders of the United Theological College at Bangalore, and a prolific contributor on many questions to journals such as the *Harvest Field*. Hirtzel was attracted by his confident argument that what was required in order to Christianize India was not the imposition of any intellectual system of theological dogma, but the sharing of a spiritual life. The task of the Christian was to evangelize and not to proselytize; something that was to be achieved through example, through education and through the rationalization of the Hindu perspective. In a succession of books written for the general reader, Lucas repeats a broad and simple argument, no less critical than Hogg of Hinduism as a system of ideas, but outrunning the most eupeptic believer in the providential benignity of historical evolution and its religious momentum.[63]

Lucas's indictment of Hinduism reinforces the main points. Religion is the chief constituent, the all-pervading atmosphere of India. But it is a religion that fatally divides the Hindu from reality, the appeal of facts never penetrating the illusive world of the seen. It is a religion of ideals, unable to appreciate the objective significance, for example, of the practice of suttee, the immolation of widows. The doctrine of *karma*, investing this life with the formal consequences of a previous one, destroys the category of individuality, and so the conception of the manhood and individuality of Christ is not easily accessible to the Hindu, nor is the sense of individual responsibility, the 'character and individuality which it is the supreme purpose of life to evolve.'[64] History, as a revelation of God's providential dealings with the human race is practically unknown to the Hindu, because evolutionary theory, the clearest evidence of the Divine mind, is quite inconsistent with the notion of *karma*.[65] What the Hindu misses is the most fundamental sense of the concrete, the morally consequential nature of social life in which the Divine is immanent, for 'the basis of Eastern thought is the reality of God; the basis of Western thought is the reality of the Universe.'[66]

If India is to take her rightful place amongst the nations of the world, the Hindu must realise that the world in which he lives and moves and has his being is essentially God's world, a cosmos of order, not a chaos of confusion; that the material is a fitting, and in fact the only expression in time of the mind and will of God; that moral law is an indication of the character of God, and that human life is the field of the Divine activity. This is the message which Christianity has to give, and its reception means a new India, risen from the dead past, and taking a foremost place in the life and well being as in the thought of the race.[67]

Conversion is not the way to bring this complex and dynamic society to its fulfilment. Lucas uses a telling image in connection with the mass movements which were of some importance in south India and in parts of the north. The mass movement does not depend on acts of individual choice, and it is, of necessity, at the moment of 'conversion' only nominally Christian, motivated by the simple and laudable desire to better conditions for the caste group. But 'the Hindu can only advance as he moves in companies,' so 'the missionary can bring the ship (which the people will not leave) to port with all souls on board.'[68] The same principle might also be right for the all-important caste Hindus of the colleges, but it cannot be realized by their conversion, only in the foreseeable future through education and the moulding of its Christian citizenship. Thus the deeper structural principle of caste, which is a religious, organic hierarchy of 'companies', may provide the vehicle for corporate evolution, under the tutorial guidance of a political regime in which it is acknowledged that the Englishman symbolizes justice and incorruptibility.

It would be wrong to suggest that the opinions of theologians and missionaries on Christianity in India were by and large uniform, with only occasional intractable exceptions such as Hogg. But it was appropriate at the end of the International Missionary Council of April 1928 that it fell to William Temple, then Bishop of Manchester, to perform a task that seemed to come easily to him, of 'formulating a "message" which with consummate skill and artistry wove together the views of the conflicting parties in such a way as to convince all (temporarily at least) that everyone's opinion was being taken seriously.'[69] In fact, there was no consensus, but Temple's own preference was for oneness, wholeness, for the principle of the 'universality of Christ' in the encounter between religions, and he invariably fastened on the grounds for consensus rather than division in debates such as this, as he did in the context of British domestic politics in the 1920s. He was an appropriate spokesman, for there was among missionary thinkers concerned with India a central tendency to the theological response, consensual and evolutionary, as articulated by Farquhar, the early Andrews, Lucas and others. It locked perfectly into the socially concerned, optimistic idealism of Temple's own post-First World War social theology.

The response to this 'sympathy' movement in England could be a troubled one. The *Church Times* reviewer of Sidney Cave's *Redemption, Hindu and Christian,* describes the book as an important and admirable addition to the series edited by Farquhar, puts some hope in the 'national devotion of heart of India,' and in *bhakti's* capacity to produce saints but, whilst acknowledging Cave's respectful summary of the great books of India, notes that the western mind must come away with some feelings of despair at Hinduism's curious capacity for holding contradictory propositions, its obscurity and its vagueness.[70] But all these reservations follow the standard orientalist assumption that the social and political incoherence of the East is a direct consequence of its hitherto unredeemed religion.

The central tendency of this 'theological' response is well diffused during the period between the wars. For example, Maxwell Leigh, a layman who followed in Andrews's path to teach for a time at St Stephen's, a scholar of Winchester and New College and an active layman for the Diocese, published in 1935 a small group of talks given in Winchester Cathedral.[71] He lucidly reminds his listeners of the profoundly religious nature of India, of progressive reform there, but also of the continuing strength of caste, of the measure of light in all religions in India, of Islam's bondage to the literal word of scripture, of the Hindu's deficiency of historical sense and lack of critical interest in distinguishing fact from fiction, and even that it is worth considering 'to what extent Christianity can find room for caste, *dharma* and *karma*.' He also fastens explicitly on the solvent encounter between eastern and western spirituality, and between British power and authority and Indian aspiration, in a comment on Lord Irwin's demonstration that Britain is able to combine authority and power to organize with spirituality. Irwin had met Gandhi, 'on his own ground, and by general admission, beat him on it. Lord Irwin's Viceroyalty did a very great deal to restore India's belief in British honesty and British honour.'

Theologians and Islam

The position of Islam in the literature under consideration here is a paradoxical one; it was seen as the relatively advanced religion of a relatively backward community. One could turn with relief from the Hindu pantheon to the austere simplicities to which the followers of the Prophet were committed. And if there were social complexities, Sunni against Shia, those claiming affinities with Moghul rule, and lower caste converts from Hinduism, they were rather tidy and easily intelligible beside the confusions of Hindu caste and sect. Islam under the Raj in the inter-war period accumulated associations with political violence with mounting frequency and intensity, but in itself it was a dry matter, quite unlike the critically fissionable material of Islam in the late nineteenth century. Islam falls naturally into a coda to the discussion of Hinduism. Unlike the Islam of the Middle East, South Asian Islam was never an indigenous threat scored into the European cultural memory, and it was treated in consequence with 'proprietary hauteur' rather than with a sense of danger.[72] In his essay in Bishop Montgomery's symposium contributed to the 'sympathy' or fulfilment tradition, Bishop Lefroy of Lahore, who had worked among Sunni Muslims during his time with the Cambridge Mission to Delhi, complained of the arrogant indifference of the missionary response to the Mohammedans, the hard-toned controversial literature 'intended rather to confute the enemy than to win the disguised friend,' and of the ignorance of Muslim literature and theology even among his brethren working with Muslim communities.[73] For the most part educationally backward, they were regarded as unpromising material, and a representative *Church Times* review just after the First World War of a text that refers to the more educated classes, is glad to pick up a reference to 'new signs of a vague dissatisfaction among educated Moslems,' and the 'possibility of a ray of light.'[74]

There were students of Islam in India in the tradition of receptive scholarship celebrated by Schwab. Sir Thomas Arnold, teacher and friend of the Urdu poet Muhammad Iqbal, for instance, reacted consciously against the orientalist discourse that is explored here, and is not cited as an authority in its literature.[75] But in Lefroy's account, Islam, like Hinduism, is ripening towards fulfilment in Christianity, and if it is demographically less important in British India than Hinduism, it has strengths which are entirely lacking in Hinduism and sets a challenging standard in some areas to the Christian church. In the exercise of grading religions as totalities, which is a central feature of British orientalism, Islam moves into position ahead of Hinduism. Once again, one can only note the conceptual and anthropological implications of this procedure. As Hick points out in his discussion of grading religions,[76] the comparison of religions as totalities substitutes abstract constructs for the internal diversity, across time and from situation to situation, within each of the religious traditions.

The fundamental advantage which is taken to bring Islam closer to Christianity is its core belief that there is *one* God and *one* ultimate will, and furthermore that this,

Truth about God lies at the base of one of the strongest social and political structures which the world has ever seen, and that this strength and power is due rather to a religious truth than to any maxims of political morality.

The fact that the social and political structures of Mohammedanism emerge, in this assessment, from its 'strong grasp of the reality of the Divine existence' and not from *political* maxims, has ramifying implications. One consequence is a clear consciousness of 'the absolutely fixed and objective character of truth', by contrast with the natural pantheism of the East, for,

It cannot be doubted that much of the want of firmness and stamina, in individual character and moral standards alike, which so frequently characterizes the East, is the outcome of that vagueness of thought and absence of all basis of objective truth which is of the essence of Pantheism.

The ritual of Islam itself, 'free from effiminacy' embodies the values of objectivity, regularity and corporate action:

In short, the whole undenominational idea, the hanging loose to the duty of the Body, which results in a weak and nerveless and divided Christianity, is wonderfully counteracted by this stronger side of Islam, supplying, as it does on a large scale, a living picture of what the institutional can do.

Ritual also reflects a belief in the brotherhood of believers, and their devotion to the Koran itself is an act of faith in the reality of Revelation, which they share with the faiths of the Old and New Testament.

These are powerful resources which fully account for Muslim political achievements before the arrival of the British, welding the Mohammedan hosts into an 'invincible engine of conquest,' inspiring them 'with a spirit of military subordination and discipline, as well as a contempt of death,' giving 'that firmness of determination and strength of will, and also that uncomplaining patience and submission in the presence of the bitterest misfortune, which characterise and adorn the best adherents of the creed.' As of course, though with a difference, they did the Christian warriors and administrators who in turn subdued India.

But what is missing? Fatally, the failure to see the 'moral correspondence between God's nature and ours.' Islam's acceptance of God's will as something purely arbitrary and not to be challenged, is the cause of its crippling contribution to the psychology of the East, a deadening fatalism and lack of moral impetus.

Turn the eyes to any country in which Mohammedanism has long held dominion, e.g. Turkey, Persia or Afghanistan, and see how barren they are in all that really makes for the ordered moral progress of human life—rather how entirely opposed they are to any true progress at all.

The remoteness of God, the absence of any sense of sympathy between the Divine nature and man is the mark of a religion that can, from its own internal resources, go no further, because its followers are not moved by the idea of 'the perfection of the Divine nature as the goal of man's effort.' Lacking this, many admirable features of Mohammedanism, the avoidance of drink, gambling and the like, are negative, merely virtues of denial.

This seemingly unproblematic and uncontentious placing of Islam as a system of belief was encouraged by what appeared to be evidence of the decline of Islam as a world religion and a political force, as well as by the tense and unstable relationship between Muslims and Hindus in India itself. At the end of the Great War the fate of Turkey and even the future of the Sophia Mosque in Constantinople were prominent issues for churchmen. Careful attention, particularly during the war, was given to the fuse that could have been ignited by fighting between the Indian Army and Turkish Muslims in Mesopotamia. But the Khilafat agitation in India did not last long, from 1919–22, and was too readily treated as the terminal activity of a defunctive pan-Islamic movement.[77] The complex indigenous impulses behind the movement in India were not recognized, and Gandhi's support for it was generally dismissed as an expedient bid for the support of the less rational elements in a Muslim community divided between those committed to the Raj and the incoherently disaffected. James Meston had dealt sternly with both the young Muhammadans, of 'poor education and no stability of character,' and the religious bigots among the *ulema*, mere 'professional trouble-makers', as he saw them, associated with Mohamed Ali in the United Provinces, in whom the Turkish defeat revived a 'smouldering dislike of Christians and of the British ascendancy in India.'[78]

Indian Muslims in general, as the minority community, were seen as dependent on the Raj and therefore naturally loyal to it, but also closer in spirit to the British as people of the book (*Ahi-i-Kitab*) and understandably hostile to the Hindu. Indeed, there were religious leaders such as Maulana Ashraf Ali Thanwi (d. 1943) who declared that 'it was religiously unlawful (*naja'iz*) for Muslims to forge a united front (with the Hindus) against the British because as a minority they would not be able to veto the Hindu dominance over Indian politics.'[79] There were missionaries, notably the Methodists in Muslim Hyderabad, who were more sensitive to Islam as an aggressive faith, aiming at 'the world, and no less,' and unhappy with the view of many public servants that Islam was a suitable religion for Asiatics.[80] However, the idiom of subversion and terrorism in India was primarily Hindu and any fragile tactical connections with Muslim groups collapsed with the demise of the Khalifa.[81]

The arguments that measured Islam against Hinduism, Buddhism and Christianity as a system of religious belief were systematically assembled in the double-entry account of D. A. Stewart's volume of 1920 for the Society for the Propagation of Christian Knowledge.[82] The stamp of sincerity in Mohammad's basic work, his preaching of the fundamental necessity of a saving truth, a God of righteousness, mercy and goodness as well as a God of power, a moral code, however dessicated by an automaton fatalism, an insistance on the unity of God and an intolerance of idolatry, make Islam infinitely preferable to Hinduism. And yet there are glimpses and hints of this in Hinduism, which has room for a monotheistic conception of God in the worship of Vishnu or Siva (but a God who makes no personal contact with man). The other Gods of Hinduism have little if any ethical quality to recommend them—Krishna is notorious for his amours, Siva the patron of licentiousness, and Durga, his consort, delights in murder and bloodshed.

The doctrine of *maya* drains human life of a sense of moral responsibility, and yet a moral code, *manu*, is taught, though in pursuing it the individual must rely entirely on his own efforts, for no strength reaches him from a personal God. Hinduism, like Islam, teaches a narrow escapist doctrine of salvation, and yet Hinduism can boast of the *bhakti* cults, Islam of the Shiah and Babi sects which fasten, though inadequately, on the necessity for a God who is in touch with man.

Buddhism, it was argued, with its beautiful elements, its hostility to greediness, to pride and sloth, its loving kindness, meekness, unwillingness to hurt, and filial piety, is nonetheless a fundamentally selfish faith based on man's sense of misery, not on his sense of sin and need for redemption. It is only Christianity that offers a God working within history, among and for men, pointing to the completion of history in the person of Christ, a revelation beside which the other sacred writings pale into insignificance, for the indwelling spirit of Christ binds morality, essential reasonableness, to religion. Uniquely, Christianity acknowledges a God who satisfies reason, a three-fold divine personality, infinite Spirit in a finite world without the annihilation of either, the absoluteness and infinitude of the Divine nature, the reality of a finite world, and the individuality of man.[83]

Theology, Politics and the Real World

Systems of religious belief bring the mundane and diurnal fabric of individual and social behaviour under the scrutiny of the most abstract and speculative of concepts. The particular perspectives which articulate Christians brought to bear on their own direct experience of India, certainly those who saw the encounter of faiths in terms of the dynamics of 'fulfilment', had no difficulty in locating the commonplace evidence that seemed to confirm their vision.

Indeed, Indians themselves are likely to point out that there *are* empirical differences between the ways in which East and West relate to the factually concrete, to assessments of cause and effect, even to the recognition of 'truth' in different circumstances and situations. The 'impractical' and subtle verbalism of Indian students in the mission colleges had exhausted generations of English teachers in India. Similarly, the western subordination of 'time' to purpose and organizational process did not seem to strike the 'eternal East' as a particularly worthwhile discovery. Oriental 'fatalism' has maddened practical Englishmen in every walk of life. At a different level, it is easy to identify social practices that offend against what appear to be obvious and universal standards, to see a connection with particular religious beliefs, and to draw obvious conclusions about their perversity and the validity of one's own. Gandhi himself never believed that whatever is indigenous is right, and there were Hindu religious and social practices that revolted him no less than they did his Christian friends, and for very similar reasons.

The perspective of the missionary theologians was not a crude ethnocentric endorsement of empirical fictions and distortions. There were features of Indian society, Hindu and Islamic, which they pointed to with genuine anxiety for India's future, which are still standard preoccupations, features such as 'communalism', 'corruption', and 'inefficiency'. We are inclined to turn to very different explanations of these phenomena today.

For instance, the Indian sociologist Satish Saberwal, has been developing an argument with a large historical sweep, bearing on precisely these urgent contemporary issues, and it is an argument in which a particular connection between Christianity and formal, organizational rationality is of pivotal importance. But the point of connection he makes between Christianity and practical reason has nothing to do with the English theologians' rationale. That assumed a distinctively Christian conviction that man must struggle for his salvation, in alliance with the Immanent Divine Spirit as it informs the difficult but concrete practicalities of this world. Saberwal's argument, by contrast, is a secular and structural one. The church gave European society *institutional* continuity in a period of serious political breakdown. During this period other specific technological skills associated with the growth of capitalism in the fields of science and exploration, in particular, developed into a general cultural skill, namely, 'the *accurate* recognition of external reality, social as well as physical.'[84] The European church, in conjunction with the absolutist state, constructed 'a unified cultural tradition out of disparate materials, and made a common ethic effectively available throughout the continent.' It did so, above all, by elaborating the idea of law. Its greatest divines, Aquinas, Duns Scotus and William of Occam, exercised the Aristotelian apparatus for drawing consistent inferences from diverse premises. A training in this rational analysis was used by clerics and others in the institutions of government. However diverse the purposes, principles and ambitions of the societies of the West, Europe, could therefore,

Devise early on what might be called *master codes*; codes which specify authoritatively how the lesser codes, purposes, and so forth may be safely brought into mutual order.[85]

India never had the equivalent institutions to establish this decisive advantage. It was and is, as anxious liberals and, more loudly and furiously, die-hard Tories reiterated, a highly segmented society, and one, as Saberwal points out, in which a multiplicity of codes of conduct exist at different levels, operating to communal, caste and ultimately family criteria of obligation. These are fundamentally at odds with the style of carefully established routines introduced by the British from the late 1700s. He quotes Kaviraj's elegant description:

Under the thin crust of Europeanized élite, the British had tolerated the untroubled continuance of large expanses of vernacular graft.... For each decision there was the internal distance in this large and ill-regulated machine, as it journeyed from adumbration as a policy, through its transmission, decimation and eventual ironical 'implementation', often in unrecognizable forms.[86]

The most casual reading of Indian periodicals such as *The Economic and Political Weekly* or *India Today* seems to provide ample evidence of the severe erosion since independence of the 'code' or style of legal and administrative procedure, in which all shades of opinion from the Anglo-India public had unshakeable faith, and which the theologians, with what appears from this perspective to be a confused intuition, endorsed as an essential part of the Christian legacy to India. The omnicompetent ICS man, as the manifestation of Justice in the dedicated personal ruler, is of course crucial to their interpretation of the evolutionary process.

In an important study of political and administrative continuities, David Potter discounts the standard argument that the quality of higher administrative personnel declined as the ICS was superceded by the IAS, but does so partly on the basis of a clear view, which confirms Kaviraj's summary, of the gap between myth and reality:

Because the British were so thin on the ground, they had to strike what amounted to political bargains with local collaborators who could normally rule for them...in the normal life of a district it was Indians who did most of the ruling.[87]

The social insulation of the British administrators and the backing of imperial power had sustained the illusion of an impersonal, rational system transcending political purposes other than those of the Raj itself. It had never existed.

The features of Indian society which attracted the concerned attention of missionary theologians are perfectly recognizable, then, in very different accounts. But they appear in a very different light in the context of an intellectual tradition, in Saberwal's case deriving from Max Weber and the social anthropology of Clifford Geertz and Victor Turner, which interprets religion in terms of function and social purposes rather than faith and ultimate Reality. They are given a different reading again in a Marxist tradition which is committed to the premis that the concrete conditions of life ultimately determine consciousness and not the other way round. Both secular traditions are bound to treat the encounter of faiths and the social uses of religious belief in India as a complex expression of rapidly accelerating conflicts within the colonial situation of the Raj, as racial, political and economic structures responded to changing institutional rules and the new opportunities for patronage and power sharing that these opened up. British Christianity is as much an expression of these contradictions as is Hinduism or south Asian Islam in the nationalist period.

If one cannot accept the validity of the 'theological interpretation' of the encounter of faiths, one can ask what the political consequences of that theological interpretation were.

Firstly, the comparison of religions as totalities, however scholarly the supporting detail, abstracted from the internal diversity of the religious traditions and graded them one in relation to the other. By the same token, since it was taken for granted in an idealist fashion, that the state of society was fundamentally an expression of a system of religious beliefs, rather than the other way around, whole communities and societies were being ranked or graded on this escalator of historical evolution. An Hegelian preoccupation with the evolution of ideas as an expression of social fulfilment, fed into English theology by Coleridge, Carlyle and F. D. Maurice, became in Christian thinking about the Raj the theoretical basis for confirming the shape and meaning of a political relationship.

If this sounds like a banal formula for an arrogant ethnocentrism, there are reasons for acknowledging that this framework of interpretation was in fact more subtle than it sounds, and for that reason the more powerful because, for the serious believer, historical objectivity insisted on a deep humility. For instance, the words of Bishop Montgomery, an 'evangelical High Churchman' and highly regarded Bishop of Tasmania who was greatly admired by Archbishop Cosmo Grodon Lang:[88]

Even this brief survey of the qualities of our race makes it possible to say that the world must not expect to acquire much alluvial gold from the English mine. It is a reef deep down below the surface and covered over with a very hard cap of rock which requires the drill and much dynamite; but the gold reef when reached is rich and lives down. The removal of the hard cap is the miracle that the Gospel has affected, till at length the man who was colour-blind, who used to hold in dim fashion that our Blessed Lord must have been born in London for the express benefit of his own race alone, has become one of the greatest of missionaries.... Today he is earnest in impressing upon all men the Faith of the Gospel, and it is not easy to speak too highly of the beauty of character of the English gentleman and the English lady. It is indeed one of the marvels of history that our race has become an apostle and herald of the Faith. We do not lack fibre, but more than any other, we need a broken heart, and that fracture was affected by the power of the Gospel. Just so far as it has been broken and thus has entered into the meaning of the first Beatitude (did our Lord turn westward when he uttered it?) it has its own message to give other nations regarding the miracles of grace and the virtues which are specially entrusted to it to put forward as of first importance for man.[89]

Montgomery was Secretary of the Society for the Propagation of the Gospel from 1901 to 1919, and authored a long list of 'popular' works, (e.g. *Foreign Missions, Light of Melanesia, The Church on the Prairie, Service Abroad,* etc.)

Bishop Whitehead of Madras, writing only a few years later in his *National Christianity in India*, commented on the incoherent synthesis of Hindu and Christian doctrines of the Spirit in *The Oriental Christ*, (1883) by P. C. Mozoomdar (d. 1905), K. C. Sen's closest colleague in the latter's Church of the New Dispensation. He is very cautious about the syncretic developments. He agrees vaguely with the Montgomery symposium that 'each race and nation will contribute something to the common stock,' and is averse to imposing such things as the Thirty-Nine Articles on the Indian Church, but he insists on the importance of denominationalism and 'the great questions about which the Christians of the West have quarrelled.' However, he too takes up the British failure in meekness and the absence of any scriptural justification for the reasons that lie behind this: 'the greatest defect of our English Christianity...the fact that it is so strongly national.'[90]

Finally, fulfilment theology fitted with perfect consistency into the more general pattern of religious thinking referred to earlier, which had been given an immediate and political urgency by the Great War. To recapitulate very briefly, the most active and socially concerned post-war Christianity, and this includes that of the non-denominational churches, fell into a pattern of evolutionary, organicist thought, stressing immanentist or sacramentalist assumptions. Influential and popular speakers and writers like William Temple analysed the contemporary social order in the light of beliefs stressing conciliation and good will, and co-operation rather than conflict between the social classes. They identified a threat of irrational social conflict in the new democracy emerging after the war, if it were to turn to a politics of 'rights' and 'demands' rather than 'duties' and 'obligations'. They saw hope in a society whose different orders were committed to the collective good, and condemned as pathologically irrational the more radical and socialistic demands for a redistribution of power. The Ruskinian conservatism of this perspective and its links with aspects of Gandhi's social philosophy will be considered later.

The Raj presented analogous problems on an imperial scale: great social stirrings, the possibility of deeply 'irrational', group-based outcomes, and catastrophic threats to an existing and fundamentally rational system of order and justice, the threat implicit in the nationalism of Tilak and his successors. Hence, the absolute necessity to transcend the sectional and intransigent and to create the authentically and organically national, an aspiration towards which the nationalism of Gandhi seemed at times, (to some more than to others) to be making a wavering progress. Britain and India were passing simultaneously through different phases of the one great historical unfolding.

CHAPTER 4

The Church in India

The Christian Presence in India

The abstract problems which preoccupied theologians and intellectuals about the nature of religious belief and about conflicts between systems of belief circulated in various dilutions among the lay and professional churchpeople at large, both in India and at home. The salience of such issues varied according to circumstances in India itself, since the church there consisted of an agglomeration of hierarchies and interests that had grown incrementally and without any general plan, organized round distinct purposes and struggling to adjust to different constraints. There were of course formal links and they were by no means insulated from each other, but the circumstances experienced within each of these sectors tended to produce, within a common discourse, different interpretations of the significance of Christianity to the Raj. Their own commentaries filtered through to the Anglo-India public in Britain through a variety of channels. The process of communication was both uneven and selective. This chapter is mainly concerned to generalize this range of perspectives from a review of sources containing first-hand commentary and material from the field in each sector. Of course, this material is itself the outcome of selection and editing by authors, and by the editors of the diocesan journals, college magazines, extracts from mission society letter-books and the like. By and large, it was produced for a specialized readership, but it is an important primary source for secondary commentary, some of which will be considered in later chapters.

Information and commentary did not, of course, flow only in one direction. The whole process was very much messier than that, but one can see at least the general features of a stable pattern by distinguishing and contrasting the different structures of which Christianity under the Raj consisted.

There were, firstly, the diocesan structures of the Indian Ecclesiastical Establishment (IEE), the churches of the cantonments and civil stations, broadly speaking; secondly, those of the grass-roots missionary organizations; thirdly, the system of Christian higher education, with colleges such as St Stephen's in Delhi and the Madras Christian College; and finally, the Indian Church, closely linked to the missions but increasingly invaded by 'nationalistic' impulses which were unsettling to elements in the other sectors. The colleges were of course mission foundations, but there is a clear division between missionary activity to the college élites, and the very different medical missions and teaching work in the villages. For obvious reasons there is a considerable literature on each of the last three sectors, but all four, in different ways, responded to rapidly changing political circumstances—the main concern of this account. If they can broadly be treated as distinct (though individuals could shift between them), there was also considerable variability of response within each, for which a number of reasons emerge in contemporary accounts. Strong personalities often seem to make a disproportionate impact. In the case of missions particularly, local relations with civil authorities could vary. The gospel was carried into India by tiny groups of men and women loaded with the denominational impedimenta and organizational habits of the churches and tendencies whose outriders they were, whether Lutheran, SPG, CMS, Methodist, Baptist, Roman Catholic, Congregationalist or Salvation Army. One can at best acknowledge this kind of complexity whilst attempting to assess the indirect or direct importance of the main elements to the general process of a Christian interpretation of the Raj.[1]

The India of the Ecclesiastical Establishment

The IEE was a Government Department. Chaplains were there to serve the ritual needs of the entire expatriate community at times of matrimony, birth and death, and to maintain Christian worship, for those inclined to attend, with such regularity as the distance and size of the communities permitted. There would be welfare and teaching work, as well, in the Eurasian community and in the cantonments among army personnel and their dependents. Like the ICS officers, chaplains were recruited into a regional administrative structure, the diocese, either from home or after mission experience in India, within which they were moved around with some frequency as death, retirement or furlough withdrew their brethren from service. So the society in which they spent their working years had the same movement in terms of stability, changing personnel and stable functions, as is familiar from many accounts of life in the ICS itself. They built up a sense of the diocese as the paths of individuals crossed and recrossed, but not as a relationship with a stable community: either one was moved on oneself, or others were. Unlike the civil servants, however, even those in the bureaucratic empyrean of Delhi and the provincial capitals, it was not 'India' with which they had to deal. They were, like the parish clergy at home, serving the church and the community, but in inescapable ways they were also quite obviously servicing the imperial system itself. They had a material stake in this system that was well recognized, for their pay and pension rights compared favourably with the parochial alternatives back in England. They were the clergy of the expatriate middle-class (to which they belonged) whom they conscientiously reminded of the higher purposes which justified the existence of the Raj.

One of them, the Revd G. M. Davies, a CMS deputation preacher in England after a career concluded in India in 1908 as Archdeacon of Nagpur, reflects the characteristic blend of evangelical and imperial earnestness of an Edwardian generation of chaplains in his memoir.[2] He recalls the impact of the spirituality of C. F. Andrews communicated in a service in Simla in 1904, and reflects 'tenderly' on the 'terrible temptations' through which 'many of our race have imbibed oriental influences and approximated to oriental morals more than to the true standard.' He recalls the cheers that rewarded Winston Churchill, speaking to an overflow attendance at a Church House meeting in 1908 in London, on 'The Responsibility of Churchmen to the Heathen and Moslem World': 'Without these forces we could not hold our Empire together for a score of years. We could not even have acquired it. It was Exeter Hall that won Uganda.'

But chaplains' memoirs are thin on the ground, and there can be no doubt that the main contribution of the padres to public opinion about the Raj back in England was informal, through family and private correspondence during postings, and through conversations and sermons at different stages in the never-ending process (only interrupted by the World Wars) of repatriation, leave, sick leave, and retirement. On furlough, many took holiday or deputation duty and would naturally draw on their Indian experience in sermons. Many retired from India to take over parishes at home. Little can be made of letters and talk now lost without hope of recovery, for the most part, but one can claim with confidence, that they were important and should be taken into account.

There is, as it happens, one large collection of letters which does appear to be representative of the commonplaces of chaplaincy experience in important respects. The Revd Aubrey Storrs Fox worked in the Diocese of Lahore, and he preserved, with a rare sense of the historical importance of the banal, the lengthy and regular letters home to his mother from 1911 till 1944, written before he retired to an Oxfordshire parish. Deposited on his instructions at the India Office Library, they record without literary skill or pretension the industrious routines and encounters, journeyings and sight-seeings, indispositions and servant problems and, very occasionally, the general reflections of a devout Anglo-Catholic on the Establishment. Their importance lies in the fact that there is so very little to be got from them. During a crucial period, Storrs Fox was in effect parish priest to the Viceroy in Delhi, to Irwin, who was a staunch Anglo-Catholic himself, and to Lord Willingdon, who was quite regular in attendance but clearly less congenial. And yet, in the tense period between 1929 and 1934 he makes the scrappiest of allusions to the world of nationalist and imperial politics. There has been a 'row in the Chowk,' and the Gordon Highlanders used machine guns and killed some rioters. A friend in charge of Arthur Road Gaol in Bombay has had trouble with Congress prisoners, especially women. Referring to rumours of a riot on the anniversary of the 'Mutiny', he is predictably and conventionally dismissive: 'I do not doubt that the badmashes will find everybody prepared to give them a hot reception.'[3] A mob outside the Bombay gaol had shouted that Irwin had sent Sapru and Jayakar to Mahatma Gandhi in prison, to beg Gandhi not to reduce the pay of the Viceroy and Governors, and had promised to release him if he would comply, which 'just shows the sort of pernicious rubbish with which the Congress are stuffing the uneducated.' In his one allusion to the Round Table Conferences, he has the reassurance that the army is not disaffected at present, that the police are everywhere splendid, but that one can trust no one in India, for the leopard has not had time to change his spots since the 'Mutiny' of 1857. He comments that the new taxation in the 1931 budget is 'to pay for Mr Gandhi's escapades during the past year.'

He responds to the wildlife of India and to the Moghul buildings of Delhi, but apart from a few ghostly servants, his letters are populated exclusively by his own kind. An impregnably Erastian atmosphere is conveyed by the iteration of routine detail: discussion with the Viceroy about new church furnishings and the form of a commemoration service; at Risalpur, the best church parade in his experience; problems with the Church Buildings Committee; the more alarming problem of keeping the front pew clear for their Excellencies, should they and their satellites arrive late for church; dinner with the Commander-in-Chief and talk about the roof of the new church; the prospect of a congenial posting to Peshawar. Of the missionary world ('why are missionaries always so slovenly?'), there is barely a glimpse, whilst he finds the moves towards church reunion in South India doctrinally offensive to his Anglo-Catholic belief in the apostolic succession. In October 1931, he is reading Winston Churchill's *My Early Life,* and has 'quite taken' to him:

In spite of all the nasty things one hears said about him (especially by Bishops of the Indian Church and those sort of people who think he is doing the work of the devil in stirring up bad feeling in this country towards it). Mr Gandhi seems quite the rage in England at present, but I cannot believe he will succeed in hoodwinking the united intelligence of our so-called National Government, while some of his dicta are silly enough even to rouse the suspicions of the hard-headed British Proletariat.[4]

The letters document one representative Indian career over a lengthy period, but the chaplains also left tracks of a kind in the ephemeral pages of the diocesan journals. Such publications are unlikely to command an extensive readership. Their styles vary from the bleakly functional to the self-consciously educational, and they can be vulnerable to the fads of individual editors, though not always in ways one would expect—the editorial stint of a British-Israelite cleric, the Revd Alexander Patrick, on the *Lucknow Diocesan Chronicle* for a couple of years at the end of the 1920s, gives no particular hint of his inclinations. He was to become a member of the die-hard India Defence League in the 1930s. Storrs Fox used to send the *Lahore Diocesan Magazine* home occasionally, and around the same time credits one number for being much better than usual: 'some of them have been mighty dull lately, and others mighty heretical.'[5] However, the more expansive of them do provide glimpses of the thinking part of the diocese and the assumptions and received wisdom of the leadership and the more articulate. The most suggestive material between the wars is printed in the journals of Calcutta, the 'Canterbury'—under the Metropolitan—of the Indian dioceses, and of Lucknow, Lahore and Bombay. Despite differences between them, it is possible to make a number of generalizations about the treatment of recurring preoccupations: the Empire, Hinduism and Islam, Indian nationalism, the Indian church and, finally and prominently, church involvement in political events back in England.

As one would expect, they take the imperial role of the British as self-evidently right and providential. Thus, the Lahore magazine publishes an unblushing endorsement of political deference in a review, in April 1927, of a book by 'an Indian Muhammadan' entitled *British India*, (written, according to the book's author, 'solely as a humble recognition of the great blessing British rule has conferred on India'), with the comment that it 'should have a place in every library and in every school, and we venture to suggest that it also occupy a prominent place on the Chaplain's writing table or in his revolving book case.' Less invidiously, in July 1925, there is an article by Lord Selbourne, reprinted from the conservative *Morning Post* on 'The Church and the Empire.' In 1924 the *Calcutta Diocesan Record* gives prominence to the effusions of Bishop Theodore Woods of Winchester on the 'Imperial Mission' in connection with Empire Day. Woods was an enthusiastic supporter of the ICF, with which fellow members of the Mission of Help were also associated. The Mission as was pointed out earlier, stressed the burden of imperial obligation on individuals and their occasional failures to live up to it.

There were other interweaving threads in this awareness of an imperial church. Above all, there was the army and its imperial service. Throughout 1933 the *Bombay Diocesan Magazine* published a series of extended regimental histories in each monthly issue of units that had been stationed in the diocese. These accounts came from the local Commanding Officer to Bishop Dyke Acland, Palmer's successor, formerly an SPG misionary, and Canon of the cathedral, (and also, as Bishop, the unwitting patron of M. Carritt's Communist Party contact, the Revd Michael Scott). A note in the July issue refers to the church memorials in St Mary's Poona, where many of the regiments in the British Army are represented and most of 'the battles by which a subcontinent was won to the regime of peace, justice and ordered liberty.' Calcutta too printed its regimental histories. The frontier diocese, where Englishmen were still being killed in this cause, was of course Lahore, and *The Lahore Chronicle* published a two-part essay in the same year on origins and survivals of British military history, by the chaplain at Kasauli. But Lahore was also the cathedral city for Amritsar, where General Dyer had conducted the Jallianwalla Bagh massacre in 1919, and was itself a city in which Gandhi's call for a *satyagraha* against the Rowlatt Act of 1919, an Act which had united, in a movement of striking intensity, different classes and communities, from well educated urban Hindu castes, such as Khatris and Aroras, to Muslim artisans and workers, all of whom were alienated from the administration of Sir Michael O'Dwyer.[6] So an influential book by the missionary educationist W. E. S. Holland, *The Outlook for India,* struck a raw nerve when it came out in 1926, eliciting a confused mixture of imperial piety and imperial assertion. Holland is acknowledged to be admirable on Gandhi, 'brilliant' on the religious mind of India, but,

He feels it on his conscience to make an apology to India for the English. We have no objection to that. In many particulars it needed doing. But even so, was it the best way to accomplish this purpose to make over again the cinders of the Rowlatt Act agitation and the Amritsar catastrophe, and to give over again the full details? What is the point of asking callow undergraduates in England who cannot form a judgement, to study in organized circles the details, not merely the underlying principles, of Amritsar 1919? Surely this is merely to excite a racial temper. Nor is Mr Holland fair. He has a strong bias. He refers to Sir Michael O'Dwyer's book *India as I knew It* only in the bibliography.[7]

There were various expositions of the moral basis of the Christian Empire by leading figures. Bishop Palmer of Bombay, who was much concerned with the emergence of an independent and united Indian Church, covers the common ground. He is reported speaking at length at the Indian Church Aid Association in London in June 1919. Anticipating doubts about the Montford reforms, he nevertheless reproduces a strong but deliberately general version of the Curtis argument. The only justification for autocratic rule is training in self-government; the British, 'through and through democratic,' cannot escape from the harvest for which the seed was sown by

Burke, Mill, Milton and Shakespeare, a literature breathing the spirit of freedom; to give away power is dangerous, but we must recall how God trains men, trusting us, despite our failures, with free will; the task of Christians is to develop the good will, trust and hopefulness between the communities and between rulers and ruled that will lead the Indian to self-government; citizenship in India is as yet weak because of the absence of trust, but the love of men which unites societies is insecure until it is founded in the love of God, which the oriental religions cannot teach, and which the mission schools and colleges and the Indian church can.

The air in Anglican and Free Church circles in England was at the time full of a rhetoric of co-operation, good will, and trust between groups and classes, and this was picked up in India, for instance by an ICS man, R. B. Ewbank, lecturing on co-operative ideals in this idiom in St Mary's Poona in November 1919. But it was difficult to sustain that anxious optimism in India, and we find the Metropolitan, Foss Westcott, taking a sterner line as nationalist activities get under way. The general argument remains the same, but evolutionary change promises to take place more slowly and uncertainly for Westcott in the 1930s than for Palmer just after the Great War. Even so, the Revd T. R. Milford, Secretary to the Student Christian Movement and Haileybury College's prolific correspondent from St John's College, Agra (where a hostel was financed by Haileybury), writes in the mid-1930s on Christianity and self-government closely on the track of Curtis's 'intensely interesting' *Civitas Dei*.

More surprising is the attention, occasionally quite technical, given to Hinduism, mainly as a religion but occasionally to its poetry and art. The general assumptions are Farquhar's, in a simple form, and he is referred to from time to time as an illuminating source. Acland himself wrote a monthly series of 'Notes on Hinduism', starting in December 1920 and still running in August 1921, which must have taxed the patience of his readers. He presents Hinduism as a dense conglomeration of beliefs, practices and superstitions, devoting a good deal of attention to the social organization of caste. On the inevitable *ling* he is judiciously independent (and descriptively more accurate, incidentally, than many occasional allusions of the period). 'The *Ling* is a phallic emblem; i.e. a representation of the organs of generation.' But he also notes, presumably as a general rather than a personal observation, that it does not 'call up improper thoughts, but I cannot say the same for the attentions that I have seen paid to the Nandi bail' (the recumbant ox which is a manifestation of Mahadev). There was little evidence that Acland's learned curiosity was shared by his Bombay colleagues.

Calcutta acknowledges its position at the heart of the Hindu revival[8] by taking regular notice of books on Hinduism, and not only the standard works of Whitehead and MacNicol. An Oxford University Press analysis and index of the Mahabharata is reviewed in 1935. A. J. Appasamy's *Christianity as Bhaktimarga* and *What is Moksha* are covered, with emphasis on his exploration of the Gospel according to St John.[9] A comparative study of Hinduism, Buddhism and Christianity by a priest in Ceylon, Isaac Tambyah, is noticed, and another Indian priest, the Revd Chakravarti, writes an article on *bhakti*. The Lahore journal refers its readers to Rondaldshay's widely read *The Heart of Aryavarta*, (it was awarded the Gold Medal of the Royal Empire Society), in a review by P. N. F. Young, reprinted from *Delhi*, the journal of the Cambridge Mission.[10] Young notes Ronaldshay's concentration on the fundamental insights of the higher Hinduism, the Vedanta's sense of the unity of all life, as most characteristic of India, criticises him for tending to see India as Bengal writ large, but recommends it as an 'excellent' book. Ronaldshay , who will be discussed later, makes a great deal of the 'perverted' religious basis of Bengali nationalism.

The fulfilment thesis is pervasive. The appeal of Appasamy, later a Bishop of the Church of South India, is that he is an Indian Christian, concerned, as M. M. Thomas has put it, to expand the 'Christian doctrine of immanence, showing both its points of contact with Hindu ideas of immanence and points of departure from them,' starting with the 'Johanine idea of the Word, the Eternal Mind animating the whole world, and its unique incarnation in Jesus.'[11] The process of fulfilment is also recognized in the various studies of the Christian Sadhu Sundar Singh, by Streeter, Appasamy and others, which came out in the period.

We are left in no doubt, however, that Hinduism and Hindu society have very far to travel and that the journey will not be completed on their own internal resources. In a series on 'Hindu leaders in the pulpit,' in the Bombay journal, the Revd H. H. Heaton of the SPG writes on Hindu social reform, noting, however, the unfortunate lapse of Ranade, a founder of the Prarthana Samaj, who married a child bride as his second wife in 1873, in a weak concession to family pressure and the fear of orthodox Hindus that he would chose to marry a widow, in proof of his sincerity as a social reformer.[12] Stern judgment is never far from the surface.

The failures of the British are consistently represented in the diocesan periodicals as lying with individuals, lapses of sound judgement or good conduct, but the failures of Indian society are shown as systemic and reflecting the deeply irrational nature of a Hinduism which can prepare only sluggishly for Christ.

If Christian writers at this time did little more on the communal issue than urge amelioration, unity and reconciliation, neither, it must be said, were nationalist leaders themselves able to do much more than preach. There were seventy-two communal riots between 1923 and 1926, as against sixteen between 1900 and 1922. A Unity Conference took place on 23 September 1924, before the scheduled ending of Gandhi's twenty-one day fast, which he had initiated in order to 'blackmail the conscience of his countrymen.'[13] Nehru's biographer notes that it 'passed a series of platitudinous resolutions,' and a dejected Jawaharlal Nehru was reduced to 'the preaching of unity and nonviolence, spinning and the wearing of Khaddar.' Westcott believed that 'a change of thought and temper' emerged from the conference, and his article for the Indian *Statesman* was reprinted in the Bombay and Calcutta journals. Religious differences, according to Westcott, were merely the effective means whereby 'designing persons have been able to excite the passions of ignorant and fanatical people.' References to Islam in the diocesan journals (though there are occasional references to standard texts such as Zwemmer's *The Moslem World*) are generally pragmatic and untheological.

The journals remind themselves from time to time of the church's detachment from, or elevation above 'politics', in recognition of the Establishment's official policy and its institutional position. 'It is no part of the Church's work to interfere with political conditions, any more than Our Lord interfered with the Roman Empire or its officers.'[14] Nevertheless, comment on specific political incidents and movements, and reflections with political implications in a broader sense regularly appear. The latter comfortably reproduce the discursive commentary on Hinduism and Hindu social organization, the malign dominance of the Brahmans and the intolerable suppression inflicted by the caste system on the inferior groups, and above all on the outcastes. (Brahman dominance is a universal short-hand in the orientalist discourse for all dominance by superior castes, and this of course emphasizes the corrupted religious basis of the entire system.) Thus, the political and economic reasons of pariah and low caste groups for mass conversion to Christianity are sympathetically recognized. In absolute figures, these were not at the time negligible. Whitehead's figures for Telugu converts in the Dornakal area, in his 1924 volume *Indian Problems in Religion, Education and Politics*, are striking enough. From an average conversion rate of about 3000 a year ten years earlier, the missions in this area had been faced for three years in the early 1920s with around 40,000 conversions a year. If Whitehead's enthusiasm for the spiritual opportunities represented by these figures was not perhaps too widely shared, they were accepted as symptomatic of a healthy disturbance of the caste system, however limited. Even more encouraging for some, because it was apparently a more practical, individualist and exemplary sign of escape from the social evils of rural inertia and backwardness, were the famous village 'uplift' schemes of F. L. Brayne in Gurgaon, to the south of Delhi, which could be closely followed over several months by Lahore readers. Brayne's projects will be described in more detail in the following chapter.

Just what constituted healthy evolutionary change consistent with the Christian perspective was the subject for a good deal of solicitous comment. There was no doubt in the Bombay diocesan journal of May 1921, for example, about the non-cooperation movement in 1921, or about the determination of all,

that the non-cooperation movement should not succeed in wrecking India. God moves in a mysterious way, and it may be that through non-cooperation Mr Gandhi may achieve what we can all believe he works for, the good of India—but this will be achieved through the proof of the failure of non-cooperation, through the proof which the movement has shown, that only through a spirit of co-operation, of creed with creed, caste with caste, class with class, colour with colour, can a country of diverse creeds, castes and nationalities, etc achieve the highest aims and obtain the greatest blessings.

Palmer's St Andrew's Day address for 1923, and later presented at the Oxford National Council of Missions in January 1924 as 'The

Church and Nationalism,' was reprinted as an important contribution. The organic model of social evolution familiar to Lionel Curtis and Bishop William Temple leads in summary form into his conclusions. The spirit of nationality, as against that of the nationalism that degenerates into intolerance and racial hatred, emerges when men 'transfer to their unified body corporate the affections which in primitive conditions they kept for the family or tribe.' The spirit of nationality is attached to a unit of territory, of tradition, of laws. A national church expresses that unity, draws out new possibilities as its contribution to a universal church. But a divided society is set on another kind of path. Abstract political theory, what he calls 'pure political concepts' are not the church's concern, but the Christian as a citizen must recognize that such matters must wait upon the ordained contingencies of history. We are urged today that every nation should govern itself, as natural justice or right.

I am inclined to say that we ought to challenge that position. I am unable to find any hint of an admission of that claim in our Lord's treatment of the question between his nationalist countrymen and the Roman Empire.... He admitted, not once only, the right of the Roman Empire to govern them.... Imperial rule was the only chance of preserving order in Palestine at that time...[and] those who were able to govern ought to govern....

A nation which has not attained sufficient internal unity to direct its own affairs in peace has no substantial claim to be permitted to continue an existence of perpetual anarchy, which makes it a danger to all surrounding nations.

In the politically hotter climate of Bengal in 1932, Westcott uses more uncompromising language. Faced with ceaseless opposition to constituted authority, a 'false patriotism' among Bengal youth of both sexes, the 'Government is certainly justified in using the sternest of measures' and is bound to 'uproot the enemies of the social order.' This pronouncement was part of an exchange with one of his less reliable co-religionists, an Indian Christian nationalist and Gandhian. It will be described in detail in Chapter 6.

But an Indian National Church, loyal to the British connection, was of course seen as an essential ingredient at the very least of a healthy nationalism. For the most part, the journals touch on 'Indianization' in the 1920s through a relatively exhaustive coverage of the great institutional debates of the decade over the Church's future in India. Clerical 'eccentrics' like Andrews, Jack Winslow and Elwin were able to argue for innovation outside the established church structures, in tribal work and *ashrams* like Winslow's Christa Seva Sangha, but they could on occasion be given a bumpy ride. Canon Acland was benignly ironical over Winslow's suggestion that the new Bishop of Ahmednagar and Aurungabad should present himself as a Christian 'guru', rather than as a European 'burra sahib', wondering what degree of fakir-like nakedness would be considered suitable and how the diocese would be administered by a Bishop subsisting on alms and a free rail pass.

But the major debates of the period were over the rationalization of church structures. There were two decisions to be made in conjunction: a Parliamentary modification of the Government of India Act, and a Church Assembly Measure. The effect would be to make the Church of India entirely autonomous. The Preface to Crockford's *Clerical Directory* for 1927 hopes, 'that this will prove to be very greatly to its advantage. Our only fear is lest some 300,000,000 people may take it to mean that the Raj has repudiated Christianity.' The assumption that even a substantial proportion of the population of India might be in some degree affected by events of this kind is a very bold one, but characteristic of those who believed strongly in the Christian mission of the Raj. For the scheme's partisans it was the only hope for a national Christianity in a Raj growing towards full membership in the family of nations, and Palmer in particular expounded the arguments with persistence.[15]

Finally, and with marginal and confused notes of criticism, the diocesan periodicals gave ample and appreciative coverage to the movement of social concern at home associated particularly with William Temple and the Industrial Christian Fellowship. Temple's COPEC (Conference on Politics, Economics and Citizenship) of 1924 was held up with admiration and his books reviewed, as are those of the ICF 'Messenger' Studdert Kennedy. An article by the latter, 'I Believe in the Protestant Church,' was reprinted from the *Daily Express* by the Lucknow and Lahore magazines, and the Bombay diocesan journal printed a series of lengthy extracts from his *Food for the Fed Up*. After his death in 1929, an obituary in the Calcutta *Record* described him as always in the front line trench of the Fellowship's attack on communistic atheism, as one who believed that men were never intended to be equal, though they were of equal potential value in the sight of God. The Meerut Conspiracy Case was just getting under way, and the threat of international communism seemed to some more serious in India than at home.

The message from home for the church in India is clearly spelled out. At home, the Church is developing a stirring movement of reconciliation and integration between the classes, a movement of individuals confronting the agents of darkness and confusion in the spirit of Christ. The Church in India is not matching up to this example.

> We have in this country absolutely no live enterprise for the regeneration of society. We have no social message. There are some people in England who are really keen and energetic in the attempt to bring the message of Christ to bear on industrial problems... but here they do not even exist.[16]

Inspiring examples are held up for all to see. One of the Mission of Help preachers visiting India, the Revd E. G. Southam, is identified as the 'Busman's parson', an 'honorary member of the T & G W Trade Union, who attends all their conferences and shares all their secrets,' and who is also an executive member of the ICF. Readers are told that Mr Percy Best, Managing Director of Selfridge's, (himself, though this is not picked up, a member of the ICF Council), attended one of the meetings of 'the Vicar's bus chums, to speak about the principles and spirit which underlie that great business.'

The ICF's interest in the trade unions was frankly managerial, or, in radical terminology, collaborationist, and it was loyally committed to the nation's established leadership, fallible and in need of correction though that might be. Its more liberal wing, heir to the old *Christian Social Union* tradition of Scott Holland and Gore on which the ICF had been founded, expressed anxieties about the spiritual and intellectual immaturity of the new industrial working class electorate, whilst calling for their fair and sympathetic treatment. The tone on the clerical right could be recognizably different, shriller and less tenderly concerned. The Revd Horace Skipton of the Indian Church Aid Association may even have found the ICF's rhetoric too 'socialistic', but his regular 'London Letter' to Bombay for October 1920 can be matched in the more prickly pronouncements of ICF activists.

> The working classes are in a most evil temper, partly owing to the spread of unemployment for which they themselves are mainly responsible, and partly to the tireless propaganda of Lenin and the Bolshevists, of which

indications are plentiful. Their leaders speak smooth things in Parliament and wring their hands in sorrow for calamities which they have themselves planned and brought to pass. And today's papers tell of a truculent speech by the miners' leader in which he warns his people that the Government are laying schemes to subdue them by machine guns and aeroplanes.

The ICAA, where Skipton rubbed shoulders with Lady Sydenham,[17] Arthur Hirtzel and others with strong conservative affiliations, was a sober establishment 'good cause': the rhetoric of popular confessional uplift was characteristic of the ICF. But the message from the spectrum of church opinion in England to which both belonged was unambiguous: the existing structures and institutions in which social reason is inherent are under threat from an inchoate and unreasoning mass. The sensation was entirely familiar to the official class of the Raj as it confronted the ambiguous promise of Indian nationalism.

The Missionary Predicament

The missionary church in India reported back regularly to its parent societies through annual 'letters', which seem to have been long or short, more comprehensive or less, according to the individual preferences of those responsible in the various mission stations. The letters were a general supplement to regular correspondence on specific issues, money, health and the deployment of personnel. Organizing secretaries at home selected and edited from this unsystematic but open-ended source, publishing whole letters or extracts, and producing annual reports for formal meetings, and articles for the various missionary magazines.

Overall, the letters convey a coherent but by no means uniform impression of an arena very different from that of the IEE. There were additional opportunities, rare but important, for the missions to attract outside attention. The most important between the World Wars, perhaps, was the scrutiny by the Commission on Christian Higher Education in India, chaired by A. D. Lindsay, Master of Balliol College, whose report was printed (and reprinted) in 1931. But the experience of a more obscure commission, chaired in 1919 by the Revd Alek Fraser (already famous as the Headmaster of Trinity College, Kandy (CMS), subsequently of Achimota on the Gold Coast, and later still as Headmaster of Gordonstoun School), will serve to focus attention on the inevitably contradictory signals coming from those in the mission sector primarily concerned with village India, as teachers and medical workers.[18]

The recommendations of Fraser's Village Education Commission are based on a severely critical view of the amateurism of mission education at this level, and of the inadequacy of Indian representation in its supervision. In themselves, as Fraser's biographer points out, the recommendations are bound to look commonplace at this distance in time: better supervision and training of teachers, training for community leadership and village life, Indian representation on educational committees. They were innovative at the time. But what is of interest here is the reaction of an evangelical enthusiast from the world of the major educational institutions to the struggling and fragmented field of routine mission work, the world partially encapsulated in the marginal, defeated figure of Barbie in Scott's *Raj Quartet*. Fraser's missionary philosophy was radical and uncompromising in relation to government, and had unusually demanding expectations of a Christian imperialism. For him, the missions were the Christian conscience of Empire and they were being allowed to do their task badly. His theology is reflected in the introduction of the comparative study of religion at Trinity College, with the message of Christ as the crowning summit, and in his commitment to the growth of an indigenous Christianity. His reading of history could have come straight out of Coupland's lecture notes: 'We could win our Empire both abroad and at home and rise to the heritage of Pitt, which to us is the call of God.'[19] But neither his theology nor his history offered self-fulfilling prophecies, and he would himself put a 'black picture' of avoidable failure, (in a contentious sermon preached in 1934 in Westminster Abbey), for example, against the saving but barely sufficient fact that, 'much of our rule has been Christian in the truest sense. We have sought not our own but the good of others.'[20]

Few things in his time on the subcontinent affected him as 'blacker' than the events in Amritsar in 1919, the symptom of a crass failure to recognize the Divine Purpose at work in Indian unrest. This event gave shape and coherence to the knowledge that the fulfilment of Empire does not lie in perpetual dominance, but in imperial sponsorship of the political maturity to which even an illiterate society is capable. Views of this kind implying, of course, a wide electoral franchise and a degree of sympathetic trust in the Indian nationalist leaders which, with few others in India, he shared with his friend C. F. Andrews, were sufficient to have Fraser and his wife sent to Coventry by most of the passengers on a P & O liner returning to Ceylon in 1921.[21] The imputation of disloyalty on Fraser's part touched class as well as race, for his father, Sir Andrew Fraser, a deeply religious evangelical who had strongly influenced his son's career, had been Lieutenant Governor of Bengal, (where he had narrowly escaped assassination in 1908).[22]

But Fraser's idealism must have struck even pro-nationalist missionaries as unrealistically demanding. Travelling on the 1919 Commission, he was made aware of the lonely ageing lives which are represented in one aspect of the fictional character of 'Barbie'. Miss Allan (Principal of Homerton Teacher Training College, and a member of the Commission) is 'so frank on the terrible loneliness of her staff as they grow old, and points out too the dried up spinsters as we travel round...[who] cut themselves off...become warped, narrow, hard.'[23] He and his colleagues were particularly depressed by their encounters with an incompetent neglect of health in the mission schools and the aloofness of the missionaries from the people. But the anniversary of Amritsar also made him acutely aware of the 'evils of Government', in the Punjab, and he conjured up visions of an imminent massacre of Europeans that would rival the Mutiny.

I believe a mutiny will break out in the north this hot weather, possibly from Agra to Pindi, with all the horrors of massacre and fiendish Mohammedan cruelty. They have every excuse. Bosworth Smith entered the Mohammedan zenanas and brought out their women, stood them up against a wall and took the veils from their faces.... He is a devil incarnate and he has exposed every Christian woman and every white woman to Muslim lust.... My dear, I feel just awful as an Englishman.[24]

But his report urges that circumstances in India, if it is not already too late, permit at least a more self-conscious engagement with the politics of nationalism, a deliberate detachment from establishment perspectives and a reversal of the missionaries' acceptable quietism in order to drag imperial politics back onto the right course. So he argues explicitly for political activity by the missionaries, proposing in effect that the structure of the missionary church at this level be redisigned to confront government of the kind that had exposed itself in the Punjab. The missionary must adapt, and acknowledge the demands of the Indian people for self-government both in church and state, by taking an irreversible structural step. 'Directive and administrative work should be placed in the hands of Indians, even where it is feared that there may be a considerable loss in efficiency.'[25] The report had real consequences for Indian education at this level. But the impatience behind it was directed quite generally at the failures of a Christian Raj.

The truth is, however, that the political implications of missionary activity have always been set about with contradictions and ambiguities in India, and it has generally been easier for crusading Christians such as Fraser and his friend, C. E. Tyndale-Biscoe of Kashmir, to see a return on commitment invested in the relatively insulated, and manifestly functional system of a selective school or college, than in the more exposed positions of the missionary field at large.

There were good reasons for the political inadequacy, as Fraser saw it, of the missionaries he encountered. Inevitably missionaries are drawn into identifications with particular groups and, where the victims of social discrimination are involved, to particular injustices. Whether they always realized it or not, missionary success at levels below those of the high caste Hindu depended on this kind of involvement. As Gibbs observes of C. T. E. Rhenius in the early history of the Tinevelly Mission, he 'hardly realized how much his success was due to his vehement championship of those he considered to have been wronged in lawsuits or by Government officials.'[26] But any such involvement entailed political discrimination and alignment in one form or another, and each mission had to consider the consequences of its activities. The uplift of particular groups suffering from obvious caste oppression was naturally more tolerable to officialdom than any resistance to its own demands. The line between sticking up for the oppressed, and troublesome or subversive agitation could be a fine one.[27] Where high rates of conversion could be reported in subordinate groups, missionaries realized that fortuitous circumstances had only opened up opportunities, that they might perhaps, in Lucas's image, bring whole ship loads of common caste members to harbour, but that any real understanding and consolidation of faith could only follow far behind the mere act of baptism,—hence the importance attached by them to symbolic acts such as the destruction of idols and shrines by converts, which at least marked a collective dissociation from Hinduism or animism. But in any event, for caste groups, and even tribals such as Mundas or Bhils, conversion was strategic or tactical in a desperate competitive struggle with other groups and in response to uncontrollable economic circumstances.[28] Loyalty to the mission and loyalty to the British could not be distinguished. But in the eyes of other groups touched by nationalist or communal sentiment, convert groups were identifying themselves with the foreigner. (The costs for *individual* converts were prohibitively high, complete ostracism more often than not, and such conversions were correspondingly few.)

So missionaries who saw themselves as sympathetic to Indian aspirations encountered them, if at all, in situations that were highly structured by caste and sectional competition. Canon Rivington of the SPG wrote with gratitude from Betgeri-Gadag in Bombay Diocese of a,

Lambeth resolution suggesting that European missionaries should abstain from political activities...for we are living in a district where the friction between the Brahmans and the Lengaits is growing every day, and it is often hard to act in sympathy with one party without displeasing the other.... If we are to be men of peace and go about doing good we have to take care that, while we encourage all legitimate national aspirations we do not help to foster the caste feeling that is manifesting itself so strongly.

A year later he adds that, 'Our religion...is looked on as the religion of the foreigner and the embracing of it an unpatriotic act.'[29] There are regular references in the letters to increasing inter-caste tensions within the nationalist ferment of the inter-war period.

Nevertheless, the Christianity preached by the missionaries and repudiated by nationalists was seen by the former as in itself a touchstone for what constituted legitimate national aspiration, nationalism manifesting the Divine will. It was logical, therefore, for the more independent minded to look to *Swaraj* to 'free us of those hindrances which are not of our making—the identification of the ruling race and the confusion between the church and the foreign ruling power.'[30] Under such circumstances the Revd F. C. Arnold's Kunbis of Ahmednagar could then continue their slow awakening from 'long centuries of serfdom and sleep' and separate themselves from the religious domination of the Brahman oppressors, without confusing the authenticity of their discovery of the gospel with the irrelevant underwriting of alien approval.

But what else might the achievement of Swaraj entail? For it was also logical to turn inwards and shrink from political risks that were not merely inexpedient but culpable, legally and morally. One might recognize 'legitimate national aspiration' in the immediate post-war surge of sympathy among ordinary Indian Christians for the non-cooperation movement in South India, for instance,[31] and take this as an indication of growing maturity, independence and readiness to take over responsibility. But nationalist practices inevitably contaminated all aspects of national sentiment and there were few morally safe areas for its expression. The problem had long been familiar to missionaries in Bengal. The Revd N. H. Tubbs, later Bishop of Tinevelly and Madurai, in his annual letter to the CMS for 1908, blames a contagion from the dark underside of European politics.

We cannot but hope and believe that the bomb and other fiendish weapons of European anarchy have not come to stay. They are unnatural to India and repellent to all her traditions.[32]

Writing in the period of civil disobedience, Crosthwaite of Lucknow diocese reports that:

There was a report a short time ago that the Congress folk proposed to invade Ummedpur and hoist the Congress flag over the church. We, as a mission, stand apart from all politial activity, and though many of us, in common with most Englishmen, are not without sympathy with the desire for freedom which underlies the national movement, the Congress flag has become a symbol of revolt against the Government, so that this could not be allowed.[33]

In the same year, F. C. Arnold, writing from Kolhar in Bombay diocese, reports that the movement, 'soon lost its vaunted non-violence, and the authorities have had the time of their lives in maintaining law and order. India perhaps has never seen such a widely organized campaign to bring Government into contempt'. But 'no Government in the world could have been more considerate and patient in dealing with this, so-called, non-violent movement.'

It is no business of mine as a missionary priest to deal with politics, but in fairness it must be said that all this turmoil was persistently kept alive at the very time when our great Christian Viceroy had arranged for the Round Table Conference where the Indians would have a chance of settling their own difficulties and of helping the British Parliament to frame a Constitution for India more in keeping with public opinion out here.... The brains of the movement were supplied by the Brahmans, and the money to carry it out came very largely from the Gujarati traders—Gandhi's own countrymen.

He adds, however, that paradoxically, there were increasingly frequent comments of a new interest and warmth towards Christianity, and that the movement in his experience was quite friendly to Christian mission work. Ambivalence towards Gandhi is regularly reflected in these comments, and whether or not they really reflect a change of any significance in Indian attitudes towards missionary activity, they are clearly important to an understanding of missionary reactions to nationalism during the inter-war period. Gandhi is associated with the release of violence in the nationalist movement, but he is also seen as a major contributor to a new interest in the truths of other religions, particularly of Christianity and the New Testament, from which he was known to read to his followers. Holland reports to the CMS in 1923 that Hindus are thinking as never before of Christ, whom they recognize as the inspiration and model of Gandhi. 'Never have I, during all my time in India, known Hindus so accessible, so responsive, just when one would expect them to be most angry' (because of Gandhi's imprisonment). The Revd G. B. Redman in 1925 associated the decline of the non-cooperation movement and the apparent disappearance of Gandhi's political leadership with an increase in Gandhi's spiritual leadership and a turning of attention in India to spiritual forces. Canon Banerjee from Allahabad claimed that the teaching of Christ drew crowds as never before in the bazaar for the same reason of political disappointment. The missions held by the American preacher Stanley Jones aroused considerable interest at the time. In 1927, a CMS clergyman, reporting on the outbursts of religious fanaticism and bloodshed and the permanent conditions of mistrust and suspicion created by them in the United Provinces, also claimed a surge in interest in religious teaching, Hindu *sanyasis* turning from idleness to socially useful work, a closing of Hindu ranks against Islam and Christianity, but also the incident of Dr J. N. Carpenter on his retirement speaking to the 'breathless attention' of between two and three thousand Muslims at the invitation of the head mulvie in Meerut.

Testimony of this kind cannot conceivably be read as evidence of a much hoped for, and regularly predicted, turning to Christ by large numbers in India, though William Paton of the YMCA and Stanley Jones were not alone in anticipating a great wave of conversions emerging from the period of political unrest in the early 1920s. But it reflects a positive element in an internally dissonant missionary perspective. Fraser's observations notwithstanding, the mission sector as a whole was not engaged in weary withdrawal from the fray, even though their options were more limited than perhaps he allowed. The missionary letters refer only in short-hand, as it were, to the higher theological issues or even to the fulfilment thesis, which in fact dominated missionary thinking in this period and virtually until the outbreak of the Second World War. But missionaries were bound to read these stirrings in a positive light, even if it was a light that shone only intermittently and perhaps deceptively on a flawed popular ferment, to which they were far more directly exposed than were the establishment clergy. Different aspects of the same events demanded their sympathy but also their condemnation, and one regularly comes across evidence of the stern abnegation that accepts hostility as an inevitable and even necessary element in a situation of productively fermenting change. The missionaries did not always fall back on a simple minded law-and-order position when confronted with threats to the Pax Britannica. They could distance themselves from attitudes more representative of the establishment clergy. In fact P. N. F. Young of the Cambridge Mission, writing with Agnes Ferrers long before he joined the IEE himself, explicitly takes issue with opinions expressed in the *Lahore Diocesan Magazine* of May 1919:

Historical indications seem to lead inevitably to the conclusion that the spirit of nationality, wherever it shows itself as a growth, must necessarily grow or crystallize round opposition, it may be hostility to somebody or something.... [It is] a necessary portion of the White Man's Burden, an inevitable incident of his great obligation, that he should become, in increasing measure, in and by reason of the very prosecution of his task, the object of Indian aversion, deepening at times into actual hostility.[34]

The point is made with some regularity that such hostility is often richly deserved. If India has yet to find the way towards an authentic sense of nationality, the British as often forget where it lies. The Revd N. H. Tubbs again, from a Bengal with fresh memories of Lord Curzon:

Doubtless [suspicion and misunderstanding between missionary and Indian Christian] is all part of the present national movement for independence in India, but how much, too, is due to our pride and exclusiveness, our domineering ways and cold lovelessness.[35]

It has been suggested in a number of recent case studies that missionary conformism and avoidance of politics was to a significant extent conditioned by anxiety about getting on the wrong side of a suspicious Government and that officialdom could be prompt and punitive about association with undesirable figures in the nationalist movement. Particularly during the civil disobedience period loyalty became a very sensitive issue. The authorities were also concerned as the Second World War approached about foreign, above all German, missions and it has been suggested that when war came Christian leaders were weak enough to forget their German brethren in internment, even though, for instance, the two members of the Leipzig Mission who had some association with the Nazi Party had left before the war and there were no objective grounds for suspecting the activities of others.[36] But submissive anxiety about the sharp voice of civil authority is not something conveyed by the letters. Rather one finds an unstable combination of polarities. There was an anxious scanning of events for the signs of a healthy unrest and progressive change, but this went with a deeply engrained faith in the rightness of civil authority and the structure of the Raj. With an awareness of the spiritual limitations of the Raj went a strong sense of the strategic importance of the missions at the growth point of national evolution in the educational system, and an acute anxiety that rationality could be swallowed up in the disorders of a corrupted political ferment.

Christian Colleges and the Praeparatio Evangelica

These tensions dominate the politics of Indian higher education in the inter-war period, not only in the minds of missionaries and church leaders but of all those involved in the planning and implementation of educational reform, because the Christian colleges were the leading institutions. It was in the area of Indian higher education that the Christian interpretation of the Raj had its most substantive and coherent encounter with the spirit of Indian nationalism. Lindsay was speaking 'to an age, which now seems remote, when Christianity was a live force in British intellectual life.'[37] It was to produce other confident educational apologists in 'Bruce Truscott' (Professor E. Allison Peers, Professor of Spanish at the University of Liverpool), Sir Walter Moberly, (theologian and vice-chancellor) and, as the process of evaporation advanced, the more solitary intellectualism of Spencer Leeson, (a Wykehamist, like Moberly, and the college's last clerical Headmaster; he was subsequently Bishop of Peterborough).[38] From the present position of the chaotic tranfiguration of higher education in Britain, it is easy to underrate the illusion of permanence investing this Christian civic culture in the public school and Oxbridge world.

Lindsay saw liberal education as a process within a broad inter-disciplinary context, an ideal reflected in the programmes at Keele University of which he was the first vice-chancellor. Authentically Jowett's heir at Balliol, his 'high philosophic idealism accompanied... a no less strenuous notion of social obligation,' as Gregor points out—a fusion of purposes which he also represented as an energetic and eminent supporter of the Industrial Christian Fellowship.[39] Projected onto the Indian educational scene, his perspective heavily emphasized the idea of a liberal and essentially literary education as an intrinsically Christian preparation for national development, despite references to the sciences and the socially useful. Lindsay and admirers like Dr Percival Spear who became a distinguished historian of Mughal and modern India, describe the attempted provision of a *praeparatio evangelica*, straightening the way for an India converted to the spirit of Christ,[40] 'preparing the way for the Gospel in the minds of the non-Christian intelligentsia.'[41] It was in the light of this task that Lindsay's commission urged a reconcentration of resources and a disengagement from the mere pursuit of examination results.

Higher education in India, in institutions such as Bishop's College, Calcutta, Madras Christian College, St John's College, Agra, or Union Christian College, Alwaye, (which was run by Indians), was concerned not with conversion but with the development of 'Christian values' in the educated élite, the prospective leaders of the Indian nation.[42] Its focus was less on the acquisition of what the examination system identified as knowledge, which ambitious Indians were only too eager to acquire, than on 'character', the development of the 'individual', the absorption, through competitive sport and, if at all possible, the experience of corporate life in a residential context, of qualities of leadership—a rare element accessible in its purest form to the British through the alchemy of public school life. The public school, of course, provided the model for the mission colleges, as it did for the princes of India in the appropriately opulent setting of Mayo College. The CMS Letter Book for 8 June 1921 puts the point very plainly:

We regard St John's College [Agra] rather in the light of a foundation such as those which William of Wykeham made at Winchester and at Oxford, which have proved a permanent contribution of inestimable value to the Christian educational forces of the whole of England.

Tubbs writes from the Oxford and Cambridge Hostel at Allahabad:

Our business is character-building by means of personal influence. We are with our students all day long on the hockey-ground, in their societies, and their rooms. We can bring to bear upon the men at closest range the force of Christian example and intercourse. India's destiny lies in the character of her future leaders.[43]

The problem for the Christian teacher was not academic backwardness, except where poorly schooled Muslim students were mainly involved, as in the SPG Christian College at Cawnpore (Kanpur).[44] The problem was primarily Hinduism, and, for different and more negotiable reasons, Islam. 'The caste system has crushed individuality. Hinduism does not produce character,' wrote Tubbs. But the response should not be a confrontation. Dr Miller, the famous Principal of Madras Christian College who taught a remarkably high proportion of the first generation of Indian legislators in South India, and who continued through annual letters to the College to make his presence felt for years after his retirement,[45] refused to baptize. A final gathering-in could safely be left to the Divine providence. But he assumed the validity of the fulfilment hypothesis.

If the idea of Christ as the fulfiller has become more familiar, and more agreeable to the minds of Christians in southern India, it is largely due to the teaching and influence of Dr Miller.[46]

God has given to each nation the task of elucidating certain truths, and there are even truths which the Christian nations must appropriate from the non-Christian. The Hindus have a strong sense of the omnipenetrativeness of God, but have yet to acquire a rational understanding of social organization wⁱ.ich western Christianity has drawn out of the Greek approach to knowledge and expression, from Roman law and order, from the Jewish sense of personal obligation to God, and from the freedom and energy of the barbarian races of Europe. Lacking the essential components of a Christian character as it has evolved over the centuries, Hinduism would have to take advantage of its valuable openness to outside influences, but,

The line between wisdom and unwisdom is that which separates men who would have India to grow into united selfcontrolling nationhood gradually, naturally, healthily and therefore permanently and those who wish all essential elements of government to be quickly placed in inexperienced hands, that is to say...those who would let the fire rage uncontrolled until every fabric founded in the past has been consumed.[47]

There was no doubt in his own mind, as an extreme gradualist, nor, he believed, in the minds of his former students, as to the ultimate and permanent unity of Empire or Commonwealth, that

the hopes and views concerning India already held by the thoughtful few, will become practically universal and therefore irresistible. Thus between you and me there is, and between you and public opinion in the West there will come to be, complete agreement as to the goal that must be kept steadily in view.[48]

It was in this spirit of severe but kindly discipline that Miller sat in the Madras Legislative Council,[49] and gave, as a teacher, astonishing substance to the routine encomiums of Shakespeare in the missionary colleges, in such works as *King Lear and Indian Politics,* and *Coriolanus and Present Day Indian Politics.* In his declining years he confidently believed that Indian nationalist unrest was the work of agitators, German agents and their accomplices during the Great War, but in any event the central thread of a providential history, emerging from the inner nature of things, is not to be found in French revolutionary frenzies, in Russian autocracy or in the German worship of power. 'I hope you will reflect how different are conditions in India. There the central authority has never failed to keep its face in the direction of freedom.'[50]

The name of Miller was venerated in south India in the early 1920s, but much younger men were reproducing essentially the same intellectual framework elsewhere in the network of Christian colleges. There is ample evidence that their Indian students at the very least learnt to replicate the received wisdom. In the St John's College Magazine, Anwarul Haq of Class 5A wrote in 1916 on 'The Truest Patriot of Modern India is he who drinks most deeply the spirit of the West.'

It is the practical use of theories that the ruling nation has been endeavouring to teach us for about a century...we have to learn a high efficiency in that respect.

Such examples can be multiplied without difficulty and, even allowing for the largely ideological function of the house journals of educational institutions, it seems reasonable to suppose that many students and Indian members of staff identified more than formally with a message that was so consistently promoted.[51] The ability of another student a year later to sustain a sonnet 'On the grant of commissions to Indians' with an opening invocation to,

Montagu, true child of Albion ever free...

suggests at least a degree of unembarrassed fervour about such glimpses, as the sonnet has it, 'O the rising sun'.

Miller's opposite number in Agra, the Revd T. D. Sully, can reproduce him almost word for word: the imperial idea presupposes a basis of moral character in the individual and a well developed patriotism within the nation; our country has 'its place' in the Empire; India, through Hinduism, fell into the initial error of enslaving personality to mechanism and escaping the category of moral purpose, however, (this is in a review of Farquhar's *Crown of Hinduism*) the present generation is revolting against such popular determinism; just as the Greeks, the Romans and the Teutonic races all helped to give fuller expression to the one informing spirit, so will India's ideas about the sacredness of society, the life of poverty and mystical communion with the supreme, contribute to our understanding of Christ and receive completion from Him. However, it is Hogg, rather than Farquhar, who is right in stressing the concept of *karma* as central to the crippling mechanism of Hindu thought, for *karma* treats action as involving the individual only, whereas action always involves at least two people and positive action is always concerned with service to others.

Hogg is something of an exotic importation from a Hindu south in this context. *The Madras Christian College Magazine* was in the habit of printing scholarly and technical articles on Hinduism, but this is much rarer in northern journals where there are regular and uncritical allusions to Farquhar.

St John's had quite specific links with Lionel Curtis. The Vice-Chancellor's Address to Convocation in 1918 was given by his friend Sir James Meston, who could imagine a,

No more resplendent vision…an Imperial India in a federation of nations, each working out its own destiny in harmony with the common scheme, and the whole in union with the greatest of the earth's free nations.

Here too, Curtis recruited a kindred spirit to the Round Table group. J. B. Raju, a lecturer in the college, in 1914 addressed the First National Conference of the Layman's Missionary Movement on 'Christ and the Asiatic Spirit.' His argument was that the characteristic attitude of the East is a beautiful unworldliness, a deep dissatisfaction with the real world and human life, a deep conviction of its unreality, in radical contrast to the West's intense faith in the reality of this world, and 'of our life here and now,' its supreme insistence on duty, morality and the life of action, and of Him who went about doing good. Gokhale was Raju's hero. Official eyebrows were raised by the Agra Round Table Group, but Raju was hardly a subversive influence.

The Christian colleges were a receptive milieu for the imperial Christian Whig in Curtis. M. Ruthnaswamy refers to the Agra Round Table Group in which Raju participated, in his 1928 Sastri Foundation Lectures on 'The Political Theory of the Government of India,' delivered in the Senate House of Madras Christian College.[52] The influence of the Round Table and of Curtis himself on Meston, Marris, Lord Chelmsford and others is the crux of Ruthnaswamy's narrative. In his conclusion he notes that Benjamin Jowett's saying that 'in India as in England we are apt to do things rather late' unfortunately still applies, but that the Christian colleges were at least clear why they believed the Montford reforms were doing the right things.

It is against this backdrop, sustained in editorials, speeches, prize essays, articles and even verse, that one picks up allusions to the events that excited the politically-minded youth of India, particularly in Bengal before the Great War, in the non-cooperation period immediately after it, and in the civil disobedience period of the early 1930s. Political India is treated in the magazines with considerable sympathy. In 1907 Tubbs reports from Allahabad that the advent of Bipin Chandra Pal 'seemed to carry students right off their feet,' and he has nothing but praise for the devotion and unselfishness of the new patriotic spirit. It is true that there is a note of gratitude in his reference to the Risely Circular, which the Government used in 1907 to control outward manifestations of political life among students, but,

For us...to take no interest in what is their whole interest would be indeed suicidal. We cannot be cold or unsympathetic towards them, and surely the religion of the incarnation touches all phases of life and springs of thought.[53]

In subsequent decades there are ingenious attempts to give a 'service' direction to these energies by forming paramedical groups to help the victims of riots, or to upstage in courteous confrontation the dissidents who picketed and demanded student *hartals* or strikes. There were failures. In 1930 the students of St Paul's in Calcutta proved impossible to handle when the examinations coincided with the Congress' National Week, and only ten students out of 150 sat them, but in the same year the Agra students held their ground against a mob of boys from other schools demanding closure and, 'grievously insulted', resumed work on the mob's departure. The historian of St Stephen's records that:

The normal scale of values was significantly revealed when in the autumn of 1930, the College, which had declined invitation after invitation to indulge in political *hartals,* cut lectures *en masse* to go to watch the English MCC team play cricket.'[54]

Curtis had good grounds for satisfaction with St John's. Holland's farewell address in 1933, after a brief spell as principal, was a textbook summary of the vision he shared with his colleagues, of a Christianized élite emerging out of the organic community of the colleges and initiating the transmutation of caste and community divisions, putting aside the febrile excitements of agitation and protest in order to concentrate on preparation for the tasks of national leadership lying ahead in the organic orders of nation and Empire or Commonwealth. Holland argues that it is precisely because the evolution of nation-building in India is so compressed in time that there is a unique opportunity to influence it, by building on her unique contribution the capacity for sacrifice exemplified in the bare feet and non-violence of the Mahatma, and the natural reverence for religion. (Even habitual deference to the socially conservative Brahman as a source of spiritual purity is an index of an essentially true scale of values.) On the other side of the account lie the divisions of caste, the hideous spirit of communalism, group selfishness and parochialism. It was argued that the Indian must learn from Greek democracy to see himself as existing for the state. The nepotism characteristic of Indian society derives from an institutionalized group selfishness. Her frail sense of public responsibility is the weakness of a people who have yet to learn the spirit of self-government, and to shake off the collosal negative patience valued by the oriental religions. Holland's irritability as a harried, travelling Englishman emerges in the sudden bathos of a complaint about railway clerks and porters who are 'entirely incapable of giving prompt information as to the times when trains are due to arrive or depart,' and 'police who can seldom tell you the way to anywhere.' He sighs over India's inability to plan ahead, its way of leaving everything so often to the last minute, its feebleness with fact and reality, its nerveless defeatism, 'instead of the determined preparation to secure that our will shall be done, that we shall rule over circumstance and not be ruled by them.' But finally, the account is balanced in the 'deep and abiding conviction that it will be a Christian India,' for Hinduism offers no clear light or uncompromising challenge and it is only through the influence of Christ that the religious influence of the *Bhagavad Purana* has been 'pushed half consciously into the background' and the *Bhagavad Gita* enthroned in the central place in contemporary Hinduism. In reality Christ is already India's accepted standard.[55]

Indian Christians and Indian Nationalism

In the context of this chapter only one aspect of this complex subject need be touched on, and that only briefly. Unlike the churchmen of the IEE and the missionary world, those Indian Christians who consciously and uncompromisingly rejected the intellectual fabric of British orientalism did not have a receptive audience in England and were, in any case, more concerned with the task of detaching to a whole-hearted nationalism those Indians who found themselves members of the small Christian minority. There were other important figures who were both Indian and, in their own terms, nationalist, such as Dr K. T. Paul of the Indian YMCA, who were known in England, but these figures define themselves more accurately as intermediaries, though some of them were suspected by British officials for their subversive tendencies. George Thomas notes that the district authorities in Madurai regarded it as an offence for missions supported through educational grants to entertain Paul.[56] But they were, for all that, voices sustaining the structure of orientalist discourse and endorsing its more liberal extensions. Paul (d. 1931) signed Curtis's letter along with Lucas and Hogg, and contributed to Fraser's Commission on Village Education. Like S. K. Datta (d. 1942), Principal of Foreman Christian College, Lahore, who gave evidence with him at the Round Table Conference, he can be described as 'orienting the Indian Christian community towards nationalism,'[57] but not as repudiating the imperial connection and the fulfilment theology that went with it. From the point of view of the less chauvinistic British Christians, they were seen as important ambassadorial envoys for the faith in the Indian world of Gandhian nationalism and as a bulwark against extremism. The appreciative foreword to Paul's book, *The British Connection with India*, was written by Lord Ronaldshay.[58] Paul and his YMCA associates will be discussed more fully below.

Nativistic reactions to the missionary impact had taken place in a number of areas from an early period, for instance, in Tamil Nadu in the Hindu Church of the Lord Jesus, which emerged among Nadar Christians in 1858, and in the National Church of India movement between 1886 and 1916.[59] Missionary reactions to such developments shifted along with their reactions to nationalist impulses generally. The process in Tamil Nadu has been traced in a dissertation by Vincent Kumarados.[60] He shows the class and caste implications of conversion in Tamil Nadu, missionary resistance to nativism (and the importance to the missionaries of the argument of organizational incompetence among Indians), and missionary shifts towards the Congress, moving from good will, through scepticism, to serious discussion about nationality around the *swadeshi* question, a softening of aggressive missionary endeavour, as the nationalist movement gathered momentum, and a recognition on the part of most missionaries, at least, of nationalist ideals. But he also makes it clear that an uncompromisingly nationalist Indian Christianity was a tentative and uncertain development, a point that can be made for India as a whole. Between the World Wars its claims were articulated for British readers only in rather obscure quarters. There is a clear exposition of the basic premises, for instance, by V. Chakkarai in the *Christa Seva Sangha Review* for January 1933.[61] Like Gandhi's close associate J. C. Kumarappa, the Christian editor of *Young India,* Chakkarai rejects the social imperialism of British Christianity and the Christ of western civilization. Like Butterfield, he takes the decisive step of repudiating the premises on which an understanding of the nature of history that is both Whig and Christian has been based, namely the providential fusion, accessible in its expression to the right-minded historian, of social evolution and divine intention. He sees Christianity instead as:

A tangent coming from the Infinite and touching the circle of human life at various points. Christianity is not identical with history...[and] the Kingdom of God is not a gradual betterment of the social and moral order.

The English historians, in his view, have offered a 'pretended or pretentious idealism for India,' along with a justificatory empiricism which they run out as a matter of routine, the representation of 'India' as a geographical name for an anthropological chaos, far from the 'unity' that a genuine nationalism requires, from which follows the commonplace that caste and religious rivalries must go before such unity can appear. We might as well wait, says Chakkarai, for the Greek Calends, for the reality is 'that in the world of today it is economic nationalism that is the key to our problems' and it is the Christian's predicament that he happens to live in the midst of these forces. Writing a dozen years later, Kumarappa takes the same position by simply turning round the fulfilment thesis.

Of course the pure personal religion of Jesus needs a sociological order suited to it to take root. As we have noted, except in cases such as that of the Society of Friends, it does not find a congenial well-prepared ground to germinate in western forms of modern Christianity.[62]

The authentic Christian solution to living in a world dominated by economic nationalism is the Gandhian one of 'getting away from the notion that man's life consists in the abundance of things.' Violence is intrinsic to all countries based on centralized methods of production. They have to deprive other people of freedom so that the latter may be converted into slaves to produce the raw materials they need and consume the goods they manufacture.[63]

A Christianity deriving from such a society exports a static, institutional form of religion. Farquhar, he indicates, is its characteristically patronizing theologian. Kumarappa inverts the standard arguments about western individualism (also by implication the British churchman's invocations of Personality and its evolution), and Hinduism's crushing of the individual. Western Christianity has become individualistic, comfortable and selfish, whilst the Hindu joint family system, whatever its weaknesses, gives a claim on a common purse to 'the fit and the unfit, the rich and the poor, the gifted and the incapable,' and 'is distinctly an attempt towards loving thy neighbour as thyself'. At the same time, Islam's premis of individual equality puts western 'Christian' racism to shame.

To seriously entertain this kind of position was to place oneself outside the recognizable terms of reference as far as the Christianity of the Raj was concerned. Where they were noticed at all by any but the Anglican 'eccentrics', who responded to Gandhi with a mixture of veneration and rather unreliable support, such people were regarded as a menace.

There is a formal, printed statement at Bishop's College, Calcutta, from S. K. George, a lecturer at the college, dated 31 March 1932, justifying his resignation. He explains that he had been in the bad books of the Metropolitan for some time, because he had complained of the Metropolitan's 'very unconvincing reply' to a letter from Kumarappa, in the course of the correspondence involving Gandhi (which will be discussed in detail in Chapter 6). The Metropolitan had held the threat of punitive action over him for a couple of years. On the renewal of the civil disobedience movement, George had felt obliged to resign,

believing as I do that the Indian *Satyagraha* is the Cross in action and that it gives Jesus Christ His greatest opportunity to enter the hearts of a remade India. I held it to be my highest duty both towards the College and the Church in India to identify myself entirely with this non-violent movement, based absolutely on Truth and seeking solely to establish Peace on Earth and Good Will among men. But such an attitude on my part was regarded as disloyalty to the College and therefore I had no other alternative but to leave the College to follow my own conscience at this time of my Country's need and my Lord's opportunity.[64]

CHAPTER 5

Evangelical Attitudes

School and Village

In the process of reporting back from the Raj to the Anglo-India public in Britain—from strange and challenging situations but in the light of familiar categories and assumptions—two crusading Christian imperialists stand out. They do so much less on account of any literary appeal than because their singleness of vision and intensity of purpose dramatized the significance of the facts they worked over, and because they were both, in different ways, effective publicists. What they identified as fact was, in a general sense, familiar to anyone attending to the literature of the Raj. But the strength of their moral engagement and their intensely practical interpretation of the struggle seemed in itself to be confirmation of the validity of what they had to say. They made a particularly stark and consistent use of the Christian orientalist discourse from a political position, with regard to nationalism and the future of the Empire, that was well over to the right. An evangelical severity towards the moral inadequacies of the Indian char·cter and social organization conditioned their judgment on nationalist and liberal claims as to whether India was nearing readiness for her release from imperial restraint.

Canon Cecil Tyndale-Biscoe (d.1949) went to Kashmir in 1890, where he became the principal of the CMS schools centered around Srinagar. Frank Lugard Brayne (d. 1952), a favourite nephew of the Nigerian proconsul Lord Lugard, joined the ICS in 1905. He acquired a reputation in the 1920s as Deputy Commissioner of Gurgaon, a district immediately south of Delhi, for his rural 'uplift' projects. On the strength of this reputation he was made Commissioner for Rural Reconstruction in the Punjab in the 1930s.

Tyndale-Biscoe was the more representative figure in terms of what he attempted. A school on his lines was set up by the socially conscious Maharajah of Mysore. Alek Fraser was inspired by his practical emphasis on the social service ideal in his own work at Trinity College, Kandy, and educationists like W. E. S. Holland, N. H. Tubbs and P. N. F. Young were admiring visitors to Srinagar. But everyone knew that the Kashmir schools were exceptional. When Fraser eventually visited the main city school in 1914, he wrote that it 'makes me ashamed of my work at T. C. K., simply ashamed.'[1] Brayne, also an evangelical and a no less dominating personality, was in many ways *sui generis*. There were no other rural uplift programmes that remotely matched his own at Gurgaon in scope and size. It was intended to cover some 1400 villages. However, though Tyndale-Biscoe educated literate and ambitious young men of a princely state, pupils who were almost exclusively high caste Brahmans in the early years, whilst Brayne was concerned with the illiterate and often marginal peasantry of north India, both men reflected and vigorously reinforced the same vision of a Christian imperialism; a set of personal certainties that were in all essential respects in place when both men first landed in India. Thus armed, they worked relentlessly on digesting successes and failures and interpreting their inner significance in successive publications, speeches and conversations.

By any odds Brayne, who appears to have been completely humourless, was the less engaging of the two. His civil service colleagues were well aware of his weaknesses as an administrator, but it was not so easy to challenge his public persona and the claims he made for his rural uplift movement. His work in Gurgaon and the Punjab became a standard point of reference in the press, defining both the possibilities and the obstacles with which progressive civil servants had to contend in rural India. Much the same may be said of Tyndale-Biscoe's struggle to establish the rudiments of an essentially Christian personality in the Hindu and Muslim recruits to the Kashmiri administrative élite, though it was conducted with a greater readiness to learn from the objects of his attention and a sharply contrasting absence of self-regard.

C. E. Tyndale-Biscoe

The India public was made aware of the moral struggle he was conducting in Kashmir by a couple of books and a succession of intriguing articles, and also by exceptionally intensive deputation work for the CMS. Once known, Tyndale-Biscoe tended to be asked back. In 1910 he spoke at Bradfield, his old school, where the headmaster D. H. B. Gray, formerly a Winchester don, had transformed the moral hell his guest recalled from his early school days.[2] He also spoke at Eton, Haileybury, Harrow, Malvern, Marlborough, Shrewsbury, Loreto, Felstead and Sandhurst, where he had to abandon his prepared theme, the contribution of the Christian soldier Lord Roberts as Commander-in-Chief to the imperial task in India, because Roberts was in the audience. In 1914 he spoke in fifty-eight churches and school chapels and at a hundred- and -one meetings; he spoke in 1925 in twenty-one churches, to eighty-nine audiences in halls and drawing-rooms and to sixty two schools and colleges. He visited The Revd Alwyn Williams's Winchester in 1925 and the Revd Spencer Leeson's in 1930, and his old Cambridge college, where he preached in chapel but also spoke to the rowing men in the college hall. He had coxed the Cambridge boat to victory in 1884 and, at eight stone, had won the college pairs for Jesus College with the great Steve Fairburn. Speaking to the oarsmen he may well have drawn on a favourite metaphor, which he shared in a variety of formulations with Fairburn himself: 'as you meet your stretcher so you will meet your God.' He was, in a phrase he reserved as his highest accolade, a Man among men, a uniquely buoyant figure in the tradition of muscular Christianity of the public schools and universities. 'Go there, just because the work *is* hard,' he urged the boys at Haileybury in May 1925, after expatiating on the enormous power for good that a single white man with high ideals can be in India.[3]

His first book *Kashmir in Sunlight and Shade* appeared in 1925, *50 Years against the Stream*, compiled by his son, in 1930, and his autobiography in 1951, too late to be more than a record, but repeating old tales and well rehearsed lessons. The last of these had no less than four forewords: by The Earl of Halifax (Lord Irwin), Field-Marshal Lord Birdwood of Anzac, Sheikh Abdullah (Prime Minister of Kashmir), and George Barne (Bishop of Lahore from 1932 till after Independence): a spread of tributes that well represents the scope of his preoccupation, the Kashmiri and his regeneration in the protective care of a Christian empire.[4] Lord Birdwood, who had been Commander-in-Chief in India and who became Master of Peterhouse College, Cambridge in 1931, was one of a number of gallant believers Tyndale-Biscoe ranked, along with the early military administrators of the Punjab, as among the finest guardians of Pax Britannica.[5] The introduction to his first book was written by another, his friend Major-General L. C. Dunsterville, Kipling's school-fellow and life-long friend and the model for Stalky in his *Stalky and Co*—another Non-conformist who succeeded within the larger framework of imperial loyalties.[6]

Tyndale-Biscoe has been accurately placed by Mark Girouard among the 'paladins' of English gentlemanly chivalry celebrated by Newbolt. He had a close association with some of the best known of such people, including the immensely popular Lord Roberts, Lord Baden-Powell, the founder of the scouting movement and Sir Francis Younghusband, who took steps in 1908, as British Resident in Kashmir, to protect Tyndale-Biscoe from a murder threat.[7]

There was Francis Younghusband, marching with his little escort of troops up into the remoteness of the Himalayas in order to talk face to face with the chief Lama, and writing to Newbolt of 'our race and its high destiny' and England's genius for leading Asiatics. There was Tyndale-Biscoe, who spent his life teaching Hindu boys in Kashmir to respect women, live purely, train their bodies, serve others, take cold dips and play the game....[8]

The chivalry of imperial Camelot merged easily into the Christian Orientalism of the Raj. Younghusband was much concerned with mystical experience and wrote, for instance, about Christianity's fulfilment of oriental spiritual insight in relation to Ramakrishna's ecstatic vision of Christ in 1874, when his love for the Hindu gods and the Mother Goddess (Kali) was swept aside by a manifestation of Christ as an Incarnation of the Lord.[9] Simple uncontemplative conviction and doctrinal indifference were characteristic of Tyndale-Biscoe, but he shared Younghusband's belief, elaborated in his *Dawn in India: British Purpose and Indian Aspiration,* that spiritual growth was the premis of the imperial mission.[10] Kashmiri Hinduism represented fallen man almost at his weakest, in the physical Eden of a princely state under imperial influence, but not direct British control.

Kashmir, first of all, had to be seen as the victim of sustained historical misfortune, tempting Mohammedan adventurers, like

Mahmud of Ghuzni early in the eleventh century, to establish a prolonged period of Muslim rule, at times atrociously oppressive, though less so under the early Mughals. The tables were finally turned on Islam by Ranjit Singh in 1820, and Kashmir was sold by the British after the first Sikh war in 1846 to Maharajah Gulab Singh. A Hindu minority, employing British advisers, now held power. But long oppression had unmanned the Kashmiri Hindu and left him with the most inadequate of spiritual resources. He had a long way to go and there was no time for the servant of Christ to be squeamish about taking unconventional short-cuts.

The Hinduism of the Canon's experience had no perceptible redeeming qualities. The Muslims' stand up rather better. In his first book he produced the kind of descriptive ethnography which is characteristic of many missionary accounts, but there is no gesture towards an understanding interpretation of the beliefs and practices he describes. Kali, for instance, is casually identified as merely the goddess of murder. A predatory sect of vagrant Sadhus erupts during a cholera epidemic but Tyndale-Biscoe sends the 'holy rascals' packing with the threat of his upraised stick, and there are other less violent but no less tendentiously remembered occasions on which he deflates Hindu spirituality.[11] The rituals of prayer and purification are presented as meaningless, often absurd, and regularly unclean. Indeed his struggle for the Kashmiri's salvation was organized to a great extent round deep and ultimately religious disagreements over the concepts of cleanliness and purity. Anthropologists have in recent years shed much light on the social nature of definitions of clean and unclean, of their importance in systems of religious understanding of reality, and of the ways they can reflect and sustain social relations and distinctions.[12] But the missionary, who needed a strong stomach rather than a spirit of philosophical relativism, had no reason to be ahead of his time, and was aware simply of dangerous dirt and, worse still, complete indifference to its presence. Hinduism's arbitrary categories of the pure and the impure, it was clear to the CMS principal, disengaged the Kashmiri from an understanding of physical reality and its moral implications at the most fundamental level. But it was not in a naïve attempt to reproduce godly cleanliness and the Edwardian games ethic in exotic surroundings that he developed his educational strategy. Compulsory teamwork, in putting dirt where it belonged by cleansing cesspits and alleys, and in competitive games, were different aspects of the instrument he used in an attack on a fatally flawed understanding of physical and moral reality. It was a precondition for any effective action in domestic and public life, for any rational improvement of social and, therefore, of spiritual conditions.

His manner of opening campaigns was robust. The first Brahmans to row were young masters whom he manhandled into a boat, over their objections to touching oars polluted by leather. Pushing off into the current, he assured them that they would never touch land again unless they took to the oars, and after floating under three of the city's bridges they took him at his word. The first leather football was kicked under the intimidation of men armed with singlesticks. Unhygenic ear-rings disappeared on the introduction of a game called *Hi Cockaloram, jig jig jig,* which involved climbing onto the back of your opponent and retaining your ascendancy by gripping his head between your knees but without using your hands. Pupils with unusually unwashed clothes were thrown in the river or publicly scrubbed: 'the parents say that if a boy looks clean and tidy, the devil may take a fancy to him and run off with him. Here cleanliness is not next to godliness, but just the reverse.'[13] Boys who complained that they were polluting their caste relationships by sitting side by side had their heads rubbed briskly together. One pupil was made to reflect on the correspondences between material and inner pollution by being compelled, under the eye of the school's medical officer, to eat several ounces of an obscene manuscript he had brought to school. The account of a police raid led by the principal on the local manufactory of these works is a parable in which wickedness is farcically discomfited. Behind an imaginative application of such vigorous sanctions lay the ultimate threat of expulsion and reduced chances of clerical appointment or, with those whose parents thought it demeaning for their sons to learn how to swim, stiffer fees.

The inhibiting garment in daily use, a nightshirt or *pheran* worn without undergarments, which was supposedly forced on the population by their ancient Muslim rulers, disappeared on the introduction of headstands in compulsory gymnastics. Long nails, the insignia of a caste above the indignity of manual labour, were trimmed. Having taken up the English gentleman's oar, Brahman students advanced to paddling shikaras, like low caste watermen. Thus by sudden degrees the CMS boys found themselves mobilized for an attack on the political culture of Brahman Kashmir. Their families resisted, but had eventually either to concede or withdraw their children. Enemies accumulated among officials and priests. With official assistance, and the Maharajah's tacit support, Annie Besant started a Theosophical College on the opposite side of the river, with three staff and three hundred boys enticed away in a 'mutiny' from the mission school. The surviving CMS roll of 500 increased within two years to 1600,

So we hoped that Mrs Annie Besant would again pay a visit to Srinagar. As she had promised her Brahman friends to be reborn a Brahman boy, we hoped she might find herself in our school so that we could teach her the joys of cleaning a filthy city. [14]

The second Headmaster of Annie Besant's school, a Cambridge man, was won over 'so that we were able to work together for truer education in the Kashmir State.'

The school was increasingly used as a task force for social action, in fire, flood and cholera epidemic and in the treatment of women and animals, particularly dying cows who could not be put out of lingering misery for religious reasons. The goal was a society in practical evolution towards a more righteous order, escaping the oppressive divisions of caste and bound together by the value of disinterested service and duty to the public good, as the inner spirit, good humour and resilience of the young Kashmiris earned their proper scope, and as old boys responded at home and in their callings to the evils of a corrupt society and provided future generations for the school. Conversion to Christianity was deliberately discouraged, from awareness of the complexity and ambiguity of the motives involved, but there were occasions when the impulse of Divine grace had to be acknowledged and it was necessary to accept the severe social costs of conversion for those few concerned. The masters, however, were almost all Muslim or Hindu, and the ideal CMS boy was seen as one who put careerism behind effective and socially useful work, reliability, and honesty. His Character Form Sheet gave him marks for Mind, Body and Soul. Body included manual labour. Soul included scripture, obedience, truthfulness and honesty to masters, pluck, 'colour of heart', absence of dirty tricks, self-control, cleanliness and punctuality. Judgments on a number of these qualities, incidentally, were arrived at democratically.

The struggle never ends and for the evangelical the outcome is always at risk. Tyndale-Biscoe had a bleak view of the human material he was called to work on:

> I hate having to write thus of the Kashimiri, as I am really very fond of him. I can name scores as my friends. Many have stood by me in dangers and difficulties, and a few have suffered for me, and I know many who have risked their lives in saving life, from drowning and other causes, so that I look upon them as heroes and true gentlemen, and all the more so on account of their adverse surroundings and environments. Yet, to be truthful, and I do not believe in writing lies, I must say that the ordinary Kashmiri such as I have known for thirty years is a coward, a man with no self-respect and deceitful to a degree, and I perhaps may write with a clear conscience, for I have told this to all classes of them to their faces times without number, and, to give them all credit, they never resent it, because they know it is true.[15]

In terms of social practice rather than character, he was prepared to cap anything in Katherine Mayo's Mother India from his own knowledge of Kashmir. Whitechapel, in his days there as a curate, was bad, but there one could turn to the saving grace of a Christian society and its inherently progressive institutions. Kashmir was outside the direct control of the ICS and the Government of India, and the moral frailty of its ruling élite was a chronic problem.

His complete heroes were those who had served the imperial purpose: the army officers, Residents and officials, ranging from the Lawrences and figures like Sir Robert Montgomery, to nameless subalterns on leave, and to his own brother, who once knocked a houseboat pimp into the water with a good clean English punch. They shared integrity, competence and an insight into a providential purpose awaiting its remote realization. Indigenous claims to speak with the voice of history on the part of civil disobedience activists and strikers, he simply dismissed as foolishness, a view that was shared by a high proportion of the succession of Viceroys, Governors and eminent persons on holiday for whom a visit by boat to the school was a memorable and spectacular event. He was particularly encouraged after one of these visits by Lord Lloyd, Governor of Bombay, who had also offered him the command of the training ship for the Indian Navy. He had a social background in common with Lloyd, whose brother-in-law bought the Tyndale-Biscoe family estate, Holton Park in Oxfordshire.[16]

On Independence he left for Rhodesia, noting without surprise, the massacres that accompanied partition but also that fourteen of Sheikh Abdullah's new ministers were old pupils. In his autobiography, geographical description and superficial ethnography make way for a concentration on the battle with the works of the devil and a deliberate expansion of the imperial context. In 1890 his brother Edward on the Rhodes expedition to Mashonaland had been selected to hoist the Union Jack at Fort Salisbury, an episode that had its place along with others in his vision of the Pax Britannica. Arriving at Zanzibar in 1937,

As we crossed into the harbour we saw a fleet of dhows. I pointed them out to my wife saying that if we had come into Zanzibar harbour fifty-odd years before, those dhows would probably have been full of slaves, but there were no slaves on board, and why? Because of the British Navy. I thought of the days when my brother Edward was a middy, with the East African Fleet, chasing the slave dhows and releasing their cargoes. Thank God for the British Navy.[17]

F. L. Brayne

The CMS mission school taught scripture, without angling for conversions, by relating stories from the life of Christ and pointing up their bearing on practical situations. But as Bishop Barne of Lahore pointed out in the foreword to Brayne's one explicitly religious book, *In Him was Light*, whilst for Christian villagers 'uplift is supported at every turn by words from Holy Writ and especially by the actions of Jesus Christ Himself,' few of Brayne's villagers were Christian or, except nominally, anything else.[18] Writing from his Gurgaon experience ten years earlier Brayne had gruffly observed that:

The appeal to religion, which is so useful in England, particularly with the young, is denied to government servants in India. This is one of the conditions of our service, and that is all there is to be said about it.[19]

He had to interpret the message of Holy Writ as he saw it in terms of the language of physical cleanliness, rational productivity and disinterested social service. The subliminal biblical texts, however, are run out for his Christian readers. They stress unlimited faith, Christ's delegation of power and authority to his followers to cleanse, heal and caste out devils, and the obligation to serve and to labour. As a sample will show, they are injunctions in the first instance for the uplifter rather than the uplifted. The message of the story of the loaves and fishes is that hungry people cannot pray. Material improvement and welfare will eventually make spiritual life possible, and the New Testament's lessons about waste, stewardship and the obligation to work can be learnt (*Acts* 5, i-xi, 2 *Thess* 2, x, etc) under enlightened guidance. But the moral and practical impulse must come from the Christian authority and work downwards to the helpless.

Even so faith, if it hath not works, is dead, being alone. (*James* 2, xvii)

Then he called his twelve disciples together, and gave them power and authority over all devils, and to cure diseases. (*Luke* 9, i).

Heal the sick, cleanse the lepers, raise the dead, cast out devils; freely ye have received, freely give. (*Matthew*, 10, viii)

And that servant, which knew his lord's will, and prepared not himself, neither did according to his will, shall be beaten with many stripes. (*Luke* 12, xlvii)

Be sober, be vigilant; because your adversary the devil, as a roaring lion, walketh about, seeking whom he may devour. (1 *Peter* 5, viii)

Brayne's adversaries threatened to devour him with inanition. On the one hand sat an imperial bureaucracy with a weakening sense of purpose, hanging fire on practical uplifting projects, distracted by the problems of security raised by a morbid urban nationalism. On the other spread a peasantry who lacked the education and the individual personality's power of judgment to recognize the simple interconnections of action and consequence that could transform conditions. 'All things are possible to him that believeth' (*Mark* 9, xxiii). But there were never enough believers in his political and working environment. Nevertheless, he was sustained in his struggle by a great deal of attention and applause, from Tyndale-Biscoe, for instance:

At Palwal, near Delhi, Mr F. L. Brayne was holding his huge 'uplift' gathering and had erected quite a small town of huts, booths and tents. Mr Brayne is an indefatigable worker and has been most successful in waking up the villagers in the Punjab to a healthier life in every respect. We just revelled in seeing this truly great man at his work.[20]

And recognition was earned from a steady stream of visitors and readers who were not themselves professional uplifters. Lady Hartog, for example, contributed an article to the Contemporary Review in 1928 on a visit to Gurgaon, which was an unqualified puff for Brayne. She saw him as dealing with Indian village life 'as a whole' by personal influence and in the spirit of service, building on village associations, and Boy Scout groups.[21] She was a writer in her own right, and her husband, the chemist Philip Hartog, was a founding father of the School of Oriental and African Studies, was on the Viceroy's Commission on the University of Calcutta, 1917–9, and was the first Vice Chancellor of Dacca University from 1920–5. In 1928 he chaired a committee on the growth of education in India, a project conducted in conjunction with the Simon Commission which was considered particularly productive. It analysed for the first time, for example, the wastage of the premature withdrawal of children from school, though in Hartog's view its most important stress was on the education of women and girls, a subject on which his wife contributed a piece to the *Contemporary Review* in November 1929.[22] The endorsement of the Gurgaon project in such quarters carried considerable weight, and Brayne also had, or appeared to have, strong support from outstanding officials as well. Linlithgow, the last Viceroy under whom he served in the Punjab, had carefully studied the Gurgaon experiment and reported on it to Parliament in the warmest terms.[23] Hailey described Gurgaon as a pioneer development in his foreword to Brayne's *Village Uplift in India*:

We have never made a direct and concerted attack on the problem; we have never deliberately attempted to effect that change in the psychology of the peasant, and in his social and personal habits without which it is impossible materially to improve his conditions of life.[24]

The military metaphor is appropriate to Brayne's approach and it is not surprising that Tyndale-Biscoe recognized a kindred spirit in him. A degree of righteous violence is characteristic of both. Both tried to force the pace, were indifferent or hostile to the structure of primordial loyalties in Indian society, brandished and used the big stick, did continuous battle over 'dirt', and humiliated high caste officials by forcing them to do polluting coolie work. Both were at their happiest when they could organize their forces to rise dramatically to the catastrophic occasion: Brayne's vivid account of damning a breach in a *bund* in Gurgaon has exactly the physical and moral exhilaration of the stories of floods in Kashmir which Tyndale-Biscoe and his colleagues and boys transformed into moral victories.[25] Both revered the authoritarian *ma-bap*, the maternal/paternalists of the Punjab, personified in Brayne's friend and patron Sir Michael O'Dwyer, the last Governor of the Punjab before the Montford reforms, with their contemptuous concern for the downtrodden peasant and their hostility to the new Indian middle class.

Readers of *Village Uplift in India*, or of the series of articles by Brayne that were respectfully printed in the *Lahore Diocesan Magazine* following his Punjab appointment, were presented with a simple, morally strenuous account of the problem of rural poverty.[26] The economic analysis was provided as the merest common sense: refuse pits for manure, good seed, a few good cattle (Haryana bred, with Hissar bulls), the killing of pests, abandoning the use of dung cake for fuel and the squandering of resources on jewellery and litigation. 'The evils of village life are, in the main, simple, and so must be the remedies; and so they are.'[27] All this was taken to require co-operative patterns of behaviour which he took to be consistent with the traditional nature of Indian village life. His villagers, however, resisted co-operation in the form he insisted on. And any rational entrepreneurial exploitation of economic co-operation, by the Sikh Jats of central Punjab, for instance, tended to be suppressed by the official agents of 'uplift'. For them co-operation had the organicist and public service connotations which invested its use in the consensualist rhetoric of post-First World War Britain. A drawing of the ladder of co-operation in one of his 'Socrates' books, which were widely translated into vernaculars, names the bottom rung as (manure) Pits, and others successively as Good Seed, Vaccination, Quinine, Girls' Educ. Consolid. leading up to the bushy leaves of Prosperity.[28] In the text *lambardarji* responds to Socrates' invocation of uplift:

This is doubtless a very noble idea, Socrates, but don't you think people are too selfish to respond to such an appeal?

I might have thought so until recently, but our beloved King-Emperor's son, the Prince of Wales, has recently been going round England making this very appeal.

Did it have any effect, Socrates?

I am glad to say that it had and is still having a tremendous effect. People who thought this work was only for paid officials or for padres and such-like folk are now joining in a great effort to make things better in England, and I have not the least doubt that in this country, too, there are plenty of people just waiting for such a call to join together and work for the betterment of their fellowmen.

Identifying the systemic features and potentialities of rural life and its transformation posed no difficulty. The problem was one of communicating the first glimmerings of a sense of man's duty to his neighbour and his community, a psychological and, in the evangelical perspective, a religious transformation that had to be engineered without the supporting sanction of religious authority.

Brayne's model, of course, had to be historical and English, and the comparison with England dictated his general answer to 'the inertia of centuries' in India. All the resources of the state must be brought to bear on the rural problem, because in rural India structures of leadership and example did not exist, nor did the structures of voluntary associational life, in which the independent individual acknowledges his corporate obligations. Books were scarce and illiteracy common. 'There is no parson or doctor and seldom a squire and—more important still—the wives and daughters of these rural leaders are invisible.' As Clive Dewey points out in an extended comparative assessment of Brayne and Sir Malcolm Darling, an early draft of which he has generously allowed me to draw on, Brayne transposed to his massive 'parish' of Gurgaon the intensities of his father's spartan rectories in Norfolk and Somerset, the practical exercise of the rector's authority in the self-sustaining associational life of the parish, the view of the rural community as nothing if not an organic moral whole.[29] By an act of will he had to bring these structural necessities into existence: moving from village to village, he created 'panchayat', rural reconstruction centre, co-operative and Boy Scout troop. He preached at villagers and bullied his subordinates into taking the first steps that he believed would lead to material progress and spiritual growth.

The extensive contemporary literature on rural economies is still far from any consensual and comprehensive understanding of its dynamics and the factors that inhibit economic development or trigger the process of growth. The study of Palanpur by Bliss and Stern, who were aware of their geographical proximity to Brayne's Gurgaon (though all significant traces of Brayne's labours disappeared very soon after his departure from the district in 1927), makes cautious use of a number of different models:

Disagreement over general views of the way a poor rural economy functions often forms the basis of the most heated divisions between social scientists discussing development, and these views differ sharply in their implications for policy. The differences between the positions lie in the assumed importance of 'rational' economic behaviour on the part of individuals, the view of the competitiveness and efficiency of markets and the distribution of power and wealth, and the role of institutions, cultures, and belief.[30]

The alternative speculations can only be tested against systematically collected evidence, and whilst this and many other studies find evidence of a (risk-averse) maximizing rationality in 'peasant' economies, they show that other factors must account for considerable and uneven variations, even when differences of caste, wealth and education are taken into account. Attitudes towards uncertainty itself differ, but there are also variable levels of enthusiasm, skill, knowledge, entrepreneurship, indolence, and fatalism. The limited range of factors that crowded out Brayne's canvas—ignorance and the 'inertia of centuries'—cannot be ignored, but equally cannot be understood without a suspension of ethnocentric assumptions, and except in terms of complex structural relationships and the factors identified by Bliss and Stern. These include patterns of land tenure, family and caste organization, local political hierarchies, markets for different factors, long-term indebtedness and the cultural histories of different groups. All of them were conditioned over a long period by the economic and political objectives of the Raj. In the north, specifically, there was the confused evolution of the 'Punjab Tradition', its preoccupation with a mass base in rural support for the Raj, and with legislative interventions over rights to land and the alienation of land which had different consequences for different groups in the population.[31] Brayne shared the political premises of Sir Michael O'Dwyer, who in a sense rounded the tradition off.

To be fair to Brayne, the individualism which he inherited from his evangelical roots, and which is taken to be the basis for co-operative social evolution in the villages, has survived vigorously in the rural development literature, albeit derived from different premises. Social scientists who have focused their attention on the economic rationality of the individual 'peasant' in specific situations have, unlike Brayne, recognized that the cultivator may have a valid rationale, for his 'undesirable practices', particularly in a 'rational' preference for security over increased production. They do not suppose that hectoring and compulsion are productive long-term instruments of rural development. They tend, nonetheless, to be concerned with adjusting incentives at the margins and making limited inroads on the larger structural facts (caste, the impact of agricultural policies on caste and local leadership, class dominance in relations of production, through indebtedness, mechanization and the rest). And it would be absurd to blame Brayne for failing to arrive at insights into the Indian village as 'a *conjuncture* of much wider relationships and processes,' which include the imperial economic imperatives and the history of offical interventions to which he himself belonged.[32]

Brayne's approach to the problems, however, was in no sense a balance of speculative uncertainties. What is distinctive about a commitment to rural uplift founded, like his, on normative judgments about categories of people, is its hermetic defence against any kind of intellectual challenge from outside itself and the facility with which it falls into the construction of factual connections that do not exist. As Dewey points out, he was woefully blind to the hard-won practical rationality of his peasants and indifferent to the perspectives and priorities that went with it. In fact the irrelevance of all his agricultural 'improvements' to circumstances in Gurgaon was already well known: the iron soil-inverting ploughs, the Hissar bulls, the application of organic manure to arid soil. He was well aware of different attitudes to work on the part of different caste groups, but read them as symptoms of moral development, of different degrees of backwardness and recalcitrance. His quantitative exploration of the elements he was determined to reform was most inadequate. It was not conceivable to him that the criteria he was importing from his own understanding of rural England and English history were entirely inappropriate though they generated a great deal of intelligible, though suppressed, resentment.

His position on the larger political context and on the nationalist movement was a logical reflection of his vision of rural uplift. Dewey points out that Brayne hated (and that is the appropriate word) the Congress Party, as a threat to the paternalist programme supported by the Punjab Unionist Party which dominated ministerial office from 1920–46. Gandhi, who had welcomed Brayne's first book, had second thoughts. Brayne saw the Mahatma's diversion of government concern and money away from reconstruction and towards problems of law and order as a disaster, and saw the man, at the time of the Quit India Movement, as,

A saint and saboteur.... One of those people thrown up in the East from time to time with the gift of human magnetism. If their character matches the gift they become Moses, Asoka, Solon, Gaútama Buddha, Confucius. If the gift is put into the body of a vain, crooked, pettifogging bania lawyer they become—Gandhi. And waste their gift in seeking power for its own sake.[33]

Gandhi's followers were 'the scum of the mental and physical degenerates of the country.' He was not the first to associate political subversion in the East with physical degeneracy.[34]

Brayne's repertory of 'fact' and framework of interpretation, the possession by inheritance of a universal and ultimate truth, blocked any valid understanding. The very general acceptability of his authority as an expert indicates that, in however loose a form, his version of this repertory and framework was widely shared.

CHAPTER 6

Gandhi and the Problem of Authentic Nationalism

The Question of Providence

The idea of a Divine Providence is no longer a serviceable category in political history or political commentary. But explicitly and implicitly it was regularly invoked in the work of imperial historians writing in the early decades of this century, notably in the works of C. P. Lucas and H. E. Egerton, who looked back to a starting point for their tradition of interpretation in the large generalizations of J. R. Seeley's *Expansion of England* (1883). In fact, for churchmen like Andrews and Holland, imperial history continued to mean Seeley, and the Broad Church gloss upon him of Foss Westcott, Bishop of Durham and father of the Metropolitan of India. Both Seeley and Foss Westcott saw expansion as the essential characteristic of English life under providential dispensation, and described the morality of the state as the expression of an organic national community of individuals united in service to the whole.[1] The conclusion to Egerton's *A Short History of British Colonial Policy* (1887) acknowledged, behind the accidents and mistakes of history,

An unseen superintending Providence controlling the development of the Anglo-Saxon race.... Wiser in this than our fathers, we recognize that the tie which unites us under a common Crown is not [a] slight and temporary thing.[2]

Similar invocations with a range of inflections crop up regularly in run of the mill commentary of every kind right across the political spectrum. It sometimes appeared as a ritual, but nonetheless revealing formalism, but more significantly as a core element in a network of ideas. Confronted from different positions, the issue is whether the concrete insertions of a superintending Providence into the historical process can be identified, and distinguished from the accidents and confusions that accompany them. Which individuals, which processes represent the leading edge of unfolding purpose, and how completely do they do so? Different answers reflect the emphases given to associated elements in the framework of interpretation. A complacent emphasis, such as Egerton's, on the privileged mission of the Anglo-Saxon, is challenged by 'renegade' polemicists like C. F. Andrews as an error with devilish consequences. Their 'history' is identified more positively with an indigenous Indian 'spirit', Christian in essence if not in name, which the British connection had released but now threatens to stifle. Elsewhere, the benign processes of order, rationality, and evolution, are set against the stubborn abnegation of material values in Gandhian politics. Gandhi in particular, and Indian nationalism in general, figure as essentially valid, or invalid, or unfortunately ambivalent manifestations of the superintending but vulnerable reality loosely identified as providence; an intelligible history that struggles against human inadequacies to shed its confusions.

In a general sense this chapter and the next explore the category of a 'Christian' providence, and its inflections and discursive connections within this framework, as an approach to a representation of 'India' available to the Anglo-India public in Britain. The emphasis initially is on the liberal side of the ideological spectrum, moving in the next chapter to providentialist arguments on the right. The orientalism of the Raj was produced by intellectuals, to use the word in a broad Gramscian sense, in many different situations, and it is of less importance to identify specific paths of influence and response than the large pattern of ideas within which the arguments between left and right, for instance, took place.[3] Missionary commentary both emerged from and confirmed this pattern. The missionary may have been a 'man on the spot' whose testimony carried weight back at home, but he had gone out to India with mental equipment that had formidable institutional support and was well aware of the expectations of his British constituency. The ICS cadres, following the early socialization of family and public school, were no less self-consciously prepared for their task. Those in senior positions by the 1920s had been required by the civil service examiners to engage with current academic controversy, to absorb the historical relativism that had become fashionable, and to assimilate the sense of the importance of particular circumstances which went with the increasingly evolutionary view of religion held by orientalist academics.[4]

It will be possible, nevertheless, to see some of the ways in which the categories of the discourse were most actively maintained, by leading 'authorities', by the journalism that served a circumscribed attentive public, and by the educational system. Somewhat different individuals and groups inhabit these various spheres of activity, but they overlap and interact. The conflicts of understanding were less sharp than some of those involved imagined at the time.

The most pressing struggles for Brayne and Tyndale-Biscoe were immediate and local. They had, in the first instance, to be forcefully persuasive with state and government officialdom, before addressing themselves to the problem of generating more indirect support for their projects through the public at home. But this too was a very important aspect of their work. Much the same can be said of a substantial group of articulate Christians associated with the YMCA in India. An American initiative, the YMCA was important because it was recognized in England as a Christian bridgehead that would be vital to the authentic success of the nationalist campaign. It was itself involved in many practical schemes, including rural uplift and education, and had to negotiate official displeasure and suspicion as a result of its activities. On 18 February 1927, for instance, the European Association passed a resolution, listing thirteen allegations, in 'grave disapproval' of the 'political' activities of the YMCA and its secretaries. At the same time the YMCA was an international organization. Though its serial publication *The Young Men of India (YMI)* did not have a significant British circulation, it provided a forum which brought together both western and Indian Christians in the development of a position on nationalism and British imperialism that was attractive to liberals who were uneasy with the potentially unruly commitments of such as Andrews and Elwin. This was sufficiently radical to alarm elements in the expatriate community, but it fell short of the 'extremism' of Gandhi's closer Christian associates. For that reason it was taken by many to represent a truer understanding of the providential signifiance of the Raj, one rooted in an Indian consciousness but not the outcome of racial hostility or political negativism. The perspective and the activities of the Indian YMCA were advertised and endorsed by the *Times*

India correspondent Valentine Chirol.

K. T. Paul, the journal's most distinguished editor (and one of the Indian signatories to Curtis's letter in 1916), was a delegate to the Round Table Conference, along with S. K. Datta, Principal of Forman Christian College, Lahore, and a former assistant secretary of the YMCA. Both were laymen and well known in England through their links with the vigorous Student Christian Movement of the period and from contacts with leading churchmen. The SCM press published Paul's book *The British Connection with India* in 1927.[5] Paul and Datta and the YMCA intellectuals generally developed a response to Indian nationalism and the Gandhian movement that was familiar to politicians and leading clerics like Lang, Temple and Bishop Bell of Chichester, and to more interested church people.[6] For the general reading public in Britain they were more distant figures. But the issues they raised were familiar to readers of the church press in England, to which we now turn.

Not the most powerful sector of the press, it represented a significant element of the Anglo-India public nonetheless, and incidentally provided a record of the ways in which India formed a preoccupation in the churchmanship of important lay figures. Among these were Chirol and Ronaldshay (subsequently Marquess of Zetland) both of whom made major contributions to the literature on the Raj. Their explorations of the purpose and meaning of the Raj will be dicussed along with others, ranging from pillars of the ICS establishment to Andrews and his Quaker friends.

This chapter concludes with some consideration of the influences directed specifically at the main pool of recruitment for future servants of the Raj, containing the potential ICS candidates, businessmen, soldiers and clergy who went out to India, but also their contemporaries who remained more or less attentive members of the Anglo-India public at home.

What is being ignored here, apart from incidental references, is the imaginative literature of the Raj. There were authors, like Nehru's friend Edward Thompson, who were driven by their experience of India from commentary to fiction and even verse.[7] Thompson cannot be ignored as a significantly ambivalent commentator on the Raj. But imaginative writing raises particular problems of assessment and there is little to be gained from cursory allusion to it. However Allen Greenberger's study *The British Image of India* shows that there are close parallels between literary fictions and informative commentary, in the use of stereotype and the exploitation of the standard orientalist preoccupations, racial, religious, sexual and, more especially from around the turn of the century, political. The orientalist discourse was pervasive.[8]

The British Connection

The idea of an Indian spiritual renaissance stimulated by a Christian *praeparatio evangelica,* as it was entertained in this century by missionaries, educationists and others, was a modern modification of a notion with roots deep in the British connection. The earliest 'theology of national renaissance' was pioneered by Alexander Duff, John Wilson and William Miller.[9] Its workings were seen in the early reform movement and the assimilation of 'Christian' values by westernized intellectuals such as Roy and Ranade. But it failed to develop as the evangelicals prayed that it might, and the idea had a different set of resonances in the nationalist India with which figures such as Andrews, Mayhew and the mission college principals were concerned. Apart, of course, from the Syrian Christians in Kerala, there was now a numerically significant but proportionally small population of Indian Christian 'converts', culturally dependent on the western missions and for obvious reasons facing an uncertain political future. There was also a small, but politically significant category of non-Christian Indians who were in part the cultural products of self-consciously Christian western higher education. In the new theology of nationalism, the illiterate and semi-literate Christian communities, particularly the converts of the mass movements, were a responsibility, even a burden on the church. But Christian higher education for the future élites, both Christian and non-Christian could be seen as the safe conduit that would channel floodwaters of the new national spirit into the areas where they were most needed.

The files of *The Young Men of India* for the inter-war period contain cognate arguments about nationalism, which display differences, however, that locate them clearly at the eastern or the western end of the British connection. Even the most general Indian discussions of the nature of Christian *dharma* in a caste society, and the antinomies of nation and community, convey a sense of urgency and an awareness of the substantive structures of caste and community which seldom comes through in the British essays. But at the same time K. T. Paul's argument, for instance, was very recognizable. It presented itself to the white liberal Christian intelligence as authentically distinct, as indigenous and, therefore, natural, but was also reassuringly familiar: a complex of universal truths which could transform the inherited social configurations of the East then undergoing a process of assimilation and adaptation.

Thus, for example, the distinguished historian of India, Percival Spear, wrote two papers from St Stephen's College in the early 1930s for *YMI,* on the state, the individual and nationalism, and one on Nazi rule in Germany.[10] They are very much the work of an expatriate missionary scholar. His theory of the state is that of the Christian Hegelianism which then permeated the thinking of the socially concerned British churchmen of the period,[11] and the historiography he shared with Curtis is implicit in it. Bosanquet and T. H. Green, (ancillary presences in the work of several Indian contributors[12]), defined the state's moral claim on its citizens this way:

Essentially it is the organized embodiment of the aspirations of society—conscious or unconscious—towards the Good Life. If it strays from these purposes or is manipulated by a group for selfish ends, it is no longer an expression of the universal will and can rest only upon inertia or upon force—the motives of apathy or fear.

In Green's words, 'Will, not Force, is the basis of the State.' Furthermore, we can take it that 'All states occupy some rung on this ladder of aspiration.' But then again all states are imperfect, to the point of aberration in the case of those nineteenth century European states which 'abandoned the pursuit of life for power or pleasure or wealth.' So, for the individual who is tempted to resist the state on valid grounds, the ethical considerations are difficult and the burden of proof lies with him, though there are relatively clear situations where what was previously enjoyed has been wrongly taken away and where resistance is right. Spear's interesting choice of examples juxtaposes Gandhi's Bardoli No-tax campaign of 1928 with the British Combination Laws, the Revocation of the Edict of Nantes, and the French separation of church and state in 1905.

[But] to disobey the State is not a light thing to be lightly undertaken; the State is like a vessel carrying society through the ocean of confusion; every act of disobedience is a tiny hole driven into its side which imperceptibly weakens its buoyancy, and which, if the wrecker is too destructive or proves intransigent when the captain remedies his grievance, may finally involve the destruction of all.

It was a message for the times, which the church had already been preaching to the 'wreckers' in British industrial relations.

The special problem of the Indian situation from this perspective was that of identifying the particular compound of material and spiritual forces that might represent a true desire for unity and the achievement of corporate personality. The Christian spirit is the only touchstone by which those forces that move disinterestedly towards ever larger unity can be recognized. They can only express themselves within the given forms of a particular culture and, of course, only imperfectly.

This argument was adapted by K. T. Paul to the realities of the Indian situation as he saw them, a society in which social being is defined by caste and community rather than by government, and in which the colonial state is both good and bad, ripe for transformation into a larger unity but yet not an evil to be rejected outright.

Dharma is duty and not right; it is enforced by the will of society and not by the authority of a central government. In both these particulars it differs radically from the conception of citizenship in the West.... The principle of *dharma* which conserved our culture through the centuries of chaos is a spiritual inheritance of infinite value. [13]

But according to this view the colonial state had itself in a fundamental historical sense, rescued Indian culture from the centuries of chaos, and had prepared the way for a *dharma* that was to look outward from caste and community towards national service. This impulse was embodied in the dyarchy legislation:

Sir William Duke and Lionel Curtis set out the best that the West could say out of its experience. Vocal India, educated in the same lore as Duke and Curtis, and knowing no other, hailed the scheme with genuine welcome. As one who welcomed the dyarchic proposal, followed its progress with intimate interest and finally hailed the India Act with enthusiasm, I may say that the glamour of it was complete. It even seemed the one venue, with no alternative, to sure progress toward a worthwhile *Swarajiya*. [14]

Even the massacre at Jallianwala Bagh, though it shook him severely, failed to destroy Paul's conviction that India's grasp on its potential future could only be sustained through the organic link with the western Christianity of the British connection. His analysis consists of a running commentary on a familiar narrative, picking first on the authentic impulse or transition and then on the aberration which succeeded it, accompanied it or threatened to undo it. Among such aberrations were the Rowlatt Act and the Amritsar tragedy, which drastically weakened the moral force of the dyarchy project. Earlier, Curzon's religious sense of imperial mission and his administrative brilliance had been pinned down by the Bengal partition, a millstone of his own making. At the level of moral evolution:

The new emphasis on personality is warranted to operate as a corrective to the exaggerated advantages which [Indian] society has taken over the individual. But where individualism sinks down insidiously to undermine the conscience in this regard, there is every danger of a devastating social revolution leading to the *adharma* (collapse of the sense of moral restraints and duties in the mind of the people) and confusion so constantly held up as a warning by the seers of India.[15]

But *dharma* of caste, in spite of everything, is able to evolve into *dharma* of nation in the spirit of authentic nationalism. This, in turn, will depend on the evolution of the Empire into a larger co-operative order and partnership in which material interest is expertly organized to serve the common good.

Gandhi's ambivalence for Paul and his associates hinged on this last point to a significant extent. In addition, there was disagreement over the practical consequences of the weapon of *satyagraha,* and over its strengths and limitations where large population were unable to meet its exacting criteria without on occasion slipping into violence and disorder.

Paul, himself an experienced administrator as the founder and Secretary of the National Missionary Society and in YMCA rural reconstruction projects, was alive to the need for the management and guidance of the disinterested British expert, specifically in relation to the bases for economic development and industrialization in India. Economic realism, for him, lay not with Gandhi but with those like Sir George Schuster, Finance Member of the Indian Government from 1928 to 1934 and subsequently MP (1938–45), who put their instrumental reason to the service of the British connection and the international community.[16] Schuster, who had directed a variety of companies in the decade before the Great War, was to write his book *Christianity and Human Relations in Industry* under the auspices of the ICF in the early 1950s.[17] Paul had recognized in him a saving combination of Christian faith and expert public-spirited practicality. Schuster's contribution to *India and Democracy* (1941, with Guy Wint) was to graft an argument, (in the spirit of progressive caution characteristic of Curtis, whom Paul so much admired) about the wise supervision of a private enterprise economy in India on to a Whiggish argument about the immaturity of her political institutions. Schuster was clear that India had come to benefit from the British connection, and he saw the Act of 1935 as a swift road to material and civic development, an essentially spiritual evolution in its accession of organic corporate rationality.[18] (Schuster's reading of the Act, the theme of his correspondence with Bishop Bell of Chichester, will be discussed in the next chapter.) For Paul, it was a human consequence of Gandhi's concentration on other aspects of the truth that made him blind to this.[19] The Mahatma could see that a premise of national development had to be that of economic independence, but he slighted the logical imperative of partnership in an advancing world economy.

Paul's second problem, the paradoxes of *satyagraha,* simultaneously transcending the reality of the state and threatening its legitimacy, were of course central to any response to Gandhi. The colonial state acknowledged them, Paul suggests, in Mr Justice Broomfield's famous address to the court at Gandhi's trial in Ahmedabad on 18 March 1922.

The silence of Jesus, that non-cooperation *in excelsis,* made a profound impression on the magistrate. Henceforth he tried, however feebly, to save the perplexing prisoner. But the 'system' had tied him hand and foot. He could only wash his hands in futility, and hand over the accused to the extreme penalty of law.[20]

The allusion to Pilate is of course not accidental.

But there were intermittencies in Gandhi's imitation of Christ. Paul had reported characteristically after the visit of the Prince of Wales in 1921:

The Viceroy pursued steadily the policy more than once explained by Lord Chelmsford in Britain, to let non-cooperation have a fair chance to work itself out and be thrown away by India as no longer needed or as no longer tenable.

First Class Blunder

This trend was broken seriously, and now perhaps irremediably, by certain surprising blunders. Mr Gandhi, though saintly in life and strikingly astute in the discernment of men and events, is strangely susceptible to tragedy. This has led him into certain first-class blunders in leadership, such as have disconcerted *his own loyal followers*. The first great blunder was the idea of burning foreign cloth: and it was a grotesque misreading of Indian psychology....

Then there was the colossal blunder, most far-reaching in its damage, the attitude towards the Prince. It was a fearful mis-estimate of the psychology of the Britisher....

Then came the fateful 17th of November: Calcutta a dead city, Bombay ablaze in violence. The absolutely complete *hartal* (strike) which I saw in Calcutta... was brought about in the same way as a religious feast or fast is again and again secured in India: through an effectual spread of authoritative opinion and desire from mouth to mouth.... The question was rightly asked a hundred times, a thousand times, in Calcutta homes, 'Who is really ruling India today, Reading or Gandhi?.' It was an amazing situation and highly disconcerting.

Meantime Bombay was ablaze. Hooligans or no hooligans, it was perfectly clear that non-violence could not be guaranteed by Mr Gandhi....[21]

The issue of non-cooperation and Gandhian political techniques was pressing for those concerned with Indian Christians precisely because of the appeal to many of them of such a Christlike national leader. In 1921 YMI published the results of an attempt by half a dozen leading Christians in Madras to analyse non-cooperation in the light of the spirit of Christ. The group, which included Paul, had reported on their deliberations to the Madras Christian conference in February. It represented a balance of prior judgments: some supporters, some conditional supporters and some critics.[22] Differences of stress on the life and example of Christ put an overall consensus out of reach, but they were at least able to break down the text of Gandhi's resolution at the special session of Congress in September 1920 into 'Christian' and 'non-Christian' elements.

It had been passed by a Congress that had, in the face of the Congress veterans, 'turned Gandhian. Its pseudo-English veneer had worn off.'[23] Gandhi identified four methods of non-cooperation: the renunciation of titles, the withdrawal of students from schools and colleges, the abandonment of legal practice and the boycott of the reformed Councils. There were two additions to be introduced at a later stage, namely tampering with the Army and the Services, and the refusal to pay taxes.

The Madras group of Christians unanimously recognized the national movement in its spirit as 'one of the most daring attempts made in human history to apply the Sermon on the Mount to the politics of a nation striving to gain freedom,' and they followed Gandhi's own teaching on the 'stages' of his resolution as 'mainly instruments to turn the searchlight upon ourselves. Non-cooperation is self-discipline and is only indirectly a political weapon.' Their doubts arose over the mixture of elements in the movement and in its methods. Unquestionably Christian elements were the 'democratic' spirit of free development into independence and also the movement's self-sacrifice and discipline, 'something very like the Spirit of Jesus Christ.' There were other elements, valid though less intrinsically Christian, such as resentment at British racial arrogance and shame at the 'slave mentality' of Indians under colonial rule. But there were also evil elements: hatred, wilful blindness to the good that has come to India and continues to come through the British connection, historical mythologies about India's past, errors of perspective and factual understanding about the legitimacy of British rule and its reforms. The central objection was that in reality non-cooperation cannot use authentic 'soul-force'. Non-cooperation in truth 'despairs of persuasion and proposes to compel by reducing the government to impotence.' For a doubtful outcome it sacrifices other goods. School strikes mean mental starvation and moral breakdown and indiscipline. Christ, under a despotic government with no appeal to Rome and no Jewish participation, in a position probably 'even more acute politically than that which obtains in India today,' had resisted the temptation to lead a Jewish non-cooperation movement. Instead, He reproved his own people 'for their irreligious sham and for their abuses of the temple, and sought to uplift them by preaching to them the ideals of righteousness, truth and love.' The significance of the Roman parallel, which is constantly drawn by Paul and others, was a matter of debate, but the group agreed that the movement was laden with possibilities for evil.

The Indian YMCA transcended denominations and institutional church interests. Under Farquhar's direction it produced books and pamphlets that were widely read in the Anglo-India public in England.

Indigenous, international and practical in its orientation, it could be seen to represent those who were self-critically in touch with nationalism's authentic spirit, going along with the political movement, but only within the limits of a political and historical realism that saw organic constitutionalism as the main vehicle for providential design. This, in broad terms was the view taken by the church press of all denominations in England, though they could be much more suspicious of Gandhi's motives and intentions than leading Indian Christians like Paul and Susil Rudra, (Andrew's friend and Principal of St Stephen's) allowed themselves to be.

The Church Press in Britain

The annual meetings of the missionary societies provided staple material from India for the church papers. The extent of the other coverage of the Raj and its political problems reflected the cycles of nationalist activity and communal relations, particularly with regard to the non-cooperation period of the early 1920s and the Round Table Conferences and civil disobedience period a decade later, and the incidence of Hindu-Muslim communal violence. But the three leading papers which will be drawn on here were all conscientiously attentive to India—the Anglo-Catholic *Church Times,* the *Guardian,* edited in the 1920s by F. A. Iremonger, Temple's biographer and the BBC's Director of Religion in the 1930s, and *The Methodist Recorder,* still recognizably heir to the imperial strain in Wesleyanism.[24]

Each paper reflected a range of views round the central tendency of a particular constituency. Thus, Edward Thompson, returning with an MC from service as chaplain in Mesopotamia and Palestine to act as principal of the Wesleyan College at Bankura in western Bengal, was already in 1918 providing the *Recorder* with the characteristic oscillations of hope and anxiety of his unusually independent intelligence in two pieces on the urgent need for Indian missions.[25] He drew hope from a naturalized Christianity, *bhakti,* and dramatic readings from Tulsidas. He wrote with anxiety about the Church's failure to survive the test of war, the 'maggots in the brain' that gradually consume the vitality of lonely and isolated expatriates, the confrontation in India of patriotism and Christianity and western 'progress'. He saw the possibility of another mutiny, exacerbated by British racial attitudes—a 'genuine war of independence' (as he saw the mutiny of 1857 to be in some areas). He even described the Methodists, invoking Cobbett, as the enemies of political progress. But Thompson's ambivalence about the British side of the Raj stands out from more predictable commentary in the *Recorder*. From outside the Methodist ministry, the Revd Garfield Williams, a more prominent publicist at the time as prospective CMS Secretary in charge of Foreign Educational Work, is closer to the norm. 'Why had God made a present of India to the British nation? Any other country might possibly have exploited it, drawn upon its raw material, and returned their manufactured goods. But "God's whisper came to us." What was God's purpose?'[26]

Each journal had its characteristic bias. The Anglo-Catholic *Church Times* took a sterner and more exclusivist view of the limitations of Hinduism. The *Recorder,* which in domestic politics was strongly behind Temple's COPEC and the interdenominational ICF, reflected the concentration of Methodist missions in princely and Muslim India. But there is also in these papers a common pattern of commentary and reaction in reporting, feature articles and reviews throughout the inter-war period. All were committed to the priority of the constitutional process itself as the instrument fashioned by reason for the unfolding of the imperial mission. All seized on evidence of an informing spirit, which struggled against aberrations in the Indian legacy, bringing to life the instruments of reason, through the 'saintliness' of Gandhi, the Christian viceroyalty of Lord Irwin, and the pragmatic sacramentalism of missionary and administrative activity. Among so many correspondents over a lengthy period there were obviously disagreements and inconsistencies. But a review of representative material across the confusions of contemporary events reveals a simple intellectual structure behind the interweaving themes, defining the issues and setting the limits of any debate.

The large vision of an Empire under Divine providence is strongly sustained. Bishop Headlam of Gloucester figures in a tradition of Empire Day sermons, celebrating the 'organic growth' of the Empire, at St Paul's in 1928, stressing the need to be strong enough for our task by maintaining armaments ('such things always seem to me a religious obligation'). A year later the Bishop of Exeter, C. E. Curzon, noted with foreboding 'an increasing tendency to boastfulness' about the Empire,[27] and underlined its higher, providential significance. The Cambridge University Ramsden Sermon

by Bishop Frodsham in 1919 had dwelt on the increasing inter-
nationalism of the British Empire, and its unselfish response to
nationalism. 'May not the roots of the claim of a people for corporate
self-realization be a blind groping after the bigger life anticipated
by the Founder of the Faith.' The task of a Christian Empire was
to empower the human race to realize its destiny. In India this was
to take the form of fostering a national unity which may leave the
people materially worse off, but which would, notwithstanding,
be a 'real' movement, a fulfilment of the British connection. *The
Methodist Recorder* associated Empire Day with the 'spiritual birthday'
of John Wesley on 24 May 1738, contrasting the moral enthusiasm
of that period in England with the mere revolutionary enthusiasm
in France. Three pages of reporting on Wesley's Day and Empire
Day in 1924 included a speech on India by Edgar Thompson: 'What
is our Indian Empire saying? We have grown up, give us our
liberty.... We cannot hold an Empire by force, but only by good
will and mutual service.'[28] Edgar Thompson and Frodsham are
some distance on the political spectrum from the conservative
Headlam but all consecrate the imperial purpose.[29]

    Some version of the fulfilment argument is standard when it
comes to the religions of South Asia, and it is to familiar concerns
in this area that discussions of nationalism constantly return. A
Guardian review of MacKenzie's *Hindu Ethics* (in Farquhar's YMCA
series) in 1923, acknowledges that the reality of caste brotherhood
puts English Christianity to shame, and that Hinduism has something to teach us in the interpretation and practice of the passive
virtues. But it goes on to balance the 'strains of lofty morality' in
Hinduism against its personal selfishness and the 'grossest phallicism'
of its texts, which MacKenzie neglects, though 'it is notoriously
present in the Shastras and elsewhere, and the lingam in well nigh
every temple is a standing witness to it.' In Hinduism 'the religious
man does not require to manifest his religion in a good life.'[30] The
implication is that a sound state cannot be sustained by such a religion.

    The publication of Katherine Mayo's *Mother India* in 1927 brought
out the standard arguments in their variety. *The Guardian* editor
offered to take up a reader's suggestion to reprint for distribution
to church groups a long and fulsome review by R. Ellis Roberts,
which dwelt on the horrors of Hinduism, the 'profound unbrotherli-
ness of the Hindu' outside caste, and the distressing hatred of men

like Tagore and Gandhi for qualities in Christianity and western civilization from which they profited.[31] A correspondence on Indian spirituality followed, the level of which was raised decisively by an argument from Stanley Cook of Cambridge University, an eminent scholar in semitic and Old Testament studies, on behalf of the insights of comparative religion. This was in turn assimilated at a scholarly level to the fulfilment thesis, by the biblical authority Canon Lukyn Williams of Ely. He concluded that, like Bishop Westcott, one 'can only welcome fresh evidence that Gentiles begin to grasp doctrines and practise ceremonies of which the real significance was only apparent after the coming of Christ.' Other correspondents too pointed to the importance of some knowledge of comparative social anthropology for those serving the Raj, and did so within the strongly normative fulfilment language.[32] For the methodists in 1932 Scott Lidgett applauded the timeliness and importance of Edward Thompson's Fernley lecture in Manchester on 'The Cross and Hindu Thought,' dwelling on Hinduism's merely partial incarnations, the contrasts of Hebrew and Hindu understandings of sacrifice, suffering and divine love, and Hinduism's deterioration into 'loathsome eroticism'.[33] And yet, we are repeatedly told, the best of India is yearning for Christ and potentially coming to completion in Christianity.

Gandhi's appearance at the end of the First World War on a political stage set with these orientalist properties was inevitably problematic. Edward Thompson knew Gandhi personally (as he did Tagore, whom he translated) and it was a measure of his detachment, which was not shared by Andrews and other friends of the Mahatma, that he did not describe him as a 'saint'. But in general it was as a 'saint', true or false, that he was assimilated to the discourse. Gandhi, it was often observed, had seen and lived by the truth of the message of the New Testament in so far as he lived a life of redemptive suffering, of ascetic and gentle courage dedicated even to the ultimate advantage of his 'enemies'. We may 'dislike Mahatma Gandhi's political activities, his warped and distorted views of British motives, mistrust his influence, hold him responsible for much unrest and violence,' but we must acknowledge the purity of his ideals, his devotion to his country, and the austerity and blamelessness of his personal life.[34] He embraced poverty and the Sermon on the Mount with literal consistency and modest good humour, in a way that reminded the West of its tradition of medieval saints and of the rarity and obscurity of such expressions of faith in modern times.

Gandhi was not the only well-known figure to stimulate envy of the non-material spirituality of the East, and guilt at the West's failure to live up to its own religious professions. The Christian *sadhu* Sundar Singh, by birth a Sikh, visited England and was the subject of a number of books.[35] He represented the possibility of an unqualified commitment to Christianity, tapping a source of Indian spirituality uncontaminated by Hinduism, which he rejected not for its grossser manifestations, but for its philosophic pantheism, the doctrine of *karma,* its path of knowledge and its morbid and life-denying asceticism. Such men were needed 'to keep things right on the Indian side,'[36] because Gandhian nationalism could be disastrous for Christianity in India and therefore for India herself. Gandhi's saintliness was thoroughly sacramental, concerned with this world. To that extent it was Christian and western, but sadly only to that extent. It was,

a mistake to count Gandhi as entirely Christian in the western sense of the word. He goes beyond and also stays behind...the eight beatitudes, without counting anything save their truth and beauty. The story is one for the Christian world to meditate with sorrow and with joy.[37]

The providential motions of fulfilment worked ambiguously through this Christlike figure by fits and compelling starts. In a long article for the *Guardian,* Holland had asked why, when Gandhi was arrested, tried and sentenced, did India not 'run red from one end to the other':

One could almost hear a pin drop, as it were, in the political world of India. What was the reason?...India felt she was watching the man who came nearer than any other Indian had ever come to her Indian ideal; and that at that supreme moment that man had for his guidance and inspiration the example and teaching of Jesus Christ.[38]

In August 1925 P. N. F. Young reported with relief that 'Mr Gandhi, reverting to his true role of social reformer with his campaign against "untouchability", has lost enormously in political prestige.' He had lost a political sense of direction with the 'unquestionable failure' of 'soul force' to achieve political power.[39]

One of Holland's critics, a retired officer from the Indian police, blamed Hinduism squarely for Gandhi's retrogressive policies: 'India will never become a nation until it has one religion—the Christian Religion.'[40] Christianity alone could challenge caste and it was caste that smothered national spirit. But there were subtler and more appreciative assessments in the church press of Gandhi's attitude to caste, particularly in the light of his assaults on 'untouchability' and western missionary 'uplift' of converted outcastes. These did not absolve him from errors, but brought his social theory as well as his personal qualities within the scope of the model of structural change which was assumed by the organicist theory of social evolution. Percival Spear summed them up many years after leaving his final posts as government whip in the Legislative Assembly of 1943 and deputy-secretary in the Information Department of the main secretariat in New Delhi:

> The burden of Gandhi's teaching was, 'Thou shalt love thy neighbour as thyself.' This principle inspired his 'Untouchable' campaign, his various reform movements, and his doctrine of soul-force itself. It was behind his disregard of caste taboos (though not of caste distinction itself). Some see in Gandhi a subtle reactionary because of his recognition of caste in general; but I think it is nearer the truth to call him a social revolutionary (no doubt subtle also) because he sought to transmute the basis of caste from hierarchy (higher and lower) to function (service to the community). The sum total of Gandhi's work as I see it, was to bring back into the Hindu fold the value of service to one's fellowmen.[41]

Behind this judgment lies the 'Christian socialism' of F. D. Maurice and the conservative economic historian the Revd William Cunningham (d. 1919).[42] Gandhi's own sympathetic encounter with this strain in British social thought was through the morally strenuous functional order proposed in Ruskin's *Unto This Last,* which was, after the *Gita* and Tolstoy's *Kingdom,* the third formative book of Gandhi's early years in South Africa. It was also a text with almost apocryphal status for the social theology of Maurice's conservative heirs among the liberal churchpeople who supported the ICF.[43] In this relation Gandhi is seen as social reformer rather than politician, pursuing tested truths from the Christian tradition about the social dynamics of authentic organic progress.

The subversive political implications of *satyagraha,* however, were a deeply disturbing counterpart to these commonplaces. They thrust the Metropolitan back onto a more defensive normative argument during the civil disobedience period. Westcott's own reflections in response to a letter from J. C. Kumarappa were reproduced in India in the *Madras Diocesan Magazine* and the *Bombay Diocesan Magazine,* which decided against printing anything from the ensuing correspondence on both sides, 'in view of the fact that special efforts are being made at the present time to bring about peace in the political world, and such controversy would not be likely to assist this end.'[44] Westcott repeated his arguments in his Bishop's Letter in the *Calcutta Diocesan Record.* His letter to Kumarappa appeared, but again by itself, in the *Church Times* of 30 May 1930, as a response to a letter from 'an Indian Christian'. Kumarappa, who reproduced the whole correspondence in *Young India* in June 1930, had grounds for complaint about the suppression of his own effective contribution.

He had written to Westcott asking him to come out against 'atrocities' inflicted on civil disobedience volunteers and to urge the Government to use Christian and non-violent methods over the satyagrahis. Westcott's reply opens with Christ's rejection of the temptation to lead a nationalist movement against Rome, and proceeds to attack civil disobedience.

You seem to assert that our Lord would have approved of civil disobedience. When I look to nature, I find that what we call 'Natural Law' is absolutely fixed and reliable. On that fixity of law depends our power of carrying on our daily work and the research student depends on it for making further discoveries....Can we expect that Jesus Christ, who came to reveal the character of God could so utterly repudiate the revelation of God given in nature? We know he did not, for again and again he exhorted his disciples to obey the law...'Let every soul be in subjection to the higher powers, for there is no power but of God: the powers that be are ordained of God. Whosoever, therefore, resisteth the power, resisteth the ordinance of God: and they that resist shall receive to themselves damnation. For rulers are not a terror to the good but to the evil,' (*Romans,* 13, i-iii).

He then turns to 'our Lord's injunction to the individual which forbade him to retaliate for a wrong done to him.' This Kumarappa had misread. Christ 'was not dealing at the time with the question of the maintenance of law and order in the state, which finds its true parallel in the natural order of the physical universe.' Non-violence is a rule only for personal behaviour.

Kumarappa was, or affected to be, amazed at this *ex cathedra* pronouncement. He clearly enjoyed writing his reply, which begins 'Dear Brother Westcott,' (Westcott had opened with 'My dear Sir'), and ends with 'you will allow me to follow Matthew 23, viii and address you 'Brother' and sign myself yours fraternally'(Westcott had concluded with 'Yours faithfully'). He had not asked Westcott for support for the civil disobedience campaign but against the callousness of authority. The Roman analogy was invalid. There are biblical quotations to be deployed on Christ's civil disobedience against the law of the sabbath.

You appear to have terribly confused ideas of 'law and Nature', and man made laws, and attribute the same potency and virtue to both alike. Law in Science is but the observed uniform order of sequence ...even in natural law there is nothing that is 'absolutely reliable' as you so innocently imagine.

Westcott, he pointed out, had conveniently refused to discuss specific immoral laws.

Westcott was no scholar, and his ideas about law and Nature appear to derive less from his third class degree in the Cambridge Natural Science tripos than from Joseph Butler's *Analogy of Religion,* written almost exactly two hundred years previously, in 1736, a significant echo from 'the Met's' training in theology. Butler's argument, in a rationalist age, had effectively allowed 'Nature' to absorb 'Revelation'. Knowledge of the lawfulness of Nature, which he assumed included the moral and social order, can only be achieved through habits of perception and action, in other words with maturity. Thus, says Butler,

the subordinations to which [children] are accustomed in domestic life, teach them self-government in common behaviour abroad, and prepare them for subjection and obedience to civil authority.[45]

Westcott was clumsily indicating that Gandhi's civil disobedience doctrine was a claim to true Revelation that subverted the only framework within which valid understanding of God's purposes can be learned. In a complex moral world individual conscience is a public issue and must express itself through the subaltern acceptance of civil authority (Nature). Nature is the instrument, for Westcott as for Butler, of a *Christian* God, and it was a Christian civil and imperial order, whatever its limitations, that Gandhi presumed to challenge.[46] There were bishops in England who would have handled the issue with greater sophistication. They would not have disputed the Metropolitan's general conclusion.

Gandhi and Westcott, incidentally, conducted a mutually solicitous correspondence for many years, in which Westcott applauded Gandhi's 'constructive' work on communalism and uplift and rebuked his activities outside the law and his use of fasting as moral blackmail.[47]

But it was the layman Lord Irwin who provided at a critical period the perfect foil for Gandhi. There was nothing new in considering the Viceroy as the representative of a Christian Empire. Ripon was regularly held up in this light and the loyal churchmanship of Harding and Chelmsford was commended. (Reading's appointment was initially criticized partly because he was a Jew, and therefore a provocation to the Indian Muslims, but partly also for his morally dubious involvement in the Marconi scandal.[48]) Edward Wood, most notably in the *Church Times,* which saw itself as the guardian of the kind of high churchmanship he and his father, Lord Halifax, were associated with, was a viceregal paladin uniquely qualified to test the authenticity of the claims of Gandhi and the nationalists. He was seen as an adroit man of affairs, a conciliator, wielding the legitimate authority of Empire in the light of a Christian insight into its significance. (His critics described him as the 'holy fox'.) He could pick out and respond to authentic and constructive pressures and yet embody the valid authority to which St Paul refers in his letter to the Romans. So he was defended with vigour by the church papers against the Rothermere press and the political right, and indeed with venom where the *Church Times* could associate political error with heretical religion, as in the case of the evangelical troublemaker and prayer-book controversialist Joynson-Hicks (Lord Brentford).[49] The image of Gandhi remained enigmatic and volatile. Irwin was taken by one writer to have believed initially that the Mahatma was 'pure gold', only to find the 'feet of clay' and a 'ready tool for unscrupulous politicians.'[50] More typically he was taken by another to have understood him better than this, as no 'eccentric William Morris', but a man in particular social circumstances with a well thought out philosophy, who 'may be blazing a trail towards a Christian civilization.'[51] Irwin was able to recognize,

that Gandhi symbolised and summed up a real response on the part of dumb millions of Indians to the lessons of liberty and self-consciousness taught to them from the West, and he insisted on looking for the best in a man who is as sincere as he is difficult.[52]

Above all it was seen that both in India and in England Irwin was leading public opinion clear of the minefields of imperial shibboleths, by patient discussion and bold initiative when the occasion demanded, and by the uncompromising exercise of authority when it did not. Throughout the period there was solid support in the church press for the constitutional initiatives to which he was committed. The composition of the Simon Commission, described by Gopal as the 'first and greatest mistake of Irwin's viceroyalty'[53] was endorsed as manifestly right. The evolutionary advance the Commission proposed from dyarchy to full provincial autonomy, Irwin's Dominion Status pronouncement and the Round Table programme of 'federation, responsibility and safeguards,' were seen as no less authentic responses to the promptings of history. There was some anxiety that the federal principle which had emerged from the conference to surprise a political world conflicted with Seeley's sweeping vision of a unitary and organic nation as the outcome to be looked for, but such anxiety was muted. Irwin in his own way was taken to match Gandhi's personal claim to a life submitted to the guidance of religious conviction. He topped him comfortably when it came to the public and historic implications of that guidance, as the Christian helmsman of a Christian Empire.

India and the Thoughtful Reader

As late as the mid-1950s, the Student Christian Movement Press published Max Warren's *Caesar, the Beloved Enemy*, an argument on behalf of a 'theology of imperialism' that summarized assumptions and practices which were widespread in that body of commentary on the Raj which had been written for the general reader in the previous half century.[54] Warren argues that imperialism is of course ambiguous, but that successive imperialisms have made their contribution to a vision of a time when the 'earth shall be filled with the knowledge of God,' by developing the capacities of the areas dependent on them. Imperialism is a preparation. St Paul's *'civis Romanus sum'* is a commitment to a prospective human unity, to be achieved over time by the instruments of imperialism, legal, technical and intellectual, and by the expression through laws of the organic service ideal (or what the theologian Paul Tillich has called vocational consciousness). The benefits of Empire are means to a greater end.

The literature on the Raj which shared this Christian vision of imperialism is quite substantial, notwithstanding the constant complaints about the general indifference to India back in England which were voiced by a concerned minority. It varies greatly in the quality of its information and in intensity of involvement. Characteristic foci shift over time, for instance from narrative history of successive emperors and viceroys to a more functional analysis of the structures of the Raj, of the broad social divisions in Indian society, of caste, race and religion, and those of the imperial superstructure itself. Those who accepted the theology of Empire balanced the constructive and the obstructive elements in different ways, but there is a predictable repertory of imperial means, and of obstructions to the realization of imperialism's greater end. The writers discussed here represent this spectrum. All of them are unfashionable now, and most of them have no general readership. Some, like Bevan, Andrews and the Quakers gave prominence to their Christian point of departure. In others, like Chirol and Ronaldshay, both of whom were widely regarded as authorities, it was less overt.

A standard work from an earlier period, Captain L. J. Trotter's strongly dynastic and viceregal *History of India,* first published by the SPCK in 1874 (and revised by Trotter in 1899) was brought up to the Durbar of 1911 with minimal alterations by the Reader in Indian History at Oxford, the Revd W. H. Hutton (and published in 1917).[55] It concludes with Curzon's rumbling peroration:

If our Empire were to end to-morrow, I do not think we need be ashamed of its epitaph. It would have done its duty to India, and justified its mission to mankind. But it is not going to end. It is not a moribund organism.... Let no man admit the craven fear that those who have won India cannot hold it, or that we have only made India to our own or to its unmaking. That is not the true reading of history. That is not my forecast of the future. To me the message is carved in granite; it is hewn out of the rock of doom—that our work is righteous and that it shall endure.

Shameless grandiloquence was not the normal ICS style, but even Sir Bampfylde Fuller's solidly factual and well-illustrated textbook in Pitman's 'All Red' series concludes with a reference to the Indian's special sensitivity to 'the Unseen Forces' represented by the King

Emperor.[56] As one would expect from a former element in the 'steel frame' of the ICS, he is cautiously progressive and nuanced, while resting the imperial mission on the controlled management of institutional change. Fuller was, however, notorious for suggesting that Islam was the 'favourite wife' of the Raj and his text stresses the influence of the Gospels on the teachings of the Prophet and the fact that 'Our Lord is held in very high reverence' by Mohammedans. Despite their social backwardness, the religious proximity of Islam to Christianity gave it a privileged position in the imperial context.

Other texts endorse Warren's argument with more cursory reference to fact and broader attention to the unfolding pattern of a Christian imperial history. The general structure of the argument is one they share with Curtis, though they generally manage to be briefer. In a sequence of unpublished 'Indian chapters' dating from the time of Curtis's involvement in India, his friend and Round Table associate Philip Kerr set out their shared commonplaces, sketching out the tentative providentialism characteristic of a number of writers of the inter-war period. Kerr starts with the comparative failure of Hindu and Muslim to produce peace by the 1750s and ends on the essential need for improvement, under a strong government, of the Indian's poor capacity for showing responsibility towards the whole community. He takes in the fundamentally different eastern and western conceptions of life, the necessary creation of the Empire to avoid misrule in India, the instruction of the East in western methods, through law, unity and education, and the Indian incapacity, as yet, for self-rule. British administration and Commonwealth, if premature self-rule can be avoided, will draw out of the Raj a future for the human race which will be closer to that promised 'knowledge of God'.[57] Such phrases do not appear in the sketch, but Kerr, like Curtis, thought in such terms, and 'always tried to correlate his political with his religious ideas.'[58] Years later, making a Mansion House speech to raise money for work in Madras, Serampore and elsewhere which had been recommended by the Lindsay Commission, and speaking with a confidence in a set of shared general assumptions about the imperial mission unimaginable at the Mansion House in later years, he made a condensed statement of elements in the Christian position.

For while we may differ about our denominational tenets, I think all in this room will agree that the success of the colleges in doing the great work which lies open before them will depend upon the degree to which they express, in the words of St Paul, 'that mind which was also in Christ Jesus.' For it is that spirit which is the answer to the forces of bigotry and communal pride, of intolerant nationalism and class feeling, of sensualism and atheism, which are so arrogant and menacing in the contemporary world, both in India and elsewhere.[59]

His reference to 'denominational tenets' would have reminded his listeners of his own strong commitment to Christian Science.

The skeletal structure of these 'Indian chapters' is filled out in texts by other authors. Edwyn Bevan's *Indian Nationalism* was already out in 1914, and another book, *Thoughts on India's Discontents* appeared in 1929. Bevan, a double first from New College, had been involved in preparatory work for the British delegation to the Paris Peace Conference at the end of the Great War, and already had other books to his credit. He wrote *Christianity* for the Oxford Home University series, and gave the Gifford Lectures in Edinburgh in 1933–4.[60]

What, he asks, is the moral justification for the Raj, beyond a crude reading of Darwin? It is for the good of the greatest number, the ruled, and the fact that 'the best part, the conscience of the nation, sanctions it' is evidence of that.[61] The Empire brought the British character and the spiritual influence of tradition to a riven society. A steel frame 'in contrast with the natural freedom of the body, is always an evil; but in contrast with the condition of a broken or dislocated body without it, it may be a necessary evil.'[62] The image of the crippled body in the steel frame keeps recurring. Patience is the best preparation for its release. That is to say that the extremists are right, that emancipation from alien rule extends far wider and deeper than politics, into the gradual acquisition of the rational skills of ruler, administrator and businessman, and depends too upon the construction of a unitary society. But the extremists fail to grasp how that may be done. India would be dismembered by more powerful neighbouring states if it achieved independence before it was ready and if it ceased to be a co-operative component of the Empire. The purpose of the Raj is to give an evolutionary substance to the extremists' impatient insight, notwithstanding the 'very ugly fact' of the destructive rudeness and the assumption of superiority of individual Englishmen.[63]

The ugly fact of behaviour out of tune with 'British character' and the spirit of the Christian tradition is a preoccupation also of his later book, but there, shortly before the civil disobedience period, he also explains the *appearance* of arrogance in terms of British realism about the threats to imperial fulfilment. Altruism, anxiety about the effects of British withdrawal, leaving an under-developed economy and an untrained society at the mercy of foreign powers,—these can take the appearance of a will to dominate. Some-how, as Coupland and the Round Table writers remind him, the impending struggle between European and non-European must be avoided, so that 'Knowledge, knowledge, knowledge' can pass co-operatively from the one side to the other, and be applied by the state.[64]

But in this book too, after a decade of Gandhian nationalism, he dwells on the religious basis of British rule and the distorted religious basis of an inadequate Indian society. Sacrifice and service have marked the nationalist movement, and these are the religious values of any essentially unitary social movement. They have been latent in the religions of South Asia. And yet there is the great impediment to national realization which, unlike Gandhi, the extremists over-look, and which Hinduism in particular is incapable of removing without contradicting its own inherent nature. This is the absence of a national community based on equally valued functions and a social pluralism transcending, as it must, the divisive hierarchies of social value and exclusiveness. Hinduism cannot recognize the unity in diversity of the human family. Buddhism and Islam can reach that far. But it is only in Christianity that the organic community is fully recognized for what it is. In this Gandhi himself is with Christ, but unhappily Gandhi is no longer taken by the whole national movement as a guide to action.

Bevan reproduces prosaically the discourse of Christian imperialism. Sir Francis Younghusband, who was far more widely known from a romantic career that had taken him deeply into the mysteries and spiritualities of the East,[65] was perhaps its most generous evangelist. Opening the new Society for Promoting the Study of Religions in 1924, with Zetland (Ronaldshay) as President, he proposed that:

The British Empire should be a mighty agent in leading the nations of the earth along the paths which would bring them to that fellowship in which the principal rivalry would be, not of trade or territorial expansion, but of spiritual achievement.[66]

His vision of the Christian Providence in *Dawn in India* (1930) is ingenuous and unqualified:

Finally, we must have faith in God—faith that working through us, through the Indians, and through the whole world, is a Power making for all that is best and noblest in life; and faith that what that Power is working for must in the end come about.[67]

Imperialists on the political right, who were less than convinced that the divine providence had much immediate use for indigenous Indian material, might dismiss the expansive naïvety of his vision of India's self-discovery within the Empire, but it is not the case that their particular negative judgments were necessarily more 'realistic' than his own more optimistic ones. He acknowledged the 'deep religious faith of the Bengali revolutionaries.'[68] He was not impressed by the die-hard insistence on the social fragmentation of India, stressing instead an underlying unity which was already in evidence and which the right kind of leadership could intensify. His account of Hindu-Moslem tension is both lucid and relatively subtle. Where die-hard references take for granted an inherent and ineradicable conflict that derives inevitably from the clash of fundamental religious principles, Younghusband stresses the political history of Islam in India as the religion of an invader, and points out that, at the level of the ordinary Indian, fundamental principles may be closer than the bigoted might suppose. Despite the pantheon available to him, the Hindu villager naturally speaks, like the Moslem, of the one God who has sent the rain. At regional and national levels Hindu-Moslem tensions are the product of political change and there are potential political solutions which 'nation-makers' like the Parsi MP Dadabhai Naoroji and the Mahatma himself could work for. Gandhi may or may not have turned 'Moslem grievances against the British to his own account in his campaign against British authority,' but 'he is obviously quite genuinely intent upon a reconciliation. His patriotism demands it, and his fundamental religious beliefs compel it.'[69] Younghusband is specific about the virulence of communalism but confident that the transcending national spirit will emerge.[70]

In Hinduism itself he sees the discarding of error and ripening strengths which had been given new light particularly in the Idealism of *The Hindu View of Life,* the short and accessible study of Hinduism by S. Radhakrishnan, Spalding Professor of Eastern Religion and

Ethics at All Souls from 1936–52.[71] In a few pages Younghusband sums up the Ruskinian vision which Percival Spear later identified with Gandhi's subtle social revolution, and which the social anthropologist Louis Dumont has elaborated in scholarly form in his *Homo Hierarchicus* (1966).

Hindu society is regarded as an *organic whole.*... [The four varnas, Brahmans, Kshattryas, Vaisyas and Sudras] all work together for a common end. And they are bound together by a sense of unity and social brotherhood. Each has its own specific social purpose and function, its own code and tradition. Each is a close corporation equipped with a certain traditional and independent organisation. Each observes certain usages regarding food and marriage. And each is free to pursue its own aims, free from interference. But the functions of different castes were regarded as equally important for the well-being of the whole. Each had its own perfection to contribute.[72]

A Raj that evolved of no set design (and despite the British Government's historical repugnance to dominion) which came about because of 'the inherent necessity 'there is in things to work for order,'[73] provides the conditions in which a modern organic whole can be achieved. It makes possible the recovery of an ancient vision of social order which is consistent with the Christian vision.

Younghusband was recognized for his services to the Empire, but he did not engage professionally with the politics of Indian nationalism. He made what is in many ways an attractive contribution to the orientalist literature on the Raj, but the official wardens of the Christian mission to the Empire in the upper reaches of the Anglican establishment were wary of him, and it was from the rank and file that he got more explicit support for the World Congress of Faiths which he initiated in the early 1930s.[74] His religious faith was too expansively inclusivist for the more orthodox and conventional and his philosophical idealism too simply optimistic, though he was widely regarded as a reliable link with the spirituality with which orientalism had invested the East.

Chirol, Indian correspondent of the Times, and Ronaldshay, Governor of Bengal (1917–22) and Secretary of State after Samuel Hoare in 1935, were directly and intimately engaged by the nationalist movement. Their main books were widely read and regularly cited. Both were highly informed, and strenuously concerned with the imperial mission, and their very consistent output must have had a considerable impact on opinion in the Anglo-Indian public. Both took a particular interest in the work of the missions and of organized religion in India. A *Guardian* review of Ronaldshay's *India: A Bird's Eye View,* observed with approval that it was 'written by one who many hope will succeed Lord Reading as Viceroy.'[75] The same paper's review of Chirol's *India* is headed 'A sage on India.'[76] Both appeared on the platform at major meetings of the missionary societies.

Their reviewers in the church papers stressed the importance they attach in their explanations to the psychology of Indian nationalism. What commentators meant by that, since they were able to take it for granted that the books were written unequivocally from a Christian imperialist position, was that both writers were much concerned with the social and political implications of the fundamental divide between Hinduism and Christianity as systems of belief. Of the two authors, Chirol is less inclined to accept that the modern purification and revival of Hinduism's underlying concepts will supercede its more sinister political effects at other levels. He makes a great deal of the morbid sensuality of Hinduism and its corruption of a right relationship with the real world, particularly the world of politics. Ronaldshay made a determined attempt to understand the confusions of Hinduism in the light of idealist and fulfilment assumptions. The evidences of oriental sensuality he is prepared to take as they come, 'human nature being what it is,' but he explores at length the deep pessimism which he sees darkening the Indian's vision of life, his unsacramental rejection of reality and inability to recognize that spiritual advance can only be pursued through the practicalities of social existence.

Chirol's *Indian Unrest,* which was put together in 1910 from his articles to the *Times,* describes the extreme nationalists as primarily a Brahman fraction representing the most morbid aspects of Hindu revivalism—which had been stimulated to some degree by irresponsible western attacks on Christian morality by such free-wheeling thinkers as Bradlaugh, Besant and the western disciples of Vivekananda, in their tracts on 'The Evil of Continence' and the like. He recognizes in Tilak and his followers a genuine desire to mitigate the evils and hardships of the poor, but these good causes were 'perverted into anti-Britishness' by the militant Brahmans of the Deccan, notably of the Chitpavan caste. His account (a second-hand one) of those charged with the murder of Mr Jackson of Nasik graphically illustrates the conjunction of religious, psychological and political pathology by which Chirol saw British rule being threatened.

[A. L. Kanhere's] appearance was puny, undergrown and effiminate, and his small, narrow, and elongated head markedly prognathous, but he exercised over some of his companions a passionate, if unnatural, fascination, which I have been told by one who was present at the trial, betrayed itself shamelessly in their attitude and the glances they exchanged with him during the proceedings. Distorted pride of race and of caste combined with neuroticism and eroticism appear to have co-operated here in producing as complete a type of moral perversion as the records of criminal pathology can well show.[77]

Nasik was a stronghold of Hinduism and therefore exceptionally 'favourable for such morbid growths.' Such events, like the revival of the 'often obscene and horrible rites' of the Kali cults, were the pathological reaction to imperial rule of a caste society in which the ideas of democracy are inherently meaningless. Thus the main effect of the Arya Samaj in the Punjab was to increase the power of the moneylenders and landlords who were the ringleaders in the agitations of 1907. In reality, representative institutions in India are bound to become 'machines operated by and for the benefit of, an extremely limited and domineering oligarchy' sustained by the ritual rigidities of caste.[78] The moral austerities of some aspects of the Hindu revival, in the Arya *gurukals* or seminaries, must be seen in this context, as the disciplines of a religious order which consolidates caste structures, and is, most fatally, militantly anti-Moslem.

The only response that will count in the end must be mounted by the resources of Christianity. Using Bishop Whitehead's figures and projections, he looks to the reclamation of whole populations from the depressed castes, achieving a new independence and status through conversion and the uplifting social effects that follow it, where missionary resources are sufficient for the task. In the Christian missions the Government has 'an admirable organisation ready to hand, which merely requires encouragement and support.' The hour is at hand for a great and combined effort.[79] Among the educated the problem is to elicit the substantial basis of a common denominator between the different religious groups, and to develop the capacity to recognize political and economic realities, to perceive the fact, for instance, that real *swadeshi* means economic development and that it was promoted by British teaching and enterprise well before the nationalist politicians perverted the cry to seditious purposes.[80]

India Old and New was published after early experience of Gandhian nationalism in 1921. The psychological argument is to some extent overtaken in this connection by the 'great constitutional experiment' of the Montford reforms. Here Chirol aligns himself explicitly with the close co-operation between Indian Christians and broad-minded Englishmen in the Indian YMCA, and shares their uncertainties about the nationalist movement and its leader. Gandhi is the great religious and social reformer, plunging dangerously into political agitation, sensitive to the blot of untouchability, but insensitive to the deadly forces that will in reality be released by the idealistic use of *ahimsa*. And of course there are the ambivalences of British rule, which has become obsessed with mechanical efficiency at the expense of the principle of co-operation, with a consequent loss of faith in the British Empire's mission.

The psychology that caught the attention of Ronaldshay took him into a rather intensive study of Hinduism, primarily in Bengal, on which he drew for *India: A Bird's-Eye View* and *The Heart of Aryavarta*, the book of which he was particularly proud because it was well received by the 'experts'.[81] As he summed it up in his President's address to the Birmingham and Midland Institute in 1930, it was characteristic of Hindu psychology to grasp abstract ideas rather than concrete proposals, and to ignore practical steps.[82] That point, applied to economic and industrial development in India, would have been readily absorbed by his hard-headed audience, as would his standard paean, repeated in the 1935 Cust Foundation Lecture at Nottingham University, to the 'fine flowering of the administrative genius of the British people' in the setting of the Raj.[83]

Less prosaic was his consistent thesis that this deficiency was the obverse of India's extraordinary achievements in religion, philosophy, literature and art. Of these fields he had some detailed knowledge and he wrote with assurance and the occasional rhetorical elevation about India's groping struggle 'from that long and brooding night of barbarism which lies behind the first faint light of civilisation's dawn.'[84] This has taken Hinduism an extraordinary distance. Thus, for most advaitist Vedantins the concept of *maya* is in fact close to St Paul's Christian doctrine that the things which are seen are temporal, only relatively real, and that it is the things which are unseen that are eternal and absolutely real. But what Hinduism adds to this, with the standard interpretation of the doctrine of *karma* and the rest, is a machinery of despair that removes real hope and any sense of responsibility for one's actions. On the other hand, the actual sense of the unseen eternal realities has atrophied in the West whilst remaining an object of strenuous pursuit in Hinduism.

His references to providence were more urbane than Young-husband's—'there has been at work some apparently purposive force, a sort of Arabian Nights genie of history....'[85] History consists of enactments with (retrospectively) inevitable consequences. But his argument for imperial co-operation extends well beyond a co-operative convergence on the rational dispositions of constitutional and economic change. The Raj represents a marriage of distinct social qualities, which are essential in combination for human progress but unevenly distributed between the partners to it.

Their successful liaison is threatened by the radical conflict between Hinduism and Islam. The 'insensate violence' that results from this conflict can be controlled by the Raj, but the Raj can only mediate between the two religions, through its own realization, which is as yet inadequate, of a Christianity which transcends both.[86]

All these writers spoke in some sense from within the establishment. There were other concerned, and often critical voices from outside it. C. F. Andrews, particularly over the period of the Round Table Conferences when making his case for a more rapid and substantial constitutional advance, also spoke and wrote in terms of psychology but within parameters very different than those of Chirol and Ronaldshay.[87] His argument came down to an assertion that the time was ripe for the transformation of the imperial connection, not only because India had already reached a level of organic unity that demanded this historical liberation, but also because the pro-longed retention of imperial control had already done grievous damage to the moral integrity of Britain itself. Andrews effectively turned around the arguments about untouchability and caste division and applied them to the social distance between British and Indian, and to British arrogance and racial superiority. It was the British denial of 'love' and the entrenched structures of its authority which were the true impediments to the authentic future that was so close to realization. Delay would push the younger generation of Indians into violence and error, with the inevitable consequence of repression, and the British would be responsible for thwarting the divine intention. Andrews's radicalism was a function of his perceptions of an 'organic' unity, both at the level of the Raj as a decaying co-operative process and also within the transformations of Indian society itself. He saw the moral degeneration of British imperialism in the die-hard opposition to constitutional reform, and the lineaments of fulfilment in the many aspects of a national awakening in India. To seize the psychological moment would be to liberate *both* partners to the Raj into a more promising future.

For Christian imperialists of the establishment Andrews was infected with a Gandhian lack of realism, though he did not disguise his criticisms of Gandhi himself, particularly over the political and potentially violent use of *satyagraha* and the symbolic burning of foreign cloth. But for Irwin, who responded to a kindred spirit in Andrews, the biblical language of unity had rather different connotations. 'We are all members of one body,' and there is no divorcing the interests of Great Britain and the federation of Indian interests, but the 'Indian nation-state' is a hollow phrase unless it is based on unity between the communities and a shared identity of purpose. For Irwin, in the final analysis Gandhi's actions and influence could not stand up to this test.[88] India's unity was still inchoate. Irwin and Andrews both lived as Christians in the same world and under the same Providence, but Andrews saw corruption where Irwin was bound to see responsibility, and a new spirit where Irwin suspected mixtures of authentic idealism and short-sighted sectional interest. Andrews used his access to Irwin assiduously, and for this reason the '"fox" element'[89] was regularly called into play in Irwin's treatment of Andrews and his radical enthusiasms.

Their disagreements, however, were accomodated comfortably within the discursive framework. Andrews's attempts to shift emphases in the interpretation of imperial reality were respectfully treated, and reached a substantial audience. C. P. Scott brought him to the Liberal and non-conformist public in England by printing his reports in the *Manchester Guardian* from 1923. His books were published in cheap editions by Allen and Unwin and the SCM press and were widely read. He appeared regularly in periodicals. Realists might dismiss as wishful thinking his hopes for Hindu-Moslem 'unity', but his critique of Mayo's obsessions and distortions, though it initially appeared as a series in *Young India* and only in 1930 in England,[90] was a better informed and more balanced account of her themes, from child marriage to animal sacrifice at Kalighat in Calcutta. Its effect was to strengthen his broad argument about the process of fulfilment as a ripening moral and religious evolution, with political consequences which he identified particularly with the personality of Gandhi.

William Temple's foreword to *The Dawn of Indian Freedom,* which was written as a contribution to the atmosphere of the Round Table conference by two other Anglican irregulars, Winslow and Elwin, illustrates the uneasy blend of acceptance and caution that could be inspired in leading churchmen by the writers who most closely identified themselves with the Mahatma. With carefully turned incoherence Temple wished simply 'to make it clear that I am neither commending nor criticizing the contents of this book otherwise than as a contribution to the English understanding of the Indian mind. But for this, which is the first necessity, I believe that it has a peculiar value.'[91] A larger validity would excuse any minor excesses of the righteous partisan. The book's framework is not challenged, though its accents and immediate implications might be.

Temple's reticence is easily accounted for by their uncritically spiritual treatment of complex political events. On the first page the Gandhi-Irwin pact of 4 March 1931 is described as a miracle won by the faith and goodness of two profoundly religious men. Gandhi himself is the incarnation of moral energy. The different facets of his nature are compared favourably with Wesley, the prophets of the Ramakrishna Mission, the great Brahmo-Samajists, St Francis, F. D. Maurice, Tolstoy and Newman. The *satyagraha* movement quite simply 'represents the application of the teaching and spirit of Jesus to the spheres of politics and international relations,' however imperfectly realized in practice, and the different *satyagraha* campaigns are compared in terms of their moral success. In this climate Winslow,

cannot believe that the communal problem is really so difficult of solution. Amongst the younger men it hardly exists. The national bond is for them so strong that it overrides communal differences....[92]

And the Church in India, which has been slow to learn the lesson of Temple's great COPEC Conference, that Christianity also covers politics, can address itself to the task of becoming an Indian church, following K. T. Paul's lead in rejecting communal representation through a separate electorate for Christians and working for the reconciliation of all religions in India.

The Dawn of Indian Freedom is interesting for its timing and for its emotional and entirely uncritical acceptance of the Mahatma as a type of Christ, but its arguments are representative of a group of authors more or less close to Gandhi and to Andrews. For all of them, Maurice and Seeley were authoritative, as Marjorie Sykes has pointed out.[93] Seeley had set the broad agenda for action in India. Half way through the Second World War, one of these authors, the Quaker John Hoyland, reproduced the fulfilment argument in his *Indian Crisis,* dwelling on the reactionary implications of the *karma* doctrine, but noting the 'heart-hunger' it represents. He described Gandhi's ethical purging of Hinduism with the intellectual assistance of Radhakrishnan and his manifestation of the spirit of Christ in Indian garb. He outlines the truncated Maurician 'honeymoon period' in the 1930s, when Indian ministries 'were proceeding hot-foot with the task of bringing about, by peaceful and constitutional methods, a profound social revolution,' especially in connection with money-lending, land tenure and prohibition, under the 'fostering care of a foreign imperialism.' He too noted the 'disastrous' communal electorates and the reactionary twist they were bound to give to the spiritual resource of the 'mighty bond of brotherhood in Islam.'[94]

The Quaker group voiced the anxieties of those who were most uneasy about a collapse, concurrently moral and pragmatic, of imperial control. For the 'responsible' middle ground, The Royal Institute of International Affairs (Chatham House) published in 1941 what Meston in his foreword described as a 'thoroughly objective study...authoritative and comprehensive,' entitled *Modern India and the West.*[95] It was edited by O'Malley, and its Indian contributors included Radhakrishnan on Hinduism and the West, and Yusuf Ali on the westernization of Islam. At some 800 pages it represents, at a time of global crisis, a self-conscious stock-taking of the orientalism of the Raj fostered by the Institute Curtis and Meston had helped to establish. Arthur Mayhew's contribution on 'The Christian Ethic and India' is an indication of his standing as an authority on Christianity and the Raj which dated from his *Christianity and the Government of India* (1929). This was published after seven years teaching classics at Eton,[96] and followed a career as Director of Public Instruction in the Central Provinces. It identifies a 'balanced' position that received less vociferous but more general support than that of Andrews and the Quakers and the Christa Seva Sangha. Mayhew sympathized with those,

who felt a strong desire to take their stand with Mr Gandhi. He had undoubtedly inspired India and individual Indians with a sense of national dignity and personal responsibility. Such a fact was in itself Christian. More than this, 'he turned the eyes of India to the Cross,' he quickened interest in the personality of Christ; 'for the first time in Indian history a nation for the attainment of its ends substituted suffering for force.'[97]

But such phrases he can apply only to an 'all too short but glorious stage' in Gandhi's career up to 1921. Thereafter, his fatal deficiencies inevitably appeared. Christianity in the western world had produced:

Not so much a new code of morals as a type of character endowed with sufficient driving power to translate into legislative and administrative action principles that had already commended themselves in theory to the noblest representatives of other philosophies and religions.

Christianity meant the embodiment of ideas in action. It had been a drastic error on the part of the British in India not to make it clear that their actions as rulers had been Christian actions and had been carried out because of a collective commitment to the Christian faith. For in India,

what may be found wanting is the hopefulness and energy, the faith that is idealism in action, the frank recognition of facts and the insight into reality, that characterise the really Christian attitude towards life.[98]

Gandhi is irredeemably Hindu in that:

He has never shown any ability, nor, one might almost add, any desire, to test his ideas in the light of actual facts or to adapt his action to circumstances as revealed by history or science.[99]

History includes the historical basis of Christianity, in the Incarnation of Christ, a kind of validation Hinduism cannot claim for itself. History too 'shows the importance of humble-minded attention to facts and the infinite capacity of the inspired soul for progress.'

With this emphasis, he is bound to see less in Hinduism than in the 'virility and hopefulness' of Islam. Islam indeed 'may yet do more for the social and moral progress of her peoples than Hinduism'. A sacramental sense of reality informs British rule, behind our absurd reticence, but that is what we have so far failed to transmit in a measure sufficient to discharge our imperial obligations. We have failed collectively to make sufficient acknowledgment of supernatural authority, and we have put too much faith in the development of the co-operative capacities of human nature within evolving political institutions. This is a criticism he also levels at Curtis's faith in the organic and progressive conjunction of co-operation and democracy, in an otherwise appreciative essay on *Civitas Dei*.[100]

The Public Schools and the Raj

Mayhew summarized his argument about Gandhi and the nationalist movement for the boys at Haileybury on the first Sunday of the Summer Term of 1930.[101] Introduced as former Director of Public Instruction, Central Provinces of India, recently Master at Eton College, and Joint Secretary to the Advisory Committee for Education in the Colonies, his talk stressed particularly the eastern weakness with facts, the need for contact with Englishmen and the unifying strength of Christianity.

Haileybury was very familiar with occasions of this kind. Talks by Tyndale-Biscoe on his regular visits, by English and Indian members of staff from St John's College, Agra, (the Revd E. F. Bonhote, who became Headmaster in 1934 had taught at St John's from 1914 to 1917), and the annual letters and reports from Holland, Sully and others at St John's, where Haileybury supported a hostel, take up a great deal of space in the college magazine. The institutional link with Christian education in India, and of course Haileybury's particular tradition of Indian service, account for the unusual prominence of the Raj in its house journal. Other institutions higher up the pecking order of the public schools took their position as imperial nurseries more for granted: the inspirational rhetoric of Winchester's *The Wykehamist* is less frequent and less overt than that of *The Haileyburian* and *The Cheltonian,* for instance. But India and Empire received regular attention in all the major schools from which the bulk of the ICS recruits were drawn, and the rhetoric of Christian service was always to hand.

This was true at the level of what would now be called career advice. Recruitment into the ICS declined in the 1920s. In a succession of addresses at a number of public schools Lord Lee of Fareham extolled the career opportunities it offered. In addition to being President of the Cheltenham College Council he was Chairman of the 1923 Commission on ICS pay and conditions and was personally responsible for repairing the opportunity structure. But he simultaneously described consecration to the public service as the highest form of applied Christianity.[102] The work of his Commission was itself an applied and practical recognition of the historical purpose of the 'steel frame'. During this crisis, *The Wykehamist* printed an article solicited from one of the relatively numerous serving officers who had been educated at Winchester. It went into the extremely favourable financial prospects for recruits in great detail, advising, nonetheless, against joining the service on career grounds because of future uncertainties. Notwithstanding this advice, however, it concluded with a booming pastiche of Kipling:

If then, you wish to do great and honourable service, the greater and more honourable because you may have to bear the outward badge of failure and dishonour: if you are willing to face danger without the reward of open heroism: if you can devote yourself, careless of self, to the maintenance of a great tradition—join the ICS.[103]

The correspondence that ensued dwelt on the practicalities of security and pension, but fully endorsed the spirit in which this piece had been written.

In addition to informative exhortation from outside the schools, there were often veterans from the Raj on the staff. Bonhote himself had broken into a long career as a school master at Rugby to go to Agra on a short-term contract. Mayhew taught at Eton, Garfield Williams at Rugby. At Winchester, which boasted among its alumni a Viceroy in Lord Chelmsford and an Under Secretary of State and imperial historian in Sir Charles Lucas (d. 1930),[104] the formidable Housemaster W. D. Monro had gone as a missionary with a Cambridge degree in Oriental Languages to Ranaghat from 1896–1902 and was to return to India to see out the Raj in his old age as a chaplain under Bishop Barne in the Lahore Diocese. He stayed on as a pastor in the Church of South India, where he died in 1958. In 1930, on the eve of the Round Table Conference he spoke at the school debating society on the motion that 'This House has no faith in self-government in India,' and the *Wykehamist's* reporter succeeded in compressing his position, that of a Christian die-hard, into one authoritative paragraph. The motion was won by 31 votes to 6.[105]

These were exceedingly conservative institutions, in some cases running on energies released by distant institutional reforms under inspiring Headmasters like Arnold of Rugby and Moberly of Winchester.[106] Thomas Arnold, as Richard Brent has shown, had in fact been as important to liberal Anglicanism in general as to the public schools through the Victorian and Edwardian periods, in helping to shift the concerns of British churchmen away from questions of doctrinal orthodoxy and the saving of souls, and towards the pervasive and general contribution of Christianity to the foundation and development of world civilization.[107] Inevitably this meant an attenuation of credal issues. But the articles of belief continued to be affirmed with confidence, if less rigorously explored, until well after the Second World War.[108] They could, in a sense, be believed the more easily because they were largely left alone after an intensive but routine working over at the time of a boy's Confirmation, at the age of fourteen or fifteen. The service ideal of the English gentleman, implicitly interdenominational as a result of the social emphasis given to faith by Arnold and others, cannot be disengaged from its religious roots.

The service ideal lends itself to description in terms of gentlemanly norms and values, the class stance of *noblesse oblige*. But it is a mistake to underestimate the strength of the idea of a Christian foundation and its public significance within the public school communities themselves. However vaguely, the public school man identified himself and his kind as Christian gentlemen and his school as a repository and protector of the values of a Christian civilization. He was constantly reminded, by visiting authorities like Lord Lee and by the ideologues of the place like Monro, that gentlemanly behaviour at the very least routinized the elements of a practical Christianity.

The idea of service applied of course to the full range of occupations open to the public school man. But the substantive preparation for these vocations was not for the most part what we would now describe as vocational. For the budding proconsul or district officer the experience of school discipline and hierarchy, the rough approximations to the *ma-bap* relationship fostered by the prefectorial system, were more important than the academic curricula. As far as knowledge of the Empire and the Raj were concerned, it was the Whig, Christian historiography to which boys were exposed. A standard text latterly was D. C. Somervell's *The British Empire,* first published in 1930 and in its seventh edition in 1948. Somervell, master at Repton from 1909 to 1918 and thereafter at Tonbridge, was a prolific text-book writer and the editor of the standard abridgment of Toynbee's *A Study of History* in the 1940s. The further reading he cites includes: on India, the report of the Simon commission, Chirol, Sir W. Lawrence, and K. T. Paul; on the Far East and tropical Africa, Coupland and Lugard, and in general, Lucas, Egerton and above all, Lionel Curtis's *The Commonwealth of Nations.*

Somervell was disturbed by the weaknesses of the public school curriculum as a training in the understanding of politics. At Repton, in partnership with his colleague Victor Gollancz, he pioneered an experiment in the teaching of political ideas and issues, which was widely noticed, and even imitated at Eton. Gollancz's enthusiasms, his pacifism in particular, proved too much for a school struggling in wartime to recover from the headmastership of William Temple under another and more institutionally minded future Archbishop of Canterbury, Geoffrey Fisher. He was sacked. Sommervell resigned and the experiments ended.[109] But their book *Political Education at a Public School* in 1918 was an essay in liberal and, for Somervell, Christian enthusiasm rather than radicalism. He proposed Curtis's early work as a set text.

One of the present writers happened to wish to interest a good classical sixth form boy in the British Empire, and handed him *The Commonwealth of Nations.* The first chapter, it will be remembered, is entirely devoted to Greece and Rome, tracing the Athenian, Macedonian and Roman experiments in Imperialism as a prelude to the study of the British. On reaching the end of that long chapter, the boy remarked, 'I never dreamt that Greek and Roman history were so wildly interesting.'[110]

Somervell had been introduced to Curtis's book by Temple. His own text was an attempt to remedy the too cursory treatment of imperial progress, particularly over the previous hundred years, in the ordinary school courses of British history. For those who were exposed to his survey, it was a systematic academic confirmation of those more fragmentary signals they received from a variety of sources. Such sources will often have included family connections and even the instructive obituaries of outstanding servants of the Raj in the school magazines, which consciously measured individual careers against the tradition the schools represented.[111] The tone of such tradition was set by the major, or so-called 'Great Public Schools', to which all those who have been referred to here belonged.[112]

The public schools, of course, also produced Christian imperialists who took up political positions well to the right of those inspired by the arguments set out by Curtis. It is to that vision of providence, in one sense more radical and in another more reactionary, that we can now turn.

CHAPTER 7

God's Providence and the Die-hards

Defenders of the Faith

Bishop Headlam's belief that it was a religious obligation to maintain military strength was out of tune with the pacifism that became fashionable in the inter-war period. But it was a belief of the Anglican mainstream, at least, to which Christian liberals were ambiguously committed. There were a few radical Christians like George Lansbury, for whom disarmament and pacifism were entailed in any serious commitment to the Christian faith. But Lansbury is impressive because he was content to fight on the 'naïve' political and religious platform of hostility to any kind of enforced dominance, on the grounds that all such dominance is unbrotherly and exploitative. In imperial affairs this meant unqualified support for Indian independence in Parliament, where he spoke regularly on India, and in *The Daily Herald,* which he edited. In domestic politics it put him across the barricades from the forces of institutional religion, including those supporting the conservative Christian socialism which found political expression between the World Wars in the ICF.[1] His opponents had a Pauline faith in 'the powers that be' which he saw no reason to share. Among them were leading churchmen who even more emphatically agreed with Headlam that, authorities had a religious obligation to be decisive and confident in the use of force.

In 1926 the Bishop of St Albans, the Rt. Revd Michael Furze, proposed a vote of thanks to Lord Allenby at the Haileybury Speech Day for the truths he had just set out about military preparedness and the Empire and for 'being a good man of God.'[2] After affirming his hatred of war itself, Allenby had added that,

unless we have a living, united British Empire, unless it continues and grows, it dies. In determining your future the greatest ambition should be the maintenance of the might of the Empire to which you belong.

Seven years later, when the *Morning Post* was voicing opposition to the India White Paper, the Archdeacon of Chester, the Ven. W. L. P. Cox, author of *Christian Ethics and Peace Problems* (1919) and *Anglican Essays* (1923), wrote to attack the 'signal mistake' in 'shilly shallying' in India. The Roman Empire, he reminded the *Morning Post*, had encouraged local self-government but kept law and order.[3] He could look back to Christian soldiers who had preceded Allenby as defenders of the Faith, including Major General Sir John Maurice, author in 1897 of *National Defences* in Macmillan's 'The English Citizen' series, and successor to his father F. D. Maurice as Principal of the Working Men's College.[4]

Maurice's analysis is technical and strictly professional. Updated versions of his consideration of the Russian threat to the North-West Frontier appeared in the *Indian Empire Review (IER)*, the journal of die-hard opposition to Government policy promoted by the Indian Empire Society. Lord Sydenham was an acknowledged authority on the topic. But the IER, under the influence notably of Lord Sydenham, Claud Jacob, the Society's chairman, and Louis Stuart, its secretary, aimed to provide its readers with what they considered a comprehensive coverage of the whole debate on India, partly in its own editorials and articles, but also by recommending or condemning other published contributions to the debate. Favoured texts were advertised as required reading for all serious supporters, whose names were printed in the modest accretions to formal membership of the Society, which peaked between February and September 1933.[5] Books that 'should be in Clubs, Messes and Institutes,' for instance, included a succession of pot-boilers by Sir George MacMunn (on the Council of the Society), whose titles announce tone and perspective no less than content, *The Religions and Hidden Cults of India, The Underworld of India, The Martial Races of India* and, by a 'British India Merchant', *India on the Brink* and *A Searchlight on Gandhi. 50 Years Against the Stream* by E. D. Tyndale-Biscoe was strongly recommended. His father Canon Tyndale-Biscoe was an early addition to the membership of the Society, whilst he himself contributed an article on raising up a backward race in Kashmir. The review of Irwin's *Some Aspects of the Indian Problem* acknowledged his good faith but rejected his political judgments, and a certain amount of other work, such as *Educational Policy in India* by F. F. Monk of St John's, Agra, was noticed in order to be judiciously put down. On the other hand, the *IER* covered even ephemeral publications emerging from the political right and spoke in its commentaries for a body of opinion far larger than the formal membership of the Society itself..So the bluff military wisdom about lines of defence and supply on the North-West Frontier appear there in a more complex debate.

A striking feature of this deposit of imperial jingoism is its theological content and the twist it gives to the orientalism that has been discussed so far. For those who shaped die-hard opinion, the theme of military defence and law and order had deeper implications than any pragmatic calculation about the traditional Russian menace or the mere management of security in the subcontinent. Russia's loss, for instance, to an atheistic Bolshevism was recognized as evidence of the omnipresent tendencies in human nature towards disorder and wickedness. Die-hard theology on the nature of man is in fact more soundly orthodox than the social and personal ameliorism which conservatives despised in liberal churchmen. Die-hards saw the institutions of the imperial order, including of course, the church, as the divine weapons in a Miltonic battle between the forces of light and of darkness. The 'sell-out' in India was, however, the clearest evidence that they are themselves corrupted by the fallen nature of man; the weak or seditious enemy within is even more dangerous than the satanic force without. The agents of the British state were threatening to abandon its historical purpose, with catastrophic consequences for the future of mankind.

The *IER* gave serious attention to the spread of material which sought to sustain this perspective. It ranged from mere hot air, a pamphlet by 'Ag Recter' (a Miss Rochester of Tunbridge Wells), *India, a Reflection, Suggestion and Appeal,* to the scholarship of the polyglot Monier Williams's 1889 volume *Modern India and the Indians.*[6] The vapourings of a classic 'Miss Tunbridge Wells' cannot have stirred the hard-bitten managers of the India Defence League, which operated during the White Paper agitation in conjunction with the Society, but they were well aware of the religiose elements in their constituency and she was delivering the right message:

India is ours. It has been given to us: it is the 'Land of our Behest' a sacred trust, and neither the people at Home, nor our fellow-subjects in India have, nor can have any 'Mandate' for the severance of the two properties.

And in conclusion:

Being 'fellow workers with Christ' His Son we may, one and all hasten the time when 'all shall know him' and the Kingdoms of this world shall become 'the Kingdom of Christ.'

The invocation of Monier Williams is a cue for a tirade on the nature of the East. Ornamenting with his own crusty recollections the supporting page references from his learned authority, 'Senex' runs through the inventory from *karma* to 'filthy practices' in one of his regular contributions, and quotes Williams on all that is 'false, impure and utterly deplorable in their religious systems.' 'Yet our polite Cabinet Ministers profess to treat these wretches as on an equal footing for governmental purposes with Christian Britons. Is this not to crucify Christ afresh?' Regular readers of the *IER* were taken time and again through different versions of these arguments.

Dorothy Crisp was one of the die-hard's popular authorities on the general theme of Empire, with a repetitious sequence of volumes in the 1930s, following *The Rebirth of Conservatism*. She quotes Bodin on Property as the reward of merit, and Prependary Gough, 'in his fine sermon in the Guard's Chapel':

We are forgetting to be strong in the Lord, and we are tending to be sentimentally weak—not in the Lord—and at the same time to be losing our hold on the great principles.... Weakness is almost exulted in. Any attempt to energise the nation by appeals to a masculine and imperial spirit—however gracious and human the purposes to which it is invited to devote its energies—is becoming increasingly regarded as 'unchristian'.[7]

Her Christ viewed this world as a battle ground of good and evil, and 'offered a hard but strictly practical and commonsense path.' The British in their recognition of this are a 'peculiarly religious people', and though their organized religion has come to a low pass, it is not yet beyond redemption. Thus by 1935, even William Temple, after years of preaching pacifism in the company of clerics like Canon Sheppard, could discover that in a righteous cause, as when Christ drove the money-changers from the Temple, it is right to fight. She calls on the 'sense of proportion on warfare' of another Christian soldier, Brigadier-General Sir Henry Page Croft MP, Churchill's ally over India and rearmament.[8] Britain alone, it is clear to Croft and the die-hard stalwarts, can enforce peace in this world with justice and fair dealing.[9]

Differences between the leading texts devoted more specifically to the Raj are of some interest to the connoisseur of these otherwise interchangeable productions. Captain E. Ellam, author of *Swaraj: the Problem of India,* identifies his own religious position *outside* the Christian churches, in a '*navayana*' sect of Buddhism. The term roughly means 'that which is new', but Ellam's denominational tenets are a matter of some obscurity, for the authorities I have been able to consult make no mention of a *navayana* sect in the 1920s. In any event, it was from this perspective that Ellam also wrote another study, of the superstitious accretions to Buddhism in Tibetan Lamaism.[10] He shared the anti-clericalism of other forceful figures on the right, Kipling and Page Croft among them, whose sense of transcendental purpose had not been successfully engaged by the contemporary church. But it is also significant, particularly in the light of the next section of this chapter, that Ellam had a vision of the great historical movements of 'Aryan' peoples from which the British had emerged in the past. Common origins in this ethnic vortex, in his view, gave us as much right to invade India from the sea as it had given others to invade it from the north-west. His Buddhism sustained him from a tap-root of authentic aryan civilization, and provided him with an alternative vantage point from which he could make standard observations about the corruptions of a Brahmanical Hinduism, which had defeated the promise of Buddhism in South Asia. By his account, too, his *navayana* insights endorsed the familiar values of the soldiers and administrators of the Raj, the efficiency and rationality which, as we have seen, were more usually represented as a product of a distinctively Christian and western sense of reality.

The other writers of general commentary particularly favoured by contributors to the *IER* were Patricia Kendal, who had strong affinities with Mayo,[11] R. Stokes, James Johnson and Hugh Trevaskis.

Stokes's first book, *New Imperial Ideals* had the seal of die-hard approval in a foreword from Lord Lloyd. He argues the moral basis for an indirect imperial rule of the Roman model over backward countries, whose educated classes, let alone the rest, cannot truly absorb the moral ideas of the West. The analogy with Rome at its height 'is irresistible, and the hopes of permanence which it suggests are strong.' For the societies we hold in trust, democracy that is not merely a cloak for oligarchy is impossible. The organic reality of Empire is present in 'the effect of unity and grandeur on the feelings of its citizens.'[12] A second book coming out a year later reflects the urgency of the constitutional time and, in its foreword by Meston, who did not align himself politically with the right, the difficulty of locating any clear discontinuities in the spectrum of commentary on the Raj. *The Moral Issue in India* concludes that the root of India's troubles are moral evil and the helpless ignorance of the masses, who are our real responsibility. Neither of these things can be removed in any other way than by education, by which he means some kind of character-forming public school system. His strongest point is the stock die-hard argument that there is no unitary national movement. The choice is between Christian ethical principles, as hitherto, or the principles of a Hindu upper class.[13]

Both Johnson and Trevaskis were ex-ICS 'men-on-the-spot'. Johnson was in despair at the Church after the Act was passed. Only the Bishop of Exeter, whose knowledge from family connections with India enabled him to be 'faithful to his trust,' had voted against Baldwin on the India Bill. 'Have we the right to wipe out the scores of years of Christian endeavour and obliterate the teaching of our Saviour Jesus Christ? These are questions I cannot answer in the affirmative'. The bench of bishops was blind to the evidence: Hindu disregard for the truth, widow-burning, *karma*, caste, obscenity and unnatural vice, temple-prostitution, Moslem-Hindu hostility, the endemic factionalism of the villages, dacoity. He recommends a book, *The Land of the Lingam*, and notes with approval Mohammedan contempt for Hindu mythology.[14]

Trevaskis was in the Punjab ICS from 1905 till 1928, where he was inspired by the leadership of Sir Michael O'Dwyer, particularly his effective recruitment of Punjabis into the Indian Army during the First World War and his strong way with sedition after it. In the 1920s, too, there was the encouragement of Brayne's Gurgaon, and of others like Strickland and Darling who were devoted to the peasantry. But Canon Lovett of the 1922-3 Mission of Help, and founder of the Lahore Cathedral Fellowship, had also made a 'tremendous impression' on Trevaskis and he followed his father into holy orders on leaving the ICS.[15] Like Johnson he bewailed the leadership of the Church of England, deploring the 'skilful propaganda' that had infected Bishop Gore in his 'otherwise admirable *Belief in God'* of 1926. Gore had written that, the

attitude of Britons in India, whether government officials or traders, towards the native and their religions remained very far below what was to be desired in the way of sympathy.[16]

But another ideal, of authoritarian sympathy with the peasantry of the 'real' India was the inspiration of the Punjab tradition to which Trevaskis attached himself. Brayne and Tyndale-Biscoe demonstrated in practical terms how far that was from the kindly benevolence of Gore. Trevaskis recalls 'the kicks and stripes which are the lot of the English public schoolboy' as the instruments of moral training.[17] During the die-hard agitation Trevaskis had a curacy in Farnham, an area well populated with retired and serving army people, and then a 'living' near Horsham in Sussex, a rather similar catchment area. He was an active speaker and committee man for the cause.[18]

Other texts and articles in the review reflect the immediate interests of traditions of service in India; the police, the judiciary, the army and the ICS, and, of course, those of some commercial enterprises; but these are all special statements in a general argument within a discourse which assumed the existence of transcendent purposes operating through specific agencies—through the imperial structures and moral values of the Raj.[19] No doubt many supporters of die-hard resistence to the White Paper spent little time turning these more ultimate categories over in their minds, but under pressure to provide a general justification for their position this was the direction in which the discourse invited them to move.

There were others in the die-hard movement, including figures of considerable importance, for whom the Christian components of the discourse were of primary importance. Some of these were also members of the British-Israelite movement which will be discussed in the following section. However, there is no basis for suggesting that the British-Israelites as an organization and a movement had any determining influence on the course of the brawl within the Tory Party over the White Paper. A consideration of their involvement, nevertheless, does throw light on the religiosity of the right, since British-Israel only carried a particular reading of the Christian imperialist discourse to a kind of logical conclusion. The logic, in its full elaboration, even in the view of many who fully endorsed the political positions British-Israelism defended, was simply nutty, but its basis was a thoroughly respectable evangelicalism. It had a supplementary apparatus of biblical interpretation that catered for those who felt the need for a special set of insights illuminating the commonplaces which British-Israelites shared with a very much larger constituency. The Revd H. G. Harding, for many years an Assistant Secretary for the CMS, wrote about the movement to the *Guardian* from his Thames Valley parish in April 1932:

[Despite their ludicrous ethnology and philology] we owe them a great deal for their insistence on the truth that we British are the covenant people of God, a belief which inspired Kipling's *Recessional* and which seems to appeal to some deep-seated feeling in British hearts.... Where, then, is Israel to be found? Like my British-Israelite friends I say, in the British Empire, but not because of our racial origin.

British–Israel and the Raj

The man who had established the doctrinal unity and central organization of the British-Israelite movement by the mid-1880s, Edward Wheler Bird, was the son of an ICS judge, and he himself had reached a senior position in the ICS by the time he retired to Bristol in 1868. In Bristol he held official posts in several missionary societies, including the CMS, before coming upon a book by John Wilson (d. 1871) 'the acknowledged progenitor of the British-Israel movement.'[20] Bird's personal history and characteristics are representative of the main features of the movement he effectively launched. It was middle-class, appealed particularly to the tidy, pragmatic and organized minds of imperial officials and servicemen, and most effectively to the evangelical outlook, whether in the Church of England or elsewhere. As a system of belief, it invested the conflicts and the controlling machinery of British imperialism with a portentous but well-defined significance in a celebratory elaboration of the right-wing vision of the Raj. The inter-war period was its golden era.

British-Israel teaching is centrally concerned with the idea of Providence, which it offers to decode with a fortifying degree of certainty and precision. The Bible it sees as something which is far from being a complex historical accumulation of texts which are required to be read in a variety of ways and, for the British-Israelite, most reprehensibly, in terms of the language of metaphor and symbol expounded by modern scholars. It is, on the contrary, to be read as a literal guide to conduct, but also as an astonishingly complete and particular anticipation of God's providential intentions for mankind. We may grasp them imperfectly, but the Bible is crowded with predictions.

It is easy to be condescendingly dismissive of the British-Israelite mode of biblical exegesis by fastening on details construed in the manuals and journals, of which there were a number between the World Wars, including the long-standing *Covenant People* and *Banner of Israel*, both of which were absorbed in 1921 into the lavishly produced *National Message*. The *National Message* had the official sanction of a well developed national organization.[21]

A tiny study pamphlet, *British Israelism,* by C.S.,[22] for example, instances Allenby's entry into Jerusalem, on 11 December 1917. This was no less than the entry of 'Allah-Nebi', God's Prophet, anticipated under divine inspiration in *Isaiah* and in *Micah* 1, ix: 'For her wound is incurable; for it is come even unto Judah; it reacheth unto the gate of my people, even to Jerusalem.' Unwittingly, Allenby's brother officers had even provided the supplementary confirmation that brings associated texts to life and into play. They referred to him as 'the Bull': try *Ezekiel* 1, x; *Hosea* 4, xvi and 10, xi; and *Numbers* 23, xxii; 'God bringeth them forth out of Egypt; he hath as it were the strength of the wild-ox.' (Revised Version of 1885. The Authorized version has 'unicorn'.)

Such readings of detail were not canonical for followers of the movement, but counter-arguments would have to be presented within the same scholiastic conventions and there was general consensus on the implications of more significant texts, such as *Isaiah* 49, xx-xxii, which was taken to refer to the Pilgrim Fathers: 'The children of bereavement shall yet say in thine ears, The place is too strait for me: give place to me that I may dwell....'

However, the exponents of the broad, central argument of the British-Israelites, when it came to citing chapter and verse, enjoyed an embarrassment of riches in the eschatological and prognosticatory stretches of both Old and New Testaments. Furthermore, as believers in the unique reality of the world they actually inhabited and the literal pertinence of biblical prophecy to it, they were quite prepared to cite history, a particular reading of history, as validation and proof of text. After all, what is the point of reading the language of prophecy Sunday after Sunday in church if it actually prophesies nothing in particular? And where else is a Christian to turn if not to the Bible to make sense of the shattering events of modern history? How, if he does so, can he fail to recognize in the recorded word of God, at once cryptic and terribly clear, the sub-text that carries the meaning of the process of history? The British-Israelite confronts without evasion the problem of what a Christian means by 'believing in the Bible,' as many churchpeople were uneasily aware that they did not, and he could support his literalism with evidence.

The central question for the orthodox reader of the Bible is who, or what, constitutes the 'Israel' with which the prophets, Christ and St Paul were concerned. The conventional Anglican, for instance, is brought up to accept a simple fideist answer. Israel is a somewhat nebulous moral entity with which he, through the church, can identify. For the believer who has, for whatever reason, a more literal and discriminatory mind, this may not be sufficient. British-Israel offers a more precise answer from its reading of the history of God's covenant with his chosen people. The Old Testament records the neglect of the Covenant by the tribes of Judah, with a crowning repudiation in their rejection of Christ, which suspended the promises of the Covenant. Christians have believed in a freshly interpreted Covenant between God and those who accept Christ, and this is accepted through the Puritan tradition by the British-Israelite movement. But British-Israel raises the supplementary question of the status of those who were of Hebrew descent, and therefore within the Covenant, but who were not involved in the repudiation of Christ, namely the 'lost' northern tribes of Israel which were led into captivity and disappeared from history.

British-Israel assumes an extraordinary historical resurgence, in which the descendents of these lost tribes, ignorant of their own history and significance and frequently at war amongst themselves, gradually swept into Europe, with a decisive group of Normans establishing the basis for an Empire within the Covenant in the British Isles. In an objective, almost legalistic sense, the British and their collaterals constitute the basis of Israel, and it is to the British in particular and their transatlantic relatives that the task of founding the eternal Empire has most clearly been given. The proof lies in the concrete history of the British Empire. The arguments, which were familiar to every British-Israelite, were set out in the British-Israel World Federation Leaflet, no. 2, by the Revd T. H. Whitehouse, an evangelical but not a member of the Church of England.

Genesis 12, ii is only the first of many statements of the Covenant:

And I will make of thee a great nation, and I will bless thee, and make thy name great; and be thou a blessing: and I will bless them that bless thee, and him that curseth thee will I curse: and in thee shall all the families of the earth be blessed.

Clearly there is only one Israel with whom this Covenant is being kept. To the British-Israelite Great Britain *is* a great nation and divinely protected: it *has* inherited the land 'from the river of Egypt unto the great river, the river Euphrates' (*Gen.* 15, xviii); its seed *has* multiplied 'as the stars of the heaven, and as the sand which is upon the sea shore' and it *does* 'possess the gate' of its enemies (*Gen.* 22, xvii); the Empire *has* formed a federated 'company of nations' (*Gen.* 35, xi); the Empire *is* fulfilling a mission of blessing to all the nations of the earth (*Gen.* 22, xviii).

The 'gates', of course, are the strategic locations that ensure dominion and survival, specifically, for instance, Gibralter, the Khyber Pass, the Cape of Good Hope and the South-West Passage. The movement was constantly reminded of the last of these gates by the Rt. Revd Norman Stewart de Jersey, Bishop of the Falkland Islands (d. 1934), who was a fervent supporter. The Bishop was an immediate contemporary of C. F. Andrews at Pembroke College, Cambridge, graduating in 1893 and serving as a naval chaplain till 1919.

De Jersey's membership illustrates a point of central importance about the British-Israelite movement. It was not a sect, in the exclusivist sense generally given the term. Of some hundred and eighty clerics mentioned in the inter-war British-Israelite literature in connection with meetings or as authors, about half appear in *Crockford's Clerical Directory* as Church of England clergy. Most had come through evangelical training colleges, but there were other sympathizers such as Prebendary Gough and W. M. H.

Milner, who had Oxbridge careers and books to their credit.[23] Milner was preferred to the living of Buckminster with Sewstern by its patron the Earl of Dysart, one of the titled figures of whose support British-Israel was particularly proud. Another was Princess Alice of Athlone, grand-daughter of Queen Victoria and wife of the Governor General of Canada.[24]

British-Israel had a Fabian strategy for the transformation from within of a lagging church, and many a parish priest in this period found British-Israelite members of his congregation tiresomely enthusiastic churchmen. The vitality of the movement within the Church was a matter of concern to the authorities. Under the headlines 'British Empire in Prophecy' and 'God's Promises to Israel Now Being Fulfilled,' The *National Message* of 17 March 1928 printed a long report from the *Kentish Observer* on a large and representative meeting, held in the spiritual capital of the established church, at the County Hall, Canterbury. The lecturer was Mr John Leech, KC, and the occasion was presided over by Canon W. D. Springett and Canon T. B. Watkins. The choirs of St Mary Bredin and St Stephen's were there to swell the singing of 'appropriate hymns'. Leach's peroration summed up the central British-Israelite argument and earned general applause:

We know something of the mighty growth of the British Empire; no human power could have made these Islands what they are at the present time...the British Empire fulfilled absolutely and accurately the promises God gave to Abraham and his descendents. There was no other country in the world, no other kingdom or empire or power which fulfilled these great promises. Therefore, he considered he was fully justified in saying that the British Empire was foretold in prophecy. (Applause)

Sermons, books and articles were produced in order to discredit the movement,[25] but its leaders were well aware of the extent of sympathy among those who were not inclined to take on the whole apparatus of their teaching, and they were adroit at turning the impulse of imperial religiosity, the basis of their success in the 1920s and 1930s, to advantage. A reported comment of Leopold Amery's, for instance, was regularly repeated. It is quoted here with the typographical enhancement of the BIWF leaflet, 'God's Spiritual Kingdom' by A. R. H.:

Mr Amery gets it right. 'THE EMPIRE is *not external* to any of the BRITISH

NATION. It is something like the KINGDOM OF HEAVEN *within* ourselves.'

The scholarly authority of Seeley was called upon.[26] And there were contemporaries with academic credentials who could not complain if they were claimed for the movement. Sir Charles Marston, for instance, was an industrialist (Sunbeam Cycle and Motor Cycle Business, and Villiers Engineering) and an active member of the House of Laity.[27] His attack on socialism from a Christian standpoint, *The Christian Faith and Industry,* was printed by the SPCK in 1927, and in Edward Norman's view accurately represents the tendency of lay church opinion at the time.[28] Certainly it re-presented a broad section of it. Marston was associated with archaeological work at Wroxeter, and his survey of archaeological discoveries in Palestine between 1925 and 1934, *The Bible is True,* was well reviewed and was in its sixth impression by 1938. He wrote on the subject for the *Morning Post.*[29] His general conclusion from such investigations is elementary British-Israelite teaching:

Some lack the imagination to appreciate mystery in these mechanical days. Yet it abounds throughout all history, and it has be... especially operative during this war—something beyond the range of cause and effect. Part of it people used to call 'The Luck of the British Army,' I call it all 'The Guiding Hand of Providence.'... In the light of those two thousand years of history, in the light of the present war with its miraculous deliverances, we feel bound to associate the British Empire and the United States with the promises made to Abraham and his descendents.[30]

Many who did not formally identify with British-Israelites could fairly be claimed as fellow-travellers. The Revd R. G. F. Waddington,[31] addressing the British-Israelite Congress at length in 1931, recalled that,

my own Bishop of Bradford some little time ago was opening a Missionary Exhibition in the City of Bradford, and I had the honour of taking the Chair for him. The Bishop took his text from a large military map of the world that was immediately behind him on the wall at the back of the platform, and he drew attention to the fact marked on the map that we British people were in actual living contact with all the races of mankind. Now he asked the question
        'WHY, WHY HAS GOD GIVEN US OUR EMPIRE?'
why has God brought the British people into contact with all the races of

mankind, why have we this wonderful privilege and solemn responsibility? and he said: 'There is only one possible answer: "Ye are my witnesses, saith the Lord, that I am God"' and he went on in that strain for a good twenty minutes, and when he had finished I got up and congratulated him on one of the best British-Israel addresses that I had ever heard....[32]

There are various indices of *formal* membership for the movement. Wilson's estimate of 5000 active members he regards as an under-estimate in the light of the magazine circulation figures of over 10,000. More than two hundred branches between them arranged on average at least 500 meetings a month and there are many reports of high attendances. There were large numbers at the major occasions, 20,000 to the week-long Annual Congress in 1931, whilst Herbert Garrison was able to fill the Albert Hall for his lectures, with lantern slides and supporting music. During the Great War he had become popular at music halls and public meetings lecturing for the Royal Colonial Institute.[33] The geographical distribution and density of the standard branch meetings is revealing. The concentration is high in well-to-do residential areas, such as Southport and Sale in the north, and the Sussex-Surrey border in the south, and in the colonies of retired professional and service people, particularly along the coast from Bournemouth to Margate and in Wessex. There were active branches in constituencies with Conservative minorities, but some ten percent of all branches generated almost half of the meetings, and all these were in constituencies with for the most part substantial Conservative majorities. The Bedford branch was particularly vigorous. Pelling draws attention to the cheap secondary schooling there under the Harpur Trust and quotes the Victoria *County History of Bedfordshire*:

It dawned on the retired officers and Indian civilians, with families still growing and incomes diminished, that here, within fifty miles of Charing Cross, they could find cheap and pleasant habitation and a public school education for £ 9–12 per year for their sons and high school education for their daughters at the same price.[34]

For the annual Bedford conversazione in 1933, at fine premises which were shortly to prove too small, there were 160 British-Israelite members with their guests, from precisely this social background.

British-Israel flourished between the wars in this milieu, immensely respectable, devoutly respectful to a monarchy of authentic descent from the House of David and to the paraphernalia of nobility and rank, pushing to tolerated limits widely held beliefs about the mission, under providence, of the Empire in an intriguing apparatus of half-baked biblical learning. British-Israelites were discouraged from associating their religious convictions with party affiliations. When the India Defence League started its membership drive, the number of recruits with a declared British-Israelite interest was small, with a handful of senior army people, such as Colonel Hume of Terrington in Norfolk as members and in the regional organizing committees of the IDL. Some twenty clergymen, fourteen of whom appear as Anglicans in *Crockford's,* openly declared for the IDL, despite general inhibitions about clergy appearing in partisan roles.[35] Two of these were prominent British-Israelites, the oddball Revd Seton of Mounie, a former Artillery Colonel and Canon W. J. Mackean, a naval chaplain during the First World War, Commissioner for the Falklands from 1926, and licensed to preach in the Dioceses of Chichester and Rochester from 1928. But there is no shortage of evidence of British-Israel as a focus for the expression of a widely diffused right-wing Christian imperialism. Within a short span of time in the period of die-hard agitation against the White Paper, for instance, the National Message reported a series of large British-Israelite meetings at York, attended by the mayor, the sheriff, Colonel Warren, Admiral Cayley and others of like status, an afternoon meeting of the East Greenwich Women's Conservative Association, where much interest was aroused on the topic of 'The British Empire in the Bible,' and a Sheffield Mission that attracted between 800 and 900 each evening.[36]

The distinctive fundamentalism of British-Israel naturally concentrated the attention of its followers on the Bible lands as the core of a vortex of migration and conquest which, as we have seen, appeared in some sense to have been closed by the arrival of Allenby in Jersualem.[37] There were speculations about the significance of parabolic movements in the opposite direction, but India figured most strongly in relation to the fulfilment of the prophecies of the dispersion of—in our 'correct' appellation—the Brith-ish race and the benefits of trans-national federation that it had brought to others. India, of course, provided ample scope for references to the racial purity and superiority of the Anglo-Saxon stock. So the movement offered a systematization on biblical grounds, with politically reactionary implications, of a much broader orientalism. For those who attended to it in England, it reduced the Indian problem to the crudest of dimensions under a providence which, though still opaque to our weak understandings, was seen as heavily determined.

The letters of a successful ICS man, Andrew Hume, show how this framework of ideas could fit the experience of a rather distinguished individual servant of the Raj. They also illustrate the organic links between this vision of supernatural sanctions and the activities of the right-wing Anglo-India public.

To some extent, Hume's fundamentalism isolated him socially in India: the random contact at the club or at work was not usually starving for humourless Bible-punching, though he occasionally succeeded in stimulating interest. But in general, he had to share his biblical certainties—and his interest in a book by 'Discipulus' on Pyramidology, which was a supplementary prophetical source for British-Israel—with his family in England. Having discovered in Simla that General Robert Knox Hazlet's daughter, whom he shortly married, was herself a British-Israelite, he acknowledged the indifference of the General and his naval son to the belief, though he put this down to simple lack of information on their part.[38] But like another evangelical, F. L. Brayne, Hume expected to have to survive in a sea of feckless inattention and social frivolity. He had assimilated very thoroughly the toughening ambivalence characteristic of the belief, the confidence of being an agent of an imperial providence that went with an oppressive sense of the incompetence of much of the imperial leadership and the wretched inadequacy of the human material entrusted to it. He eagerly identified the real men of Empire when he came across them (the tougher ICS men, Hailey for a time, a small number of clerics, Willingdon, Lloyd, etc.), whose moral and practical intuitions about the Raj were in his view right, and his family letters bear defiant witness to his strong identification with a society of the righteous, the understanding, and the practical. This world centred on his British-Israel family in Norfolk. It included the network of churchmen (among them, as a Roman Catholic, Sir Michael O'Dwyer) which was drawn into the protests against the Bolshevik assault on Christianity in Russia, and the disgruntled constituency supporters of the Tory party, who saw themselves as cheated and outmanoeuvred by Hoare and the leadership over the 1935 legislation. Grass roots opposition to the India Act was certainly expressing a service and professional interest, but it also represented an interpretation of history and a vision of the Empire which readily crystallized round the formalism of this strain of evangelical belief.[39]

Andrew Hume came from a family that had produced many Anglo-Indians.[40] He joined the ICS in 1926 from King's College, Cambridge, as a good modern linguist, and took high marks in the Hindustani and Persian examinations.[41] He was sub-divisional officer at Roorkee, with considerable responsibilities from 1929–31, and the Officer in charge of Barelli District in 1932. In 1935 he was responsible for producing the 1933–4 'Moral and Material Progress Report' for presentation to Parliament, under pointed instructions that there was to be no gloating over the recent discomfiture of Congress and Gandhi. For five years he had major responsibilities in slum clearance and housing in Delhi and ended his career in Simla with war-time responsibilities for food and medical supplies. During his time in Barelli, he was in vigorous confrontation with Congress agitation. Sometimes criticized by his superiors for his brusqueness towards natives and even for being unpopular with the people, charges he rejoiced in, he was highly regarded for his courage and competence.

Hume mastered the art of interpreting his powers as a magistrate, in ways that were not strictly defensible, to impose social discipline on his charges.[42] Potter takes him as an example of a recognizable type of ICS officer, referring to one of his escapades as an instance of a kind of irregularity in the performance of the steel frame of British law and order, when it was under pressure, that was not uncommon.[43] The latter part of 1930, September particularly, had been a rough period in Roorkee, with liquor-shop picketing by Congress and a serious disturbance, in which Hume and his police colleague had routed a large Congress demonstration.[44] At dinner in November with Captain Billy Gough of the Gurkhas,

I whispered the names of one or two ['Congress Dictators'] in his ear and hinted that they might advantageously be interviewed by a few Gurkhas. Billy took and acted on the hint to the full....

The soldiers surprised one 'fat bania' down by the canal.

The needful consisted in whitewashing the naked bania, adminstering a certain amount of corporal chastisement and pitching him into the canal, whence he emerged more dead than alive.

The salutary effect on the district he describes as 'electric'.[45] In March of the following year, Hume was shrugging off the threat of a civil suit for Rs 6000, which had Captain Gough seriously rattled.[46]

Hume's authoritarian racism is frank and overt, and it is an extreme statement of familiar propositions. It did not touch, for instance, the martial Gurkhas, efficient and subject to the discipline provided by imperial purposes. It was based on a deep, exclusivist hostility to the Hindu. He refers with embarrassment to Hinduism's sexual morbidity, as recorded by Mayo and others.[47] However, without directly invoking the religious excuses of the doctrines of karma and maya, he is most eloquent on the Hindu's hopeless detachment from the processes of reality, as manifested in his slovenliness, incompetence and natural corruption.[48] The notion that a British form of democracy can be grafted onto the civilization that produces such a mentality, in a 'wog government', is a repudiation of logic and natural order.

You cannot have a black man shouting revolution in your face and keep any self-respect.[49]

Everyone knows perfectly well that whatever else Gandhi may be—saint possessed of true spiritual perception or not—he is certainly no politician and is entirely impractical.[50]

The Humes believed in dominion status and the rest as 'an honourable British policy for those capable and worthy to be intrusted with it.'[51] But the only justifiable and certain response to Indian nationalism was the uncompromising imposition of British authority.

This, however, was precisely what the blind and thoughtless were shirking. From Hume's perspective, Irwin was something close to a 'religious maniac',[52] who had made a greater mess of India than anyone, 'Tamerlaine not excepted'.[53] He was the associate of dangerous sentimentalists like the Master of Balliol and Andrews, who is 'always messing about Gandhi, and running down anything to do with the British,' and whose 'proper place is the Andamans.'[54] For 'the question of religion, I have always told you, is the most serious thing out here,'[55] but the Raj had failed to confront the historical disaster of Hindu civilization by establishing a state church which would institutionalize the reality of the British imperial obligation and force individual Englishman to recognize it. Rhodes, or more precisely the Rhodes of S. G. Millin's biography, whatever may have been his religious beliefs, had the intuition of the genuine statesman for the thrust of imperial destiny. Hence his unqualified approval of 'the despotism that works so well in India.'[56]

The engagement of the Hume family in the die-hard campaign, therefore, was grim but vigorous. Andrew Hume welcomed his copies of the *Indian Empire Review,* which in its first issue, incidentally, had reprinted from the British-Israelite *National Message* an article on India by the Methodist Episcopal Bishop Brenton Thoburn Badley of Bombay, which had first appeared in the New York *Christian Advocate* and the *Star News* of Pasadena.[57] This was presented as useful in dispelling the claims of nationalist propaganda. But Hume feared that the review would only be read 'by those who already agree with the opinions expressed therein.'[58] Nevertheless, he wrote a man-on-the-spot letter of outrage at Baldwin's claim that the younger generation of ICS men generally supported the reforms. This passed from his father to Lord Fermoy and Louis Stuart of the *India Defence League,* who took a 'confidential abstract'. On 3 May 1933, Hume senior wrote to Archbishop Lang, who was a member of the Joint Select Committee. The recommendations before the Committee, he complained, 'will be compelling officers who engaged to serve their King and Country under British-Christian ideals to serve in the future or to agree to serve under Brahman ideals,' though 'Mohammedan ideals will prevail provincially in a few places.' He implied that this was strongly resented.[59] The *Morning Post* of 29 May 1933 printed extracts from a letter attacking Baldwin's claim, 'from a young serving officer in the ICS'.

In its sustained and vitriolic campaign the *Morning Post* printed a number of such documents. On 26 May a dozen old India hands, including Trevaskis and Stuart, who had been a Chief Judge in Oudh, had also attacked Baldwin's claim in a joint letter.

Hume senior was an assiduous India Defence League activist and his endeavours were warmly supported from Barelli. On 20 April the *Morning Post* had printed his account of his own intervention at the Eastern Provincial Area's Conference of Conservative and Unionist Associations. The procedural details belong with an account such as Carl Bridge's of the political management of grass-roots sentiment against the White Paper and Hoare's Bill.[60] But the letter makes the standard India Defence League allegation that the party leadership did not dare to allow a genuinely open debate on the India issue. On this point the die-hards had a strong case, though the reasons for opposition to the party leadership over India were complex with some groups, and individuals such as Page Croft, holding back from Churchill's more comprehensive attack on the Baldwin Government. The India Defence League generated embarrassing expressions of support for its cause in the constituencies. Maxwell Leigh wrote as a former ICS man to the *Hampshire Chronicle* expressing his confidence in Baldwin, but Tory groups in such areas of the Tory heartland were buzzing with hostility.[61] The concluding section of this chapter turns to a strain in this opposition, which was represented in one variant by the evangelical tendency to which the Hume family belonged.

Christians and the India Act of 1935

At the 1934 Conference of the National Union of Conservative and Unionist Associations at Bristol, Brigadier-General Sir Henry Page Croft challenged what his supporters called a 'muzzling motion', to suspend judgment on the White Paper proposals, with a motion of his own denouncing them. He was defeated by the narrow margin of 23 on a vote totalling 1063. Newspaper reports of every political colour agreed that the acclamation that greeted his appearance on the platform was more impressive than any enjoyed by the regular party leadership. The vote was the outcome of an extraordinarily vigorous intra-party campaign which had taken Croft to innumerable platforms across the country from his own bailiwick in Bournemouth— 'far and away the most intellectual constituency in the country,' as he liked to describe it.[62] The rebels had caused Baldwin, Hoare and their White Paper supporters much anxiety. Local *India Defence League* groups had sprung up. Along the coast from Bournemouth, at Horsham in Sussex, Lord Winterton's local Conservative association had refused to back his position on India. The Bath association had invited Lord Lloyd to address them, and turned down the Central Office speakers. The Duchess of Atholl was able to swing the Womens' Executive of the National Union against the White Paper's Federation proposal for India by 900 to 700.[63] By May 1933 Churchill had been confident of 70 MPs.

There were various ingredients to this opposition, and the die-hard leadership of course pursued as wide a base of opposition as possible, so Croft's speeches touch on all the main issues: the threat to Lancashire cotton and commercial interests generally, the interests of expatriates in the ICS and the services, defense and the question of 'safeguards', the hijacking, by the pro-White Paper coalition, of Parliament's right to decide and, crucially, the constructive legacy of British rule over a potentially chaotic subcontinent. Croft gave a great deal of attention to the last of these. In terms of mobilizing local interest it was a more rewarding theme than such technical issues as dominion status for India, over which he also fought a sustained battle with the party leadership.[64] But it was an area on which he spoke with passionate conviction, with the confidence of an experienced politician aware of the responses available from a familiar kind of audience. The premises of a right-wing Christian imperialism were exposed more effectively and persistently, and for a wider public, by Croft than by other senior die-hard politicians who thought in the same terms, such as the aged Lord Sydenham and Lord Lloyd. For Churchill, whose thumb-nail judgments about Hinduism accorded with Katherine Mayo's, and who was to the end concerned with the political advantages to Britain of Indian disunity, especially between Muslim and Hindu, this was not an open line of approach.[65] Page Croft's role was recognized by enemies no less than friends. Lansbury and Croft on a number of occasions in the House and at the Church Congress, traded barbed compliments on their protagonist's dangerous combination of uncompromising sincerity in religious belief and political error. Viscountess Milner's Foreword to Croft's *My Life of Strife*, likens him to 'Dürer's Knight, as he rides steadily on his way through the forest.'

The church press and liberal church leaders deplored the opposition of such earnest churchmen to the White Paper. But if Edward Norman is right in thinking that Sir Charles Marston's perspective on British industrial relations represented a substantial body of lay opinion in the church, to which church leadership was insensitive, the same can surely be said of the speeches with which Page Croft, particularly, and Lord Lloyd stirred the local associations.[66]

Croft and Lloyd, who was highly regarded in Lang's milieu,[67] also made what impression they could with the same arguments on the leaders of the church. But Lang, Bishop George Kennedy Bell of Chichester and others were simultaneously being courted from the other side by the Indian Conciliation Group and by Gandhi himself, who was well aware of the importance of access to the moral high ground they could command, whilst making strenuous attempts to generate grass-roots sympathy in Britain.[68] In that particular tug-of-war, however, it was the referee, Sir Samuel Hoare, who won. The extremes were courteously fended off and the benediction of the Archbishop and the church establishment fell upon the pragmatic middle ground.

In reality, Page Croft stood no chance of swaying Archbishop Lang, a close friend of Irwin's and a pillar of the responsible establishment. But his open letter to the Archbishop of 27 April 1934 was a public challenge to the church hierarchy, with which he and his friends had long been disillusioned.[69] It expressed the 'very grave anxieties which are felt by large numbers of churchmen with reference to the proposed reforms in India.' It urged that in India 'no political considerations can compare with the strength of religious tenets,' and that these divide two fanaticisms, as the outrages committed by the Mahomedan Moplahs and the carnage of the Cawnpore (Kanpur) massacres by Hindus too clearly demonstrate. Only the example and precepts of Christianity can in the end bridge this gulf, and 'may we not claim that British government, administration and justice, based as they are on the fundamental precepts of Christianity, are a witness to the doctrines of Christ?' Christianity has been banished in Russia and many Christians foully murdered there. Now Gandhi has threatened to end Christian missions in India, so what is the future for its Christians, and, more important, what of our spiritual abdication in 'moving perhaps for all time the witness of the Cross from India?' He rounded vigorously on the critics of this attack, reverting to the Moplahs and Cawnpore and introducing fresh examples of the horrors that the departure of the Union Jack would release. He made it clear that he was not concerned with conversion, but with the historical realization of Christian principles in British political and administrative institutions. As he wrote in the *Yorkshire Post*,

The whole ideal of British laws, justice and administration, if carried out in accordance with our will and desire, would exactly interpret the Ten Commandments It is an imperfect world, but our ideal of government is the nearest approach to Christianity, and to exchange it for government which may lean towards the precepts of the Hindu religion and the ideals of the worship of Shiva or Kali is quite definitely, in my view, a "spiritual abdication".[70]

He told the readers of the *Church Times* that he believed 'that the British race is under Providence permitted to hold a great trust in the world, and that in accordance with divine plans, nations are given work to do in the advancement of civilization.' This belief had led him to break with old friends over the India issue. 'I beg ...as a humble Christian to state that when the comrades of Christendom stood by in silence and allowed the martyrdom of Christianity in Russia, my faith in the Church militant suffered a rude shock.'[71] At meetings specifically for churchpeople he underlined his disconsolate but orthodox churchmanship, on the platform with three Anglican clergymen of the Colonial and Continental Church Society, for instance:

I am not prepared to say that our race is the only chosen race, but he would be a strange individual who cannot see that our people have a great trust such as has never been given to any other race in the world...our British ideals, which are the ideals of Christianity....[72]

But his providentialist argument for the imperial obligations was prominent, whatever his audience, and he contrived to put his critics on the defensive. It was not possible to brush aside the evidence of mounting communal hostility and its ugly consequences, of Congress intransigence and disunity, and of instances of corruption and inefficiency among Indian officials. It was only too easy to read Gandhi's political signals in a complex situation in terms of oriental cunning and unreason, and to draw on the imagery of violence and barely suppressed depravity which stocked a popular conception of India. The confusion of responses to this rhetoric can come through very clearly in the imagery thrown up in the course of the die-hard agitation. An Admiral from Waltham Abbey, for instance, in the Hertfordshire Conservative association, urged support for Churchill's demand that the government should 'go forward' by stiffening up its administration 'in that great country,' adding in the next breath, in reference to Gandhi's personal attendant Mirabehn, formerly Madeleine Slade, that what he objected to was 'an Admiral's daughter rubbing Mr Gandhi's legs.'[73] But Page Croft provided his sector of the Anglo-India public with more than the visceral reflexes of the Tory clubs and shires. For imperialists, whose world was beginning to crumble, he articulated a simple position that had deep historical roots, however crudely they were interpreted, one that gave to British society a moral coherence under supernatural sanctions.[74]

Central components of that position were shared by the senior clerics who had to resist the implications of his argument. Their reality was in some ways more complex and difficult to decipher than his, the instrumentalities of God's purposes subtler and more uncertain, and they felt obliged to take up the India question despite their lack of direct knowledge. Thus Bishop Bell, in the course of his intensive correspondence with Sir George Schuster, who was in London for the Round Table Conference, recognized that:

If Gandhi holds the key so far as India is concerned, then coming to grips with him is the vital matter and worth taking risks for. If Gandhi is not important, then obviously the whole picture is altered. But I suppose that even though Gandhi is far from all powerful, there is nobody else who comes anywhere near him in ability to stand for Indian opinion and has the power,—even though I agree a restricted power—for influencing all India.[75]

They saw the India problem less in terms of a confrontation between the West and an all but unregenerate East, and more in terms of constructing a co-operative solution from a variety of progressive impulses, with powerful growth points emerging in Indian society itself. But they also had a much weaker sense of the structural conflicts that might be fundamentally intractable, and with no necessary resolution inside the constitutional rationality of an imperial framework. Communal conflict, which the die-hard Raj would simply contain, was the most obvious of these. It was almost a condition of the clerics' involvement in the issues formulated in the White Paper debates that there was a Christian, co-operative solution for 'men of good will' within an organic framework, just as they assumed such a solution within the organic framework of domestic economic and social relationships. It was appropriate that when the Round Table process got under way, it was the indefatigable director of the ICF, The Revd P. T. R. Kirk, who organized a Church House meeting proposed by Andrews and encouraged by Bell, between Gandhi and a group of bishops. Kirk had been getting

Christian spokesmen of industry and of labour to converge on a platform of co-operative good-will for years. The meeting was not a success, for 'Gandhi made a bad impression on an audience which was prepared to be sympathetic.'[76]

But for concerned church leaders, the obstruction, on this occasion as on others, had to lie with Gandhi's inability to 'see reason'. Gandhi's fast and his rejection of separate electorates in 1932, the event that vitalized his untouchability campaign and signally represented the imposition of his will on the British Government, was taken without reflection by Temple as evidence of Gandhi's sincerity, but also as another 'illustration of his hopeless detachment from actualities.'[77]

Bell, who was modestly anxious about rushing in to the chamber of wise men 'where angels fear to tread,'[78] was far more deeply engaged by the Raj than Temple. He made a sustained practical attempt to persuade Gandhi to distinguish between the rational but receptive and amenable conservatism of the White Paper group and the fire-eating of *Daily Mail* and *Morning Post,* which he took to be entirely unrepresentative of genuine British opinion. He also exercised greater intellectual independence than Lang, partly because he did not have Lang's political commitments as a member of the Joint Select Committee on the White Paper, but partly because he had neither Lang's patrician outlook nor his close friendship and dependence on Irwin. But at the end of the day, he seems to have backed away, subdued, first of all by the relentless realism of Schuster and Hoare and then, more sadly, by the Government of India's imposition of the Ordinances and the arrest of virtually the entire group that had accompanied Gandhi on his visit to the Palace at Chichester on the weekend of 10–12 October 1931.[79]

Schuster and Bell exchanged at least six thousand words in their correspondence of October 1931. The letters can be read as a serious debate, which Schuster was politely determined to win, on the locus of rationality in British dealings with Gandhi. Bell strongly resisted the standard imputation to Gandhi of oriental guile and detachment from reality. He was also prepared to put his money on the authenticity of Gandhi's 'religious belief that there is a purpose behind his coming and a purpose that he is intended to fulfill for India.'

He is obviously a good man and deeply in earnest. He is also very clearly indeed a politician and with a very firm grasp of political situations.... He did strike me as a person who was prepared quite definitely to meet argument with argument, and to see the force of reason...a tremendous belief in the power of reasoning and a real readiness to yield a position if reasons were presented to him which showed that it was a less strong position than he thought.... He has a tremendous belief in collaboration, going over the articles of a particular plan point by point.

Schuster responded to this. His earlier letters repeat the standard formulae: 'a great saint...[but] also an extremely astute politician.... It is impossible to divine what any particular Oriental is thinking or aiming at at any particular moment....' But on the 17 October he finds on rereading his last letter that,

it did not take sufficient account of the moral impression which you had formed of Gandhi during your conversations with him. This was the more unfortunate because if we could get a clear picture of Gandhi's moral and intellectual attitude and could in some way disengage the saint from the politician, it would be far easier to form a clear view of the tactical necessities and such appreciation as yours assists to this very desirable end.

But Schuster's appropriation of insight into the essential realities of the situation, and therefore of the moral implications of any practical action, is set out almost in his first paragraph. Gandhi and the other Indian politicians, he says, persist in attributing to the British Government all sorts of 'subtle and far-reaching designs.' In fact,

the policy of this Government, like that which preceded it, is perfectly simple and straightforward. It is to grant to India such degree of self-government as the Indians are willing to accept and to work, subject to the fulfilment by the Government of the responsibilities which they or their predecessors have undertaken to the Indian population and to the civilised world.

Starting from this premis, he identifies Gandhi's moves in relation to the Conference as political (he came to London in a bid to re-establish control over a movement that was becoming too strong for him). They are disingenuous (dictated by 'a group of Indian financiers who have no moral merits at all...depress the wages of their work people and make fortunes by speculations in Indian currency'). They are simply irrational (his demands with regard to the army and finance, where he knows the British have nothing to concede). They are blind to relevant facts and realities (in London, to the pressures under which the government and ministers were currently operating, and in India, to the realities of Hindu-Muslim conflict, and also to the financial or, more strictly, the currency crisis).

In his letter of 23 October to Gandhi, Bell was reduced to repeating Schuster's point about the pre-election pressures on the National Government and expressing hopes for the post-election period.

Gandhi replied from 88 Knightsbridge:

Dear Friend,

It was a great joy to receive your good letter. I knew that you were doing all you could for the cause of Indian freedom which to me is the cause of humanity. I am not losing hope in the midst of despair. We had a nice time at Oxford.

The Oxford reference is to the celebrated but awkward meeting with Lindsay, Coupland, Lothian, Malcolm MacDonald and others.[80]

The following May, Bell was involved in attempts, prompted by H. Polak and others in the Indian Conciliation Group, to get the Ordinances relaxed, but his correspondence with Hoare ran into the sands.[81]

Lang's support over the White Paper was obviously important to Hoare, who well understood the nature of the opposition he would have to confront in the House and in the more active rank and file of the party. In a private note early in 1933 the Archbishop minuted pressure from Hoare to join the Joint Select Committee. Hoare had even raised 'the *possibility*—and no more—of my acting as Chairman.'[82] What he needed, Lang notes, was someone who was not committed in the difficult business of meeting the claims of various groups. Lang was in the event to exhaust himself on the committee.[83] Four years later Coupland told Don, the Archbishop's chaplain, that no one on the commission displayed so acute a mind. 'This is high praise from that quarter.'[84] Lang set himself the task of arriving at a general appreciation of the forces that were in tune with progressive developments and also of the particular accidents of interest and personality that were likely to obstruct that develop-ment. Inevitably, given his position and his personal links with

Irwin, Hoare and others, he assumed that reason and progress, the valid vehicles of providence, lay within the constitutional process that was being negotiated and developed by the government. There was an essential historical rationality at work, which a larger vision of co-operative development could keep sufficiently in focus, despite the perturbations introduced, on the one hand, by the fantasmal realism of cassandras of the right and, on the other, by sentimentalists like the Quakers and C. F. Andrews with his 'very unregulated belief in gesture.'[85] He was attentive to 'responsible' missionary opinion, which increasingly identified with reform and Indianization.[86] He recognized the centrality of Gandhi as the embodiment of a valid element in Indian nationalism, though his private comments were often disparaging and he seems to have leant heavily on Irwin's reservations about the Mahatma's saintliness.[87]

He did, however, attempt through Hoare and Zetland to moderate Willingdon's policy of 'ostracizing Gandhi', of which Birla, the Mahatma's financial stand-by, complained, though none of this made any impression on Willingdon.[88] But when the Viceroy came down dogmatically on Lang's public endorsement of Gandhi's concern for rural uplift, observing that 'we know that Mr Gandhi's motives are largely political' and that his enthusiasm for the *harijan* and the agricultural worker was 'of very recent origin,' Lang fought back, recalling Gandhi's warmth and sincerity on the subject and pointing out that the ostracism referred to earlier might have had something to do with the fact that Gandhi had not approached the Government in this connection.[89]

But these were minor assertions of intellectual independence. Like Bell, Lang had to accept official wisdom and confirm, as a valid interpretation of imperial obligations, the shifts and responses of government policy as it worked its way towards the large objectives that were supposedly built into the imperial situation. He had helped to see to it that the religiosity of the right and the political intuitions of Gandhi's Christian advocates could be largely discounted. His chief function, impressively enshrined in his House of Lords Speech of 13 December 1934, had been to endorse a major reformulation of the development of British trusteeship in India on behalf of the state church and with the backing of a substantial body of public opinion.[90]

CHAPTER 8

Conclusion

It can be said in favour of the die-hards that they acknowledged the inevitability and primacy of conflict in the politics of the colonial situation, however crude their understanding of its roots and however harsh their response to it. It is also true that some degree of wishful thinking was reflected in the liberal reform projects and indeed, as we see them in retrospect, in the hopes of many nationalists associated with Gandhi and Nehru, with regard to Hindu and Muslim communalism. But the die-hards expected the worst of the East. In a version of the orientalism which saw the Middle East as a mosaic of societies constrained by external power and lacking the inherently progressive social and economic structures of the West,[1] they saw South Asia as an assemblage of essentially different, socially retarded and mutually antagonistic social groups under imperial discipline. What they feared above all, were the internal weaknesses of the imperial authority—which alone represented reason, order and hope.

In 1940 Linlithgow wrote a comment to Zetland on a 'Memorandum on the Basis and Structure of Indian Government,' by Percival Spear. Spear's essay represented a belated acknowledgement of realities which had seemed self-evident to conservatives. The Viceroy praised the 'somewhat depressing accuracy' of Spear's analysis, only commenting that the author 'appears to overlook the problem of States' (i.e the existing regional divisions) and that his proposed reconstruction was hardly practical politics.[2] The impulse behind Spear's essay was the disillusionment that had crept in over some twenty years which had undermined the assumption of an *essentially* homogeneous and potentially democratic nation in India. The assumption had, he wrote, made it possible to regard communal representation as an anomaly and not as a principle, at least until

1931, and had been reinforced by the Lucknow Pact of 1916 and the non-cooperation movement of 1920–1.

Facts have gradually proved these hopes to be illusory.... We have therefore to face the fact that India is not one society with diverse surface political manifestations, nor is it one society with certain deep rooted economic or class interests; it is a true 'communitas communitatum', a group of societies, rarely geographically distinguished, but more often superimposed one upon another, or existing side by side.

The social organism remains for him by definition the *raison d'etre* of the state, but social organism will not, it is now ^lear, emerge out of a transcending nationalism, as nationalists and their supporters had argued that it was doing, or not fully, and at least not without an institutional modulation of irreducible differences between groups. We must therefore assume that the primary aim of government in India 'is to comprehend diverse societies in an organic union.' He sketches out a constitutional framework to meet this requirement. The kind of political framework he suggests has affinities with subsequent pluralist models, originating in the work of J. S. Furnivall on Indonesia,[3] but a point of departure was the Christian Guild Socialism of Figgis. In the Indian context, of course, Figgis's assumption of a fundamental Christian basis for different religions has to go, as Spear points out, but he identifies 'the fundamental divisions of the country...(as) not so much political, or economic or merely religious—though all these play their part—but cultural.'

His specific proposals depend on analytical distinctions between different levels of collective concern, and on the institutionalization of appropriately separated structures to handle them. Thus, he admits a fundamental incompatibility between the essentially aristocratic texture of Hindu culture, together with its world-renouncing doctrine of *karma,* on the one side, and the materialism and the equalitarian, if not democratic, nature of Islam. But this conflict is not all-inclusive; it generates tensions at certain levels only. There should therefore be a structure of institutions at national and provincial level which would be either more or less inclusive and representative, ranging from democratic federal institutions, concerned with the obvious common ground (defence, commerce, trade, etc.), to communitarian structures of guilds and the like. This 'guild system would so restrict the field of political action that many of the present causes of political friction between the communities would be removed.' There would of course remain occasions for conflict between culturally defined 'guilds', but these can to a degree be anticipated and guarded against: the Army would consist of units containing a mix of communal sub-units; Public Services Commissions would supervise the allocation of patronage; second chambers, representing the guilds, could filter out economically discriminating legislation; an executive and judicial structure drawing on Swiss and American experience would curtail the dominance of communal majorities.

The document seems to have travelled no further than the desks of Linlithgow and Zetland, but it is a striking attempt to accommodate an intractable world within a strictly limited theoretical development. Standard components of the Christian imperialist discourse do not appear in it. This is in itself an implicit criticism of the well-meaning concern of the generation of liberals to which Spear belonged. However, subsequent scholarship, in the tradition one can broadly describe as that of the 'Subaltern Studies' and their constructive critics, has been concerned with disintegrating the kind of 'essentialism' Spear's paper does still retain from its orientalist antecedents. Essentialist assumptions pervade imperial historiography, and are at the heart of the misrepresentation of reality enshrined in its discourse.

This argument in general terms is by no means new. The Subaltern Studies tradition, however, has been preoccupied with very detailed explorations of the languages of resistance, and only with relatively obvious features of the colonialist discourse itself as a language of dominance and control. The strategy has been to confront these élite perceptions of reality with the innumerable, other realities of subaltern and resistant groups. Another aspect of the imperialist discourse, the flexibility and strengths it derived from the western religious tradition that contributed to its formulation, has been explored here. Its comparative argument about religions, western and eastern, their standing as cultural and historical facts in relation to the development of human civilization, endorsed established judgments about specific communities and groups in India. The essentialism to which the Subaltern Studies scholars object appears as an unchallengeable component of the Whiggish, 'Christian' historiography.

Before turning to the question of these assumptions, we can note the distinctive aspect of Spear's paper, a decisive separation from the Christian historiography which dominated the discourse, though there is no loss of faith in the 'scientific' modification of constitutional systems by the imperial trustee. His paper confronts the strong possibility of decay and potentially violent disintegration of the Raj, and proposes a defensive political solution based on popular consent. It has no kind of presentiment in the evolution of Indian history, but it would, he argues, insulate the distinct and sensitive areas of cultural ('communal') concern from arbitrary external interference.

One might infer that the comparative theology consistent with his proposal would have to be something like the religious pluralism indicated by Hick, a suspension of hierarchizing judgments. It would seem to be the case, too, that the Christian would have to look for a contingent and tangential encounter between the reality of Christ and the reality of history, of the kind posited by Butterfield and Chakkarai, rather than the Whiggish providentialism laid out by Curtis and echoed even by some nationalist Christians. He would take it that God makes his presence known in human history, but that he is not using history to write what we could recognize as a progressive and ultimately consoling story.

Taken together these points represent a shift, significantly challenging the discourse, which has ramifying implications. It was the British, for instance, as Spear points out, who made educated India *consciously* democratic, on the false premise imported with Mill and Rousseau that Indian society was capable of democratic decisions because there was a fundamental unity of belief among its peoples. The right-wing of the Anglo-India public had never believed such unity existed, but others had committed themselves more or less heavily on that assumption to the natural evolution of a national political culture.

But in other respects Spear's paper seems to be anchored in the orientalist discourse. Of course, one does not intrude on a Viceroy's time with pages of detail in a document of this kind, as its author could very readily have done. Nevertheless, he does identify the causes of communal conflict in the primordial, given, essential characteristics of identifiable groups. His political solution is to compose these groups into distinct structures of one kind and another, to protect their social space, at least as regards the core areas of cultural identity, from the kind of encroachment that would trigger predictable, passively responsive and dangerous reactions. At every turn, the discourse of the Christian imperialists imposes order on its subjects through this kind of essentialist taxonomy, and identifies the causes of political friction as internal to determinate properties, values and beliefs of the different communities, as a given problem for the political culture and institutions of the organic state. Disagreements within the discursive framework have been over the question of whether larger organic loyalties would emerge to absorb the lesser.

We can generalize the distance from reality of the discourse and its characteristic Christian components in two stages. Both apply also to Spear's paper, despite the distinctions noted above. The first is concerned with the identification by the discourse of conflict in the Raj primarily in cultural (necessarily religious) terms, rather than in terms of the primacy of complex and changing economic pressures and opportunities. Obviously, this excludes the most basic general insights of the Marxist tradition. The second is concerned with the way in which the discourse identifies the cultural entities that constituted the Raj.

There is, first of all then, the connection between the discourse and the dominant social theology of the day; non-denominational and with a substantial public of its own, extending well beyond regular church goers. This provided the norm for an organic society. It excluded the category of political domination, identified class feeling and class antagonism as a failure and an aberration in a social process that was of its inherent nature built on the realization of mutualities and shared obligations. By invoking transcendant sanctions, it enhanced the pervasive language of good-will and co-operation that flowered most notably in British politics in the decade following the Great War. It was broadly speaking a middle-class language, though, without entering into contention over the scope of hegemonic values, it clearly had a much wider resonance as well. It was standard in the world of the public schools and entirely familiar to those who could also be identified as the more serious members of the Anglo-India public at home.

As we have seen, many of those who were most actively and self-consciously engaged in sustaining it felt required by their position to clarify and justify imperial structures of power as well, and they did so in closely analogous terms, both in England and in the expatriate community. In each case, domestic and imperial, it appeared that the core values associated with unity and order were under potential threat which, however sympathetically one might on occasion view radical challenge, was invested with an intrinsic irrationality. It was inchoate, incoherent in its purposes and blind to the destructive consequences of its resentful militancy. The categories both of 'class' and of 'nationalism', therefore, had to be assimilated or guided towards the main stream of a discernable historical evolution. In the case of the home country, the structural problem for this process most certainly involved the horizontal divisions of class, but these were moralized in terms of the evolution of a transcending national unity. In the case of the Raj, the problem was less manageable in a sense, because the 'communitas communitatum' simply lacked the bonding interdependences of a highly evolved industrial society. The dangerous divisions in the Raj were vertical ones, between cultures and religions, which have their own internal and 'organic' social relations, but lack any real basis for 'unity' beyond their own boundaries. The question of class conflict and class dominance in such a society could hardly be said to arise. What corresponded to it was the confrontation of the Raj by the nationalist movement, a challenge that might represent all sorts of positive energies, like the acceptably democratic energies of Britain after the First World War, but one that was also pregnant with irrational possibilities.

Those who lived with this framework were aware of an alternative, Marxist historiography, as the sinister mirror-image of their own, with its own providence in deterministic 'laws of history'. The conventional Indian Marxist historiography of the Raj does in fact provide a rather comical inversion of the Whiggish search for an authentic Indian nationalism. It has on occasion charted in a crudely teleological way the steady march of the oppressed across the centuries towards an enlightened class interest.[4] But Marxists have a genuine difficulty, as Rosalind O'Hanlon points out,

as to how we may discern, in the consciousness and practice of those we study, processes of unilinear change, real learning experiences gained in the course of struggle and resistance, and how far we should assign all change to the realm of the reversible and contingent.[5]

Everybody has problems with the owl of Minerva.[6]

Within the Christian orientalism of the Raj, these 'learning experiences' are neither admitted nor admissible, and the attempt to justify them was an assault on rational and even natural order. This is not to say, however, that the locus of economic exploitation cannot be instantly identified within the orientalist discourse. There are money-lenders, professional pleaders, rack-renters and exploitative, generally 'Brahman', castes. These all engage in violations of a 'moral economy', whose grossest excesses can at least be brought under control by the steel frame. But the language disengages the indigenous structures of economic relationships, and therefore the constantly changing pattern of social and economic class relationships, from the domination of an imperial economy which in reality both encapsulates and vigorously penetrates them. In its economic aspect, the British connection is represented as necessarily and ultimately benign, though that does not mean that it is perfect. But the structural obstacles to its influence are indigenous and not of its making. They are inherent in a caste society, which is consistently conceived of as a standing, once-for-all sort of arrangement which exists to be somehow broken down. There are, for instance, the economic expressions of Brahman, or *bania* or trading caste dominance, with their obstructive consequences, and there is the rural negativism of a peasantry conditioned under such an arrangement, against which Brayne had to contend.[7]

The imperial economy and the structures of dominance that maintain it are of course the central component, explicitly or implicitly, in any Marxist analysis of the Raj, and are taken to be primary determinants of class formation in the subcontinent. Whilst the imperialist discourse does take account of poverty and of exploitation of Indians by Indians, it is not organized to identify complex connections between the distribution of poverty and the particular incidence of exploitation, on the one hand, and the nature of the colonial situation, on the other. Thus, to take one obvious point, we now have a good idea of the extent to which modern caste relations are a creation of the Raj. They are the product of a continuous process of consolidation and division among groups competing for advantage within its political economy. They reflect the manipulation of opportunities presented by its legal and administrative procedures, for instance, the official use of precedent in settling disputes and, particularly, the social codification of successive censuses.

However, essentialism can take different forms. It must also be recognized that if Marxist theorists have identified what colonialist discourse suppresses by omission, a submerged reality in the changing relations of production, an economic base profoundly conditioned by the colonial experience, they have also, the Subaltern Studies scholars have argued, foreclosed too rapidly on the analysis of these immensely complex processes.

This brings us to the second consideration, of how the cultural entities which constituted the Raj are to be identified. Marxists have wielded the categories of class, class formation, and class consciousness on political histories of resistance and insurgency that refuse, on closer examination, to fall into place so easily. Rebellious peasants have been invested by Marxists with a new class essence. They have indeed been replaced, to quote Guha, by 'an *abstraction* called the Worker-and-Peasant, *an ideal rather than the real historical personality of the insurgent....*'[8] Whatever evidence there has been of the actual perceptions and consciousness of the peasantry assimilated to this abstraction has been construed as the local expression of a universal, emerging class awareness. Essentialism of this kind, therefore, has been identified as a problem both of an élite and of a Marxist historiography. In this way Marxist historiography has mirrored the limitations of the discourse it set out to attack.

This study has been concerned with an orientalism which has in this sense been echoed in the Marxist tradition. For, in addition to glossing over the economic basis of social reality in a language that was self-consciously concerned to hold the gates of knowledge against ungodly Marxist incursions *ex partibus infidelium,* a blinding essentialism was intrinsic to the Christian imperialist discourse. Spear himself provides a classic statement of the kind of assumption against which the Subaltern Studies project itself was directed:

At no period has there been any organic connection between the villager and the central government. He expects to receive commands; he also expects to bargain and negotiate; but he does not expect to take any initiative himself.

In the Marxist historiography that has been criticized, the villager/ peasant is transmogrified into another essential being by the onward march of history. In the discourse from which Spear half distances himself, the peasant is a clod with certain known characteristics, who can be improved by appropriate action from above. In neither case is he allowed to arrive at a definition of his predicament which is of his own origination. Such a vision might be clear to himself, invisible to the colonial eye of authority, but invisible also from the position of scholars with a supposedly privileged theoretical access to the 'meaning' of history, and only accessible with difficulty to a much more tentative and open search for neglected, and certainly inadequate evidence.

Whether the Subaltern Studies themselves have located the 'real historical personality of the insurgent,' or have created a subtler academic essentialism of their own, is a question that has itself been raised in O'Hanlon's difficult and stimulating article. But her doubts about this development in South Asian historical studies only reinforce the point that is being made here about a discourse which was articulated at a far cruder level, not entirely by scholars and not by anyone in particular, but by holders and moulders of 'knowledge' in the Anglo-India public. The discourse, particularly on the right, stressed the variety and heterogeneity of Indian society, but did so in terms of a mosaic of social fragments that fell into a limited range of patterns. It was incapable of acknowledging the extreme fluidity of the economic and social conflicts that were taking place below the level of party and communal organizations, or of recognizing the ways in which they reflected the material consequences of the British connection itself. By playing on a network of notions, of evolution, mutuality, unity, rationalization, nationality, it avoided the central reality of the Raj as a structure of domination, which operated in a whole range of ways from physical coercion, through economic constraint, to the co-optation and complicity of educated élites in the discourse itself. The task which the Subaltern Studies tradition has undertaken, and at least to some degree realized, is to understand the workings of power and domination in South Asia in categories which 'must be as multifarious and nuanced as the courses and ligaments through which power itself runs.'[9] The descriptive categories of the imperialist discourse were a more or less elaborate device for avoiding anything of the kind.

One can only point, in conclusion, to the kind of scholarship that has in recent years superceded the repertory of authoritative facts and judgments and uncertainties explored above. The broadest and most obtrusive feature of the discourse was the standard essentialist contrast between Hinduism and Islam. Mushirul Hasan quotes Ronaldshay:

The Muslims have their internecine quarrels, but these apart, the solidarity of Islam is a hard fact against which it is futile to run one's head.... It was not always realized by the constitution makers even in India itself how fundamental and far-reaching is the cleavage between the two communities.... The divisions between Muslims and Hindus are not only those due to religious belief and practice, but to a profoundly different outlook on life resulting in social systems which are the very antithesis of one another.[10]

Hasan's own analysis shows, on the contrary, that the Indian Muslims were not 'a monolithic community with common interests and aspirations.' Their common religious experiences and the value of their religious symbols were not enough to distinguish them from the rest of the community. 'Even the zealotry of religious revivalists could not halt the continuous process of cultural and social integration in the countryside.'[11] Furthermore, 'communalism' when it did emerge strongly cannot be seen as the sporadic by-product of a latent religious fanaticism. Partition and the horrors that went with it emerged out of the working of imperial politics.

Other studies, of the Moplah rebellions for instance, have shown that the accentuation of religious differences and 'communal' organization were the product of intense economic and political pressures, very often of long duration, and furthermore that they were not primarily the product of manipulation by the élite of religious symbols and of their less educated subordinates. They were the products of 'subaltern' political movements, with their own objectives and employing their own symbolic resources.

The communal sentiment or 'fanaticism' of the Moplahs was only the symptom and not the disease. The 1921 rebellion, like the uprisings that occurred throughout the nineteenth century, was in essence an expression of long-standing agrarian discontent, which was only intensified by the religious and ethnic identity of the Moplahs and by their political alienation, above all in the years between 1885 and 1920. Like those of the past, it drew its strength primarily from the poor Moplah peasantry; the rich well-to-do Moplah *kanamdars* were not the principal actors in the insurrectionary drama.[12]

The Moplah's long tradition of millenarian revolts ensured that the troubles of 1921 would automatically be written off to 'Muslim fanaticism.' Another tradition, associated with the Gaurakshini Sabhas or cow-protection societies, in the United Provinces and west Bihar, in which a small Muslim minority suffered severely at the hands of an alliance of high caste Hindu zamindars and certain lower caste groups, has been interpreted in corresponding terms, as the result of élite manipulation of 'fanatical' communal sentiment. Gyan Pandey's detailed study presents a far more complex picture and very different conclusions.[13] 'Communal' issues were injected into situations in the U.P. that were already tense with inter-*caste* rivalry, based on the most straightforward competition for scarce economic (and political) resources. Caste groups that were upwardly mobile in economic terms were changing patterns of behaviour and ritual practice—'sanskritizing', to use the term coined by Srinivas—to match those of castes higher on the scale of 'purity'. Supporting cow-protection was one way of signalling their 'sanskritizing' pretensions. There were of course revanchist elements involved in the politics of the cow, but at this level one can only say for those drawn into the competitive process by caste identification, that political and economic aspiration and anxiety had available to it a repertory of religious symbolism which performed various functions for the community, a language through which it was possible to express and direct competitive and defensive energies.

Cow-protection, which served to represent the social aspirations of certain lower caste groups, necessarily precipitated conflict with Muslims who wished to celebrate the Baqr-Id festival with the ritual slaughter of cattle, though, again, there were economic conflicts involved here as well.

Pandey notes that existing competition between Hindu castes was given focus and organization by the 1901 Census which attempted to list castes according to precedence. Bhumihars and Kayasths protested at being placed in the Vaishya *varna* along with lower castes, such as Ahirs and Kurmis, who in turn objected to the caste proximity of Hajjams (barbers) and Kahars (water-carriers). Such competition was concerned with material standing and opportunity; but these contests of local power were enacted through the subtle language of ritual purity, with outcomes that could be influenced by relations with the imperial authority.

The articulation of conflicts of power and material interest, however, also cut across both caste and communal lines. For there were political alliances between zamindars and lower castes, such as Ahirs, and there were also alliances at the upper levels between

Hindu landlords and Muslim landlords, articulating economic class interests, and involving high levels of violence against the lower orders.

Enough, perhaps, has been said by way of summary to return us finally to the question of the status of 'religion' as an analytical category in this tradition of enquiry, as a category that can be distinguished in an intelligible way from those categories of a political analysis, in which one describes relations of power, conflict and dominance. All the argument needs is the 'shallow assumption' made by Kolakowski, 'that what people mean in religious discourse is what they ostensibly mean.'[14] This is in fact precisely the premise on which the Subaltern Studies themselves were based. It is for the scholar to uncover the political and economic pressures and distresses that, for instance, precipitate rebellions and revolts, but it is for the 'subaltern' himself to reveal how this reality presents itself to him, and the beliefs, visions and projects with which he is able to confront it. He will have a discourse of his own on which to draw, containing shared definitions of the sacred and the obligations entailed in them. This is not in itself a cultural essence of which he is the vehicle and expression, but rather a resource of which he can chose to make use in order to struggle for control over his environment in highly specific circumstances.

By definition, the environment of the subaltern is coercive and hostile. But those, finally, who have coerced and imposed their will upon him, however indirectly, have done so with (among other weaponry) the tool of an alternative discourse, denying his realities and substituting theirs. They have done so in the name of their own supernatural sanctions and their own sense of the presence of the sacred, in all relations of authority and material control over those whom 'history' has subordinated to them.

Notes

CHAPTER 1

Introduction

1. '[It was] alarming and also nauseating to see Mr Gandhi, a seditious Middle Temple lawyer, now posing as a fakir of a type well known in the East, striding half-naked up the steps of the Vice-regal Palace, while he is still organizing and conducting a defiant campaign of civil disobedience, to parley on equal terms with the representative of the King-Emperor.' Winston Churchill to the West Essex Conservative Association, 23 Feb. 1931. Hence the title of Robert Bernay's excellent journalistic account of Gandhi during 1931, '*Naked Fakir*', Gollancz, 1931.

2. Michael Carritt, *A Mole in the Crown*, distributed by Central Books, 1985. Scott came to be much better known in connection with Africa. S. Evans, *Michael Scott of Africa*, 1949.

3. Lord Meath's Empire Day movement was in its prime. He himself had heavily stressed the religious, essentially spiritual concept behind it. In 1943 Archbishop William Temple was to establish the Sunday after Ascension Day as Empire Youth Sunday. John M. MacKenzie, *Propaganda and Empire: The Manipulation of British Public Opinion*, 1880–1960, Manchester University Press, 1984, p. 233 ff.

4. *Hansard*, 5 June 1919, 2305.

5. Carl Bridge, 'The British Conservative Party and All-India Federation, 1927–1940'. Ph.D. Thesis, Flinders University, 1977, p. 311. Published as *Holding India to the Empire*, Oriental, 1986. J. A. Cross, *Sir Samuel Hoare: A Political Biography*, Cape, 1977.

6. See, for example, H. F. Owen, 'Organising for the Rowlatt Satyagraha of 1919' in R. Kumar, ed., *Essays on Gandhian Politics: The Rowlatt Satyagraha of 1919*, OUP, 1971.

7. B. R. Tomlinson, *The Political Economy of the Raj*, 1914–1947, Macmillan, 1979, pp. 165–7.

8. D. A. Low, ed., *Soundings in Modern South Asian History*, Weidenfield and Nicolson, 1968; *Lion Rampant*, Cass, London, 1973. R. J. Moore, *The Crisis of Indian Unity*, 1917–1940, Oxford, 1974; *Escape from Empire*, Clarendon, 1983.

9. Bridge, 'The British Conservative Party', Ph.D. Thesis, op. cit., p. 245.

10. Ibid., p. 304.

11. Ibid., p. 34.

12. Judith Brown, *Modern India: The Origins of an Asian Democracy*, OUP, 1985. R. J. Moore, 'Recent Historical Writing on the Modern British Empire and

Commonwealth: the Later Imperial India', *Journal of Imperial and Commonwealth History*, 4, 1, Oct. 1976. Ranajit Guha, ed., *Subaltern Studies*, vols. 1–5, OUP, 1982–8: 'The traditional historiography of Indian history, whatever the radical differences of interpretation, was based on a common assumption about the power of the imperial rulers. Whether the results were good or bad, British policy decisions were seen as automatically seminal to developments in the indigenous economy and society. Modern scholarship has delighted in undermining these assumptions: from all-powerful pro-consuls of European civilisation and capitalism, British officials have become baffled victims of a complex society.' Neil Charlesworth, *Peasants and Imperial Rule: Agriculture and Agrarian Society in the Bombay Presidency*, 1850–1935, CUP, 1985.

13. C. Bridge, 'Conservatism and Indian Reform (1929–39): Towards a Pre-requisites Model of Imperial Constitution-making', *Journal of Imperial and Commonwealth History*, 4, 1, 1976.

14. A. Seal, *The Emergence of Indian Nationalism*, Cambridge, 1968.

15. G. Almond and S. Verba, *The Civic Culture*, Princeton, 1963.

16. For example, S. R. Mehrotra, *India and the Commonwealth*, 1885–1929, London, 1965.

17. P. S. Gupta, *Imperialism and the British Labour Movement*, 1914–1964, OUP, 1968.

18. Antony Copley, *Gandhi*, Blackwell, 1987, p. 23.

19. J. F. C. Watts, 'The Viceroyalty of Lord Irwin, 1926–1931: With Special Reference to the Political and Constitutional Developments'. Ph.D. Thesis, Oxford University, 1973.

20. D. Kopf, *British Orientalism and the Bengal Renaissance: The Dynamics of Indian Modernisation*, 1773–1835, Calcutta, 1969.

21. E. W. Said, *Orientalism*, Routledge and Kegan Paul, 1978.

22. Michel Foucault, *The Archaeology of Knowledge*, Tavistock, 1972.

23. Ibid., p. 46.

24. L. Curtis, *The Problem of the Commonwealth*, London, 1915; *The Commonwealth of Nations*, London, 1916; *Dyarchy*, Oxford, 1920; *Civitas Dei*, Macmillan, vol. 1, 1934, vols. 2 and 3, 1937; *With Milner in South Africa*, Oxford, 1951.

25. The die-hard Lord Sydenham wrote of 'the disastrous Mr Lionel Curtis,' and of 'one of the most crazy constitutions ever concocted,' in *Studies of an Imperialist*, Chapman and Hall, London, 1928.

26. W. Nimocks, *Milner's Young Men: The 'Kindergarten' in Edwardian Imperial Affairs*, Durham, NC, 1968; B. Semmel, *Imperialism and Social Reform: English Social-Imperialist Thought*, 1895–1914, Allen and Unwin, 1960.

27. J. E. Kendle, 'The Round Table Movement and "Home Rule all round",' *Historical Journal*, 11, 3, 1968. E. David, ed., *Charles Hobhouse, Inside Asquith's Cabinet*, Murray, 1977.

28. Gerald Studdert-Kennedy, *Dog-Collar Democracy: The Industrial Christian Fellowship*, 1919–1929, Macmillan, 1982.

29. William Temple, *Mens Creatrix*, Macmillan, 1917, pp. 211, 250.

30. *Hume Papers*, IOL, 15 Nov. 1937.

31. Foucault, *The Archaeology of Knowledge*, Tavistock, 1972, p. 200.

CHAPTER 2

Jesus Christ and The Constitution

1. V. A. Demant, *Christian Polity*, Faber, 1936; N. Micklem, *The Theology of Politics*, OUP, 1941; Maurice Reckitt, *The Christian in Politics*, SPCK, 1946.
2. E. G. Selwyn, ed., *Essays Catholic and Critical*, SPCK, 1926.
3. G. A. Studdert Kennedy's books were all published by Hodder and Stoughton, and all ran into many editions. The prose includes: *Democracy and the Dog-Collar*, 1921; *Lies, Food for the Fed Up*, 1921; *The Wicket Gate*, 1923; *The Word and the Work*, 1925; *I Pronounce Them*, (novel), 1927; *The Warrior, the Woman and the Christ*, 1928.
4. R. Niebuhr, *Discerning the Signs of the Times*, SCM, 1946, p. 129.
5. Paul Addison, *The Road to 1945*, Quartet, 1977, pp. 27, 25.
6. D. Marquand, *Ramsay MacDonald*, Cape, 1977, p. 54.
7. H. Butterfield, *Christianity and History*, Bell, 1949, p. 52.
8. Melvin Richter, *The Politics of Conscience: T. H. Green and his Age*, Weidenfeld and Nicolson, 1964: Peter Robbins, *The British Hegelians*, Garland, 1982; Gerald Studdert-Kennedy, op. cit., ch. 3 and 4.
9. H. Butterfield, *The Whig Interpretation of History*, Bell, 1931, and Pelican, 1973, p. 40.
10. H. Butterfield, *Christianity and History*, op. cit., p. 47; *The Englishman and his History*, CUP, 1944, p. 124.
11. Butterfield, *Christianity and History*, op. cit., p. 31.
12. Ibid., pp. 83, 65.
13. W. Dray, *The Philosophy of History*, Prentice-Hall, 1964, p. 98 ff.
14. R. Neibuhr, op. cit., p. 61.
15. Butterfield, *The Whig Interpretation of History*, op. cit., p. 25.
16. Ibid., p. 74.
17. Ibid., p. 24.
18. Kenyon points out that this book marks Butterfield's own conversion to a celebration of Whiggish continuities. J. Kenyon, *The History Men: The Historical Profession in England Since the Renaissance*, Weidenfeld and Nicolson, 1983, p. 273. H. Tulloch's essay leaves no excuse for continuing to accept Butterfield's characterization of Acton himself. Far from being the arch-Whig, '...Acton's entire historical career is nothing less than a sustained assault on every variety of whig present-mindedness.' *Acton*, Weidenfeld and Nicolson, 1988, p. 92.
19. J. W. Burrow, *A Liberal Descent: Victorian Historians and the English Past*, CUP, 1981, pp. 3, 300.
20. Nimocks, *Milner's Young Men*, op. cit.; D. C. Ellinwood, 'The Round Table Movement and India, 1909–1920', *Journal of Commonwealth Political Studies*, 9, 3, 1971.
21. Ronald Hyam and Ged Martin, *Reappraisals in British Imperial History*, Macmillan, 1981, p. 156.
22. R. F. Holland, *Britain and the Commonwealth Alliance, 1918–1939*, Macmillan, 1981, p. 156.

23. John Bowle, *The Imperial Achievement: The Rise and Transformation of the British Empire*, Secker and Warburg, 1974, p. 315.

24. W. David McIntyre, *The Commonwealth of Nations: Origins and Impact*, 1869–1971, OUP, 1977, pp. 171–7, 473.

25. J. M. MacKenzie, *Propaganda and Empire*, op. cit., pp. 166–8. Deborah Lavin, 'History, Morals and the Politics of Empire', J. Bossy and P. Jupp, eds., *Essays Presented to Michael Roberts*, Belfast, 1976.

26. Lothian's early interest in India, which he visited in 1911 and 1912, is discussed in Chapter 6. In 1930–1 he was Chairman of the Indian Franchise Committee and defended its 'very modest' proposals against die-hard attack, whilst himself berating civil-disobedience as the mirror-image of die-hardism. *Lothian Papers*, Scottish Record Office, Edinburgh, 1932, GD40/17/435. Lothian's enthusiastic involvement was not highly regarded by Hoare or Sir George Schuster. See, Gerard Douds, 'Lothian and the Indian Federation', John Turner, ed., *The Larger Idea: Lord Lothian and the Problem of National Sovereignty*, Historians' Press, 1988, and Bishop Bell's correspondence with Schuster, *Bell Papers*, Lambeth Palace Library.

27. Arnold Toynbee, *Acquaintances*, OUP, 1967, p. 147. Toynbee, Director of Studies at Chatham House and a friend who handled Curtis cautiously, as both a 'great man' and monomaniac, rejected his idealization of politics as the instrument of man's salvation. Nevertheless, though he was predisposed to be generous in his criticisms, he clearly took the book seriously, to the point of finding it a German translator. The question of whether publication in Germany would be permitted is raised in their correspondence.

28. It appears that Curtis was given the job in 1912 in order to restrain his embarrassing zeal for a Permanent Imperial Council. In 1913 he produced an 'egg' (Round Table jargon for discussion paper) which the moot found too radical. A revized 'egg', produced after further travel, was accepted in 1914. John Marlowe, *Milner, Apostle of Empire*, Hamilton, 1976, p. 212.

29. Carroll Quigley, 'The Round Table Group in Canada, 1908–1938', *Canadian Historical Review*, vol. 43, 3, 1962.

30. G. A. Studdert Kennedy, *Rough Rhymes of a Padre*, 1918, etc. collected in *The Sorrows of God*, 1921, and *The Unutterable Beauty*, 1927; new paperback edition Mowbray, 1983, reprinted 1987.

31. John Dunn has rescued Locke, a vastly more important and complex apologist of liberal constitutionalism, from readers who had neglected his Christian beliefs. 'What Locke trusted in was the Christian God and his own intelligence; and when it came to the crunch and the two parted company, what he proved to trust in more deeply was the God and not the intelligence.' *Western Political Theory in the Face of the Future*, CUP, 1979, p. 39. Later liberal theorists have moved their roots across into different soil, but not Curtis or those for whom he wrote.

32. Nirad C. Chaudhuri, *Hinduism*, OUP, 1979.

33. These are *practical* problems, fatally ignored by St Augustine. Curtis stressed particularly financial rationality as an instrument of Christian rule. He had persuaded Milner to engage Hichens as Treasurer of Johannesburg. Hichens's

uncompromising economic orthodoxy and 'realism' were widely recognized in the ICF and in Temple's no less interdenominational COPEC movement as a heartening example of practical Christian leadership. The Raj too boasted Christian exponents of financial management in Sir George Schuster and Sir Basil Blackett, successively Finance Members of the Indian Government. Hichens resisted the 'Prussian Toryism' of manufacturers such as Dudley Docker. British history, he believed, provided the soil for a unique flowering of 'Personality': '...It is better for a country to have a large number of small manufacturers than a few big trusts: this also accords more with the genius of our race, whose sturdy independence and self-reliance has built an Empire containing a quarter of mankind. Lionel Hichens, *Some Problems of Modern Industry*, Watt Lecture, 1918, p. 57, quoted in R. P. T. Davenport-Hines, *Dudley Docker: The Life and Times of a Trade Warrior*, CUP, 1984, pp. 7, 4, 132, 191; and see Davenport-Hines on Hichens in the *Dictionary of Business Biography*, vol. 3, pp. 198–205.

34. Sir Edward Grigg, *The Faith of an Englishman*, Macmillan, 1936, pp. 253–4.
35. There is an extensive collection of reviews in *Curtis Papers*, Bodleian, boxes 151–2. The correspondence with Harold Macmillan is also in the Curtis papers.
36. Richard Symonds, *Oxford and Empire*, Macmillan, 1986, pp. 72, 116.
37. E. S. Montagu, *An Indian Diary*, Heinemann, 1930: Nov. 10, Dec. 1, 7, 12, 24, 1917; Jan. 2, Feb. 6, 7, 16, 19, 1918.
38. Sir William Marris, *India: The Political Problem*, University College of Nottingham, Cust Memorial Lecture, 1930.
39. Review in *New Statesman*, 12 June 1943.
40. R. Coupland, *Wilberforce*, Collins, London, 1945, p. 424; undated lecture notes, *Coupland Papers*, Rhodes House, MSS Brit. Emp. s403, box 4.
41. R. Coupland, *Kirk on the Zambezi*, Oxford, 1928, p. 278.
42. R. Coupland, *The Indian Problem*, 1833–1935, OUP, 1942. A report in three parts on the constitutional problem in India, submitted to the Warden and Fellows of Nuffield College, Oxford. Also, *The Cripps Mission*, OUP, 1942; *India: A Restatement*, OUP, 1945.
43. Viscount Templewood, *Nine Troubled Years*, Collins, 1954, p. 69.
44. P. Vergili Maronis, *Opera. recognovit brevique adnotatione critica instruxit Fredericus Arturus Hirtzel*, Oxonii, E Typographeo Clarendoniano, 1900.
45. A. F. Hirtzel, *The Church, the Empire and the World: Address on the Work of the Church Abroad*, SPCK, 1919, p. 12.
46. Ibid., p. 11.
47. Ibid., p. 48.
48. Wolpert notes that since, 'Hirtzel alone kept a diary that has been preserved, his influence may in fact appear somewhat more exhalted than it was, though sufficient independent testimony by Morley (in letters to Minto and the Prime Minister) seems to corroborate the accuracy of Hirtzel's own estimate of his influence.' *Morley and India*, 1906–1910, California, 1967, p. 248.
49. Ibid., p. 55.
50. Hirtzel, *Diaries*, 23 May 1907.
51. Wolpert, *Morley and India*, op. cit., pp. 201 ff.
52. G. Prestige, *The Life of Charles Gore*, Heinemann, 1935, pp. 60 ff, 111 ff, 308 ff, 525.

53. Hirtzel, *The Church, the Empire and the World*, op. cit., p. 94; C. Gore, *Orders and Unity*, Murray, 1909; E. J. Palmer, *Papers*, Lambeth Palace; E. J. Palmer, 'The Proposed Union of Churches in South India', *Contemporary Review*, Oct. 1929; E. J. Palmer, *South India: The Meaning of the Scheme*, Winchester, 1944.

54. Hirtzel, *The Church, the Empire and the World*, op. cit., p. 32.

55. Ibid., p. 54.

56. Ibid., p. 62.

57. Ibid., p. 64.

58. Ibid., p. 24.

59. Earl of Ronaldshay, *The Life of Lord Curzon*, vol. 3, 1928, pp. 246–9. The 9th Lancers were subsequently applauded during the Durbar parade, even by official spectators, as they marched past Curzon. Wolpert, *Morley and India*, op. cit., p. 53.

60. Keir Hardie, *India: Impressions and Suggestions*, London, 1909, p. 101.

61. Edwyn Bevan, *Indian Nationalism*, Macmillan, 1914, p. 19; *Thoughts on India's Discontents*, Allen and Unwin, 1929, pp. 33, 53–4.

62. Arthur Osborn, DSO, *Must England Lose India?*, Knopf, 1930, p. 98. Katherine Mayo, *Mother India*, Cape, 1927. This ran to seven printings in 1927.

63. Hirtzel, *Diaries*, 28 August 1907.

64. Hirtzel, *The Church, the Empire and the World*, op. cit., p. 19.

65. Ellinwood, op. cit.

66. Revd David Jenks, *The Mission of Help to India, 1922–1923: Report*.

67. Gerald Studdert-Kennedy, *Dog-Collar Democracy*, op. cit., ch. 6.

68. Archbishop Davidson said of the mission: 'The stimulating and strengthening of the Church's life is obviously a matter which belongs not to India only, but to the well being of the Empire as a whole.' *Church Times*, 24 Jan. 1921.

69. Spencer H. Elliott, *A Missioner Abroad*, Jackson, 1923.

70. *Calcutta Diocesan Record*, Nov. 1922.

71. *Bombay Diocesan Magazine*, Aug. 1922.

72. Jenks, op. cit. Rawlinson arrived in India in 1921. Towards the end of the year he noted that 'race hatred is increasing, and there have lately been far more incidents between natives and white men.' F. B. Maurice, ed., *The Life of Lord Rawlinson of Trent*, Cassell, 1928, p. 302. He was by no means hostile in principle to nationalist expectations. General Maurice, who sympathetically edited his journals and letters, was the grandson of the conservative 'Christian socialist' F. D. Maurice.

73. *Bombay Diocesan Magazine*, June 1923.

74. It is not clear what the Bishop based his judgment on. In the merely statistical evidence there seems to be no very significant difference between the rank and file clergy in India and in England. In 1927 between 45 per cent and 50 per cent in each case were Oxbridge men. Proportions coming from each of the other sources, Trinity College Dublin, King's College London, Durham, the theological colleges and other universities, are much the same in England as in India. The Oxbridge preponderance conceals a shift over time that affected both India and England. The proportion of IEE men recruited from Oxford and to a slightly lesser extent from Cambridge declined sharply from 1905–10. But Oxford, though not Cambridge, became proportionally less important in church recruitment

in England at this period as well. IEE men graduating between 1910 and 1915 were substantially more likely to have come from King's, London, or the theological colleges and Durham, with TCD always close to the overall average for each generation of graduates. *Crockford's Clerical Directory*, 1927' India listings compared with a random sample of 250.

IEE men of all generations were more likely than clergy in England to have served during the Great War as temporary army padres (33 per cent to 12 per cent overall) but in the case of those graduating between 1910 and 1915 this rose to 45 per cent to 15 per cent. These proportionate differences are similar to those between Industrial Christian Fellowship activists, many of them ex-padres, and a random sample taken from the 1924 *Crockford's*. See Gerald Studdert-Kennedy, *Dog-Collar Democracy*, op. cit., ch. 6, 'The Church Public of the ICF'.

75. Ibid., Mar. 1923.
76. 'Only a few of those nearest to him knew the degree of sustenance that he drew from his faith, and how often, and with what absorption he turned to it and gained consolation from it. His religion was always present with him—the greatest reality of his life...' C. F. Adam, *Life of Lord Lloyd*, Macmillan 1948, pp. 227, 94, 190. See also, J. Charmley, *Lord Lloyd and the Decline of the British Empire*, Weidenfield, London 1989.
77. *Bombay Diocesan Magazine*, Mar. 1921.
78. Ellinwood, op. cit., p. 197.
79. *Church Times*, 13 May 1921.
80. Lord Meston, articles in *Contemporary Review*, Sept., Oct., 1921; Nov. 1922; Apr. 1924. Sir Reginald Coupland, *India: A Restatement*, op. cit., p. 115.

CHAPTER 3

Nationalism and Theology

1. Raymond Schwab, *The Oriental Renaissance: Europe's Rediscovery of India, 1660–1880*, New York, Columbia, 1984.
2. Markovitch, quoted by Schwab, op. cit., p. 451; Leo Tolstoy, 'A letter to a Hindu, 1908'; 'Gandhi Letters, 1910', *Recollections and Essays*, trans. Aylmer Maude, OUP, 1937, vol. 21; C. F. Andrews, ed., *Mahatma Gandhi at Work*, Allen and Unwin, 1931, appendix 2, 'The Revd. J. J. Doke's account of the origin of Satyagraha in Mr Gandhi's own mind'.
3. British scholars like Sir William Jones, Thomas Maurice and Charles Wilkins, did work in India. Only four of the major French orientalist scholars of the nineteenth century had visited India by 1900. Schwab, op. cit., p. 47.
4. Ibid., p. 166.
5. Ibid., p. 147.

6. D. Chattopadhyaya, *Lokayata: A Study in Ancient Indian Materialism*, People's Publishing House, 1959.

7. L. Dumont, *Homo Hierarchicus*, Weidenfeld and Nicolson, 1970, p. 23, first published by Gallimard, Paris, 1966. Dumont's study of caste is a late classic of the Oriental Renaissance, an analysis drawing heavily on a decoding of the 'learned Brahmanical tracts', and attending 'surprisingly little to the extensive empirical literature on village India and on caste in India which has emerged during the post-Independence era.' Gerald D. Berreman, 'The Brahmanical View of Caste', in T. N. Madan, ed., *Contributions to India Sociology*, New Series, 5 Dec. 1971, p. 23.

8. Schwab, op. cit., p. 166.

9. Ibid.

10. Ch. 6 'Benares on the Isis', Symonds, op. cit. On Monier-Williams's arrogant evangelical perspective see Richard Gombrich, *On Being Sanskritic: A Plea for Civilised Study and the Study of Civilisation*, Inaugural Lecture as Boden Professor of Sanskrit, 14 Oct. 1977, Clarendon Press, 1978.

11. Francis G. Hutchins, *The Illusion of Permanence: British Imperialism in India*, Princeton, New Jersey, 1967, p. 135.

12. Ibid., p. 167.

13. Ibid., p. 22.

14. Sir Malcolm Darling, *Apprentice to Power, India*, 1904–1908, Hogarth Press, 1966, p. 119; Sir George Cunningham, *Rectorial Address*, St Andrew's University, 9 Apr. 1947, appendix 1 in N. Mitchell, *Sir George Cunningham*, Blackwood, 1968. Lawrence is generally taken to have been a committed Christian. Whether he was so in fact is open to question. Hutchins, op. cit., p. 34.

15. See, for example, the Revd A. W. F. Blunt's essay in A. Lunn, *Public School Religion*, Faber, 1933. Blunt applauded the use of books like D. C. Somervell's *The History of our Religion*, in the fifth and sixth forms of some schools, but complains of the vagueness of public school religion and its substitution of the pagan ideal of a gentleman for I *Corinthians* 13.

16. Eric Stokes, *The English Utilitarians and India*, OUP, 1959.

17. Ibid., p. 192.

18. Sharpe, *Not to Destroy*, op. cit., pp. 358–60.

19. *Delhi*, the magazine of the Cambridge Mission to Delhi, editorial, July 1931; *Times*, letter, 27 Apr. 1931.

20. *Church Times*, 8 May 1931.

21. John Hick, *Problems of Religious Pluralism*, Macmillan, 1985, p. 32.

22. Dante Alighieri, *Inferno*, Canto 4, 37.

23. Raymond Panikkar, *The Unknown Christ of Hinduism*, London, 1964.

24. Thomas Hobbes, *Leviathan*, ch. 4, 'Of Speech'.

25. Bipan Chandra, *National and Colonialism in Modern India*, Orient Longman, 1979, p. 138, and 'Tilak', pp. 368–74.

26. For instance, to the Quaker John S. Hoyland, who edited *Gopal Krishna Gokhale: His Life and Speeches*, Builders of Modern India, YMCA, Calcutta, 1933. See, Stanley A. Wolpert, *Tilak and Gokhale: Revolution and Reform in the Making of Modern India*, University of California Press, 1961.

27. Chandra, op. cit., p. 369.
28. Judith Brown, *Modern India*, op. cit., p. 192.
29. D. C. Somervell, *The British Empire*, Christophers, London, p. 244. Revised editions 1938 and 1942. Somervell was to edit Toynbee's *magnum opus, The Study of History*, vols. 1–6, as a labour of love. The project was gratefully acknowledged by Toynbee and became the standard compact edition.
30. Ibid., p. 242.
31. Sharpe, *Faith Meets Faith*, op. cit., p. 19.
32. Sharpe, *Not to Destroy*, op. cit., p. 300.
33. B. Chaturvedi and Morjorie Sykes, *Charles Freer Andrews*, foreword by M. K. Gandhi, Allen and Unwin, 1949. Hugh Tinker, *The Ordeal of Love*, OUP, 1979. V. Elwin, *The Tribal World of Verrier Elwin*, OUP, 1964. In the course of a confrontation with his Bishop, Alex Wood, Bishop of Nagpur, Elwin heard Andrews described as a 'recreant priest'.
34. E. Sharpe, *The Theology of A. G. Hogg*, Christian Literature Society, Madras, 1971.
35. J. N. Farquhar, *Modern Religious Movements in India*, New York and London, 1915; *The Crown of Hinduism*, OUP, 1913. These are the main books in a prolific output. Eric Sharpe studies Farquhar's life and the development of his theology in detail in *Not to Destroy*, Lund, 1965. In his preface to *The Crown of Hinduism*, Farquhar acknowledges detailed contributions from C. F. Andrews.
36. Bishop H. H. Montgomery, ed., *Mankind and the Churches: Being an Attempt to Estimate the Responsibilities of the Great Races to the Fulness of the Church of God, by Seven Bishops*, London, 1907, p. 393. Montgomery worked for the SPG and became Bishop of Tasmania.
37. Arthur H. Nethercott, *The Last Four Lives of Annie Besant*, Hart Davies, 1963.
38. Daniel O'Connor, *The Testimony of C. F. Andrews*, The Christian Institute for the Study of Religion and Society, Bangalore, Christian Literature Society, Madras, 1974, p. 41.
39. J. Dunn, ch. 3, 'Nationalism', in *Western Political Theory in the Face of the Future*, CUP, 1979.
40. Amrit Rai, *Premchand: A Life*, translated from the Hindi by Harish Trivedi, People's Publishing House, Delhi, 1982. There is a massive collection of reports of Vivekananda's public speeches in S. P. Basu and S. B. Ghosh, eds., *Vivekananda in Indian Newapapers, 1892–1902*, Modern Book Agency, Calcutta, 1969.
41. Nirad C. Chaudhuri, *The Autobiography of an Unknown Indian*, Macmillan, 1951, reissued Hogarth Press, 1987, p. 202.
42. Charles H. Heimsath, *Indian Nationalism and Hindu Social Reform*, Princeton, 1964.
43. *St Matthew* 5, xvii.
44. Farquhar, *The Crown of Hinduism*, op. cit., p. 54.
45. Ibid., p. 61.
46. M. M. Thomas, op. cit., ch. 6, 'Vivekananda: Christ as Jivanmukta'.
47. C. F. Andrews, *The Renaissance in India*, United Council for Missionary Education, 1912, reprinted 1914.
48. Farquhar, *Crown of Hinduism*, op. cit., p. 202.
49. Eleanor Jackson, *Red Tape and the Gospel: A Study of the Significance of the Ecumenical Missionary Struggle of William Paton*, (1886–1943), Phlogiston, in association with Selly Oak Colleges, 1980.

50. Sharpe, *Not to Destroy*, op. cit., pp. 194 ff.

51. Ibid., p. 339.

52. Ibid., p. 351. The appeal of the 'fulfilment' thesis is reflected in occasional polemics against it. See, for example, S. J. Imam-ud-Din, *Gandhi and Christianity*, Rawalpindi, 1946. Published with an acknowledgement to the Revd K. W. S. Jardine, CMS Principal of Edwardes College, Peshawar. Dr Safir Akhtar kindly drew my attention to this publication.

53. *Renaissance in India*, op. cit., pp. 135 ff.

54. Ibid., p. 163.

55. S. C. Carpenter, *Theism in Modern India*, Hibbert Lecture, 1922.

56. Hugh Tinker, *Ordeal of Love*, op. cit., p. 39; and *Civil and Military Gazette*, 8 Sept. 1906.

57. *St Stephen's College Magazine*, May 1907.

58. Ibid., May 1908.

59. *Curtis Papers*, 11, 4 Aug. 1937.

60. On the important topic of games, Christianity and the British in India, see J. A. Mangan, *The Games Ethic and Imperialism*, Viking, 1985.

61. *St Stephen's College Magazine*, 'Religion and Patriotism', Feb. 1907.

62. For a very different account of the geo-political conditions from which early Buddhism emerged see D. Chattopadhyaya, *Lokayata*, op. cit., pp. 469 ff.

63. B. Lucas, *The Empire of Christ*, Macmillan, 1907; *Christ in India*, Macmillan, 1910; *Our Task in India: Shall we Proselytise Hinduism or Evangelise India?*, Macmillan, 1914.

64. B. Lucas *The Empire of Christ*, op. cit.

65. B. Lucas *Christ in India*, op. cit., p. 151.

66. Ibid., p. 101.

67. B. Lucas *The Empire of Christ*, op. cit., p. 89.

68. Ibid., p. 101.

69. Sharpe, *Faith Meets Faith*, op. cit., p. 72.

70. Sidney Cave, *Redemption, Hindu and Christian*, OUP, 1911. *Church Times*, 31 Oct. 1919.

71. Maxwell Leigh, *Advent in India*, SPCK, 1935.

72. Said, *Orientalism*, op. cit., p. 75.

73. H. H. Montgomery, ed., *Mankind and the Church*, op. cit. Montgomery's father, Sir Robert Montgomery, ended his Indian career as Lieutenant-Governor of the Punjab in 1865, where he had served under James Thomason and the Lawrences. He came from the same strongly evangelical Irish background as the latter. Brian Montgomery, *Monty's Grandfather, Sir Robert Montgomery, GCSI, KCBB, LLD, 1809–1887: A Life's Service for the Raj*, Blandford Press, 1984.

74. *Church Times*, 12 Dec. 1919, review of H. U. W. Stanton, *The Teaching of the Qu'ran*, CBU and SPCK, 1919.

75. Sir Thomas Arnold, *The Islamic Faith*, Benn, sixpenny booklet, 1928; Christian Troll, 'Sir Thomas Arnold as a student of Islam', Iqbal Academy, Birmingham, 19 November 1988, published *Iqbal Review*, Lahore, 1990.

76. Hick, 'On grading Religions', in *Problems of Religious Pluralism*, op. cit.

77. Prabha Dixit, 'Political Objectives of the Khilafat Movement in India', Mushirul Hasan, ed., *Communal and Pan-Islamic Trends in Colonial India*, Manohar, Delhi, 1981, p. 49.

78. Quoted in Aparna Basu, 'Mohamed Ali in Delhi: the *Comrade* Phase', Ibid., p. 120.
79. Mushir-ul-Haq, 'The Authority of Religion in Indian Muslim Politics', ibid., p. 363. The Maulana published a collection of questions and answers in Urdu in his journal *An-Nur* in 1930.
80. W. Goudie, review of Ballard, 'Why nor Islam?' in *Methodist Recorder*, 1 Jan. 1920. 'Islam lifts low pagan a little way no doubt, but to fix them there in a state of mental and moral stagnation.'
81. Rajat Ray, 'Revolutionaries, Pan-Islamists and Bolsheviks: Maulana Abul Kalam Azad and the Political Underworld in Calcutta, 1905–1925', in Hasan, op. cit.
82. D. A. Stewart, *The Place of Christianity Among the Great Religions of the World*, SPCK, 1920.
83. Other more or less specialized texts pursuing a common general argument include Edgar W. Thompson, *The Call in India*, Wesleyan Methodist Missionary Society, London, 1912, written for study circles to celebrate the centenary of the founding of the society; Dr Ballard, *Why Not Islam?* WMMS Bookroom, n.d.; Canon Sell, *Studies in Islam*.
84. Satish Saberwal, *India: The Roots of Crisis*, OUP, Delhi, 1986.
85. Ibid., p. 22.
86. Ibid., p. 27. From Sudipta Kaviraj, 'On the Crisis of Political Institutions in India', *Contributions to Indian Sociology*, 18, 1984, pp. 223–43.
87. David Potter, *India's Political Administrators*, 1919–1983, Clarendon, Oxford, 1986, p. 43.
88. *Bishop Montgomery: A Memoir*, by M. M. Introduction by Cosmo Cantuar, SPG, 1933.
89. H. H. Montgomery, ed., *Mankind and the Church*, op. cit., p. xvi.
90. H. Whitehead, *National Christianity in India*, Christian Literature Society for India, London, 1911. M. M. Thomas, op. cit., ch. 4, 'P. C. Mozoomdar: The Oriental Christ and the Unfolding Spirit'.

CHAPTER 4

The Church in India

1. E. R. Hambye's massive but rather inaccessible bibliography can be consulted in the India Office Library. E. R. Hambye SJ, Vidyajyoti, Delhi, *A Bibliography on Christianity in India*, The Church History Association of India, 1976, (mimeo). For a general account see M. E. Gibbs, *The Anglican Church in India*, 1600–1970, SPCK, 1972.
2. G. M. Davies, *A Chaplain in India*, London, 1933.
3. *Badmash* is standard Hindustani and Anglo-Indian for 'rogue'. Storrs Fox's plural is of course Anglicized.
4. *Storrs Fox Papers*, India Office Library, MSS Eur. 343: 5, 14 Jan.; 20 Apr.; 4 May; 14 Sept.; 1, 9 Nov., 1930: 4 Oct., 1931.

5. Ibid., 3 Feb. 1929.
6. Ravindar Kumar, 'The Rowlatt Satyagraha in Lahore' in Ravindar Kumar, ed., *Essays in the Social History of Modern India*, OUP, 1984.
7. *Lahore Chronicle*, Oct. 1926.
8. Heimsath, op. cit.; L. A. Gordon, *Bengal, the Nationalist Movement*, 1876–1940, Columbia, 1974.
9. A. J. Appasamy, *Christianity as Bhaktimarga*, Madras, 1926, London, 1927; *What is Moksha?*, 1931.
10. Earl of Ronaldshay, Second Marquess of Zetland, Governor of Bengal 1917–22, Secretary of State for India 1935–40.
11. M. M. Thomas, op. cit., p. 142.
12. Ranade's second wife became his pupil and later organized the Seva Sedan, for Women's Welfare in Poona. Heimsath, op. cit., p. 184. Mrs Rambai Ranade, *Himself, the Autobiography of a Hindu Lady*, New York, 1938.
13. Sarvepalli Gopal, *Jawaharlal Nehru, vol. 1*, 1889–1947, OUP, Delhi, 1975, pp. 85 ff.
14. *Bombay Diocesan Magazine*, Feb. 1925.
15. *Palmer Papers*, Lambeth Palace.
16. *Calcutta*, July 1922.
17. The second wife of George Sydenham Clarke, Governor of Bombay, 1907–13. He was a churchman and, at the time of his death in 1933, a leading die-hard. Sidney and Beatrice Webb were their guests in Bombay in 1912. Beatrice's account manages an astringent sympathy: 'Sir G. Clarke, whom Sidney knew twenty years ago, and who had the reputation of a liberal-minded and progressive administrator, has grown old and bitterly reactionary, both as regards Home Politics and, what is more important, as regards Indian affairs. Poor man, he looked unhappy, his eyes had that lifeless, sullen and suspicious expression which betokens disillusionment....' *Indian Diary*, OUP, 1988, p. 181.
18. Sixteen Anglo-Catholic missionaries covered the ground in summary form in E. R. Morgan, ed., *Essays Catholic and Missionary*, SPCK, 1928, stressing an inclusivist message, a fulfilment approach to other religions, cults and practices, looking for a nationalism redeemed from the spirit of domination and recognizing ambivalencies in missionary–government relations.
19. 'The duty of the Church to the Empire and the World, especially to India', *Church Congress Report*, copy in *Fraser Papers*, Rhodes House, Oxford, MSS Brit. Emp., s283.
20. 'The Burden of Empire', sermon preached in Westminster Abbey, 13 Apr. 1934, *Fraser Papers*. This sermon was followed by protests from clerics and others.
21. W. E. F. Ward, *Fraser of Trinity and Achimota*, OUP, Oxford, 1965, p. 132.
22. Cuttings from *Colombo Observer*, Fraser Papers, box 2.
23. Fraser to his wife, 1 Dec. 1919, Fraser Papers, box 8, f. 168.
24. Fraser to his wife, 6 Dec. 1919, Fraser Papers, box 8, f. 178.
25. Quoted in Ward, op. cit., p. 143.
26. Gibbs, op. cit., p. 100.
27. G. A. Oddie, *Social Protest in India: British Protestant Missionaries and Social Reform*, 1850–1900, Manohar, Delhi, 1979.
28. See, for example, the Chota Nagpur report in *SPG Series E*, 1929, that the mass movement among the Madras had fallen off in the two previous years, as a

result of agrarian unrest precipitated by tensions over the Land Settlement.

29. Ibid., 1921. For a study by a political scientist of the complex interaction between missions, Congress and the non-Brahmin movement in the south, see J. Manor, 'Testing the Barrier Between Caste and Outcaste; the Andhra Evangelical Lutheran Church in Guntur District', *Indian Church History Review,* 5, 1 June 1971.

30. *SPG Series E*, 1922.

31. *SPG Series E*, 1922.

32. *Extracts from the Annual Letters*, CMS, 1908, p. 251.

33. *SPG Series E*, Oct. 1930.

34. P. N. F. Young and Agnes Ferrer, *India in Conflict*, SPCK, 1920.

35. *CMS Annual Letters*, 1908, p. 26.

36. Paul von Tucher, *Nationalism: Case and Crisis in Missions, 1939–1949*, Selbstverlag, Erlangen, West Germany, 1980; Arthur Jayakumar, 'The British Government in India and Missionaries of non-British Societies in the Light of the Memoranda of 1919: Some Case Studies', *Indian Church History Review*, Dec. 1984, pp. 119–33; 'The Government of India's Attitude Towards Indian National Movement, a Case Study: Dr Ernest Forrester-Paton', *Church History Association of India*, 6th Triennial Conference, Oct. 1985, Alwaye, Kerala.

37. Robert Anderson, Comment on Ian Gregor, 'Liberal Education: an Outworn Ideal?', in N. Phillipson, ed., *Universities, Society and the Future*, Edinburgh University Press, 1983.

38. Bruce Truscott, *Redbrick University*, Faber, London, 1943; Walter Moberly, *The Crisis in the University*, SCM, London, 1949; Spencer Leeson, *Christian Education*, Longman, 1947; Spencer Leeson, *Christian Education Reviewed*, Longman, 1957.

39. Gerald Studdert-Kennedy, *Dog-Collar Democracy*, op. cit., pp. 76, 143.

40. T. G. P. Spear, Review of the Lindsay Commission Report, *Young Men of India*, Jan. 1932.

41. Sir George Anderson and the Rt. Revd Henry Whitehead, *Christian Education in India*, Macmillan, 1932.

42. F. F. Monk, *A History of St Stephen's College, Delhi*, YMCA, Calcutta, 1935.

43. *Extracts from the Annual Letters*, CMS, 15 Nov. 1908.

44. *SPG Series E*, Nov. 1908.

45. T. N. Cunnooswami, ed., *The Voice from Burgo Park: Principal Miller's Messages to Former Students of the Madras Christian College*, Veperey, 1922.

46. O. K. Chetty, *Dr William Miller*, Church Literature Society for India, Madras, 1924, p. 44.

47. Cunnooswami, ed., *Burgo Park*, 'Message 13' 1918, p. 168.

48. Ibid., 'Message 10', 1916.

49. Chetty, op. cit., p. 68.

50. Cunnooswami, ed., *Burgo Park*, 'Message 11' Miller more than makes up for the reticence of the *Madras Christian College Magazine*, which had a policy of avoiding political comment.

51. The Biographer of the Victorian Principal of St Stephen's claims that the College has 'drawn its members up towards Christianity, even though comparatively few of the students became Christians as a direct result of their school or college teaching.' Cecil H. Martin, *Allnutt of Delhi*, SPCK, 1922, p. 76.

52. M. Ruthnaswamy, *The Political Theory of the Government of India*, S. Sastri

Foundation Lectures, Thompson and Co., Madras, 1928. There are references to Raju in *Meston Papers*, IOL, Eur. F. 136 11, Meston to Curtis, 10 March, 16 May, 1915. Raju published *Swadeshi and Christianity: A Reply to Mr Gandhi*, enlarged from *St John's College Magazine*, 1916.

53. *CMS Annual Letters*, 1907.

54. Monk, op. cit., p. 234.

55. *St John's College Magazine*, 1932–3.

56. George Thomas, *Christian Indians and Indian Nationalism*, 1889–1956, Verlag, P. D. Lang, 1979.

57. M. M. Thomas, op. cit., p. 322.

58. K. T. Paul, *The British Connection with India*, SCM, London, 1927, reprinted Anmol Publications, Delhi, 1986.

59. K. Baago, 'The First Independence Movement Among Christians', *Indian Church History Review*, 6, 1967.

60. Vincent Kumarados, *Protestant Missionary Impact and the Quest for National Identity: Tamil Nadu Experience*, 1900–21, D. Phil. Thesis, University of Madras, 1983.

61. V. Chakkarai, 'Christianity and Nationalism', *Christa Seva Sangha Review*, Jan. 1933. There is also a slighter piece by him, 'Nationalism and Christianity', *The Young Men of India*, July 1931.

62. J. C. Kumarappa, *Christianity, its Economy and Way of Life*, Navajivan Publishing House, Ahmedabad, 1945, pp. 77 ff.

63. Ibid., p. 41.

64. File entitled 'Gandhiji etc., 1921–33 and Clergy and Politics, 1930–1, *Bishop's College Archive*, Calcutta.

CHAPTER 5

Evangelical Attitudes

1. Ward, op. cit., p. 96. In 1922–3 more than three hundred European visited the school, including the Commander-in-Chief and his Staff and the Governor of Bombay. 'Another visitor was a *sadhu* who goes about preaching for the government and against non-cooperation', *CMS Annual Reports*, 1922–3.

2. See Gerald Studdert-Kennedy, *Dog-Collar Democracy*, op. cit., p. 99.

3. *The Haileyburian*, 1925, p. 334.

4. C. E. Tyndale-Biscoe, *Kashmir in Sunlight and Shade*, Seeley, London, 1925; E. D. Tyndale-Biscoe, *Fifty Years Against the Stream: The Story of a School in Kashmir*, 1880–1930, Wesleyan Mission Press, Mysore, 1930; C. E. Tyndale-Biscoe, *Tyndale-Biscoe of Kashmir: An Autobiography*, Seeley, 1951. Pamphlets: *Character Building in Kashmir*, CMS, 1896; *A Mission School and Social Service*, CMS, 1910; *A Valiant Man of Kashmir*, CMS, 1910, (on a Kashmiri Mohammedan convert to Christianity—Samuel Bakkal).

5. Lord Birdwood, *Khaki to Gown*, Ward Lock, 1940.

6. R. Kipling, *Stalky and Co.*, Macmillan, 1899: Major General L. C. Dunsterville, *The Adventures of the Dunster Force*, Arnold, London, 1920; Lord Birkenhead, *Rudyard Kipling*, Weidenfeld and Nicolson, 1978; Angus Wilson, *The Strange Ride of Rudyard Kipling*, Secker and Warburg, 1977, Granada, 1979, 64 ff. Both Sir John Lawrence and General John Nicholson had been British Agents in Kashmir.

7. C. E. Tyndale-Biscoe, *Tyndale-Biscoe*, op. cit., pp. 105 ff.

8. Mark Girouard, *The Return to Camelot: Chivalry and the English Gentleman*, Yale, 1981, p. 273:

> These were paladins, these were Craven's peers
> These with him shall be crowned in story and song
> Crowned with the glitter of steel and the glimmer of tears,
> Princes of courtesy, merciful, proud and strong.

Sir Henry Newbolt, 'Craven'. As Girouard points out, 'The Knight's Prayer' is printed on the first page of the Canon's autobiography.

9. Sir Francis Younghusband, *Modern Mystics*, Murray, 1935, ch. 1, 'Hindu Mystics: Keshub Chander Sen, Ramakrishna and Vivekananda'.

10. Francis Younghusband, *Dawn in India: British Purpose and Indian Aspiration*, Murray, London, 1930.

11. Chaudhuri, *Hinduism*, op. cit., pp. 164 ff.

12. Mary Douglas, *Purity and Danger*, Routledge and Kegan Paul, 1966; Louis Dumont, *Homo Hierarchicus*, Weidenfeld and Nicolson, 1966; McKim Marriott and R. Inden, 'Caste Systems', *Encyclopaedia Britannica*, 15th edn., vol. 3, pp. 982–91.

13. Tyndale-Biscoe, *50 Years Against the Stream*, op. cit., p. 11.

14. C. E. Tyndale-Biscoe, *Tyndale-Biscoe*, op. cit., p. 77.

15. Tyndale-Biscoe, *Kashmir in Sunlight and Shade*, op. cit., p. 79.

16. C. E. Tyndale-Biscoe, *Tyndale-Biscoe*, op. cit., p. 192.

17. Ibid., p. 250.

18. F. L. Brayne, *In Him was Light*, OUP, 1933.

19. F. L. Brayne, *The Indian and the English Village*, OUP, 1933, p. 13.

20. C. E. Tyndale-Biscoe, *Tyndale-Biscoe*, op. cit., p. 215.

21. Lady Hartog, 'Indian Village Uplift: A Visit to Gurgaon', *Contemporary Review*, Sept. 1928. The entire Simon Commission visited 'the Gurgaon District, justly rendered famous by the enterprise of the District Commissioner Mr Brayne.' Edward Cadogan, *The India We Saw*, op. cit., pp. 48–53.

22. Mabel Hartog, *Living India*, Blackie, 1935, written at the request of the Imperial Studies Committee of the Royal Empire Society. Brayne was her principal informant on rural development. Her condensed factual account marginalizes Gandhian nationalism and the Congress Party. P. J. Hartog, *A Memoir*, Constable, London, 1949.

23. Royal Commission on Agriculture in India, (chairman, Lord Linlithgow), *Report*, Government of India, Calcutta, 1928, pp. 502–3.

24. Sir Malcolm Hailey, foreword to *Village Uplift in India*, Pioneer Press, Allahabad, 1927. C. F. Strickland of the ICS endorsed Brayne as a matter of course: 'A reputation extending beyond the limits of India.... The 'clodhopper' is rapidly becoming a new man. It remains to prove whether he will live up to his new ideals, and whether the same reformation can be carried out in other districts and other provinces. Talking—or legislation—alone will not suffice, and the

Indian politician, however genuinely patriotic, tends to be satisfied when he has passed a new law.' In 'Co-operation and the Rural Problem of India' *Quarterly Journal of Economics*, May 1929, p. 530.

25. 'The Rajput zaildar roared himself hoarse giving orders, encouragement, and, when needed, abuse. I provided two drummers who kept up a lively beat all day; it had the same effect on the workers as the bagpipes have on a Highlander. They were like ants. The men ran up in two lines, one on each side of the breach.... At last came the crisis. The gap was only ten or fifteen feet wide....' Undated note, *Brayne Papers*, India Office Library.

'(Dr Arthur Neve) pluckily got into the nearest boat; it happened to be an iron bath tub, which he handled most skillfully. I fortunately had my canoe handy and in these craft we entered the house.... On the top shelf were Mr Knowles's most valuable translations of the Bible into Kashmiri... as the canoe left the study, the ceiling-high bookshelf fell over into the flood....' C. E. Tyndale-Biscoe, *Tyndale-Biscoe*, op. cit., p. 63.

26. In January 1934 the editor of the *Lahore Diocesan Magazine* welcomed the tardy recognition of the importance of rural development and education by the appointment of Brayne as Commissioner of Rural Reconstruction, and noted that his writing and work were already famous. Brayne wrote articles on his standard themes in successive issues. The magazine also carried an article in this period on the Tyndale-Biscoe schools, and printed Kipling's 'new hymn', 'The Engineer'. Brayne, like Bishop Barne, spoke for a practical and earnest Christian constituency in official, military and business circles. Many of them, and there were a number from much further afield than the Punjab, sent their sons to the last of the Tyndale-Biscoe Schools in Kashmir, a prep school started for English boys by the Canon's son in 1940 and run under the CMS schools' motto, 'In All Things Be Men.' E. D. Tyndale-Biscoe, *The Story of Sheikh Bagh*, Wesley Press, Mysore, n.d.

27. Brayne, *The Indian and the English Village*, op. cit.

28. F. L. Brayne, *Socrates Persists in India*, London, 1933, p. 10. Other titles are *Socrates in an Indian Village*, Lahore, 1929, London, 1931; *Socrates at School*, (with W. M. Ryburn), Bombay, 1933. He was regularly reviewed in CMS and SPG Reports.

29. Clive Dewey, *Anglo-Indian Attitudes*, (forthcoming).

30. C. J. Bliss and N. H. Stern, *Palanpur: The Economy of an Indian Village*, OUP, 1982, p. 51.

31. P. H. M. van den Dungen, *The Punjab Tradition*, Allen and Unwin, 1972.

32. John Harriss, *Capitalism and Peasant Farming: Agrarian Structure and Ideology in Northern Tamil Nadu*, OUP, 1982, p. 17.

33. Quoted in Dewey, op. cit. (forthcoming).

34. See, for example, Sir Valentine Chirol's references to the accused at the trial for the murder of the Collector of Nasik, in ch. 3 of *Indian Unrest*, Macmillan, London, 1910, quoted below, ch. 6.

CHAPTER 6

Gandhi and The Problem of Authentic Nationalism

1. R. T. Shannon, 'John Seeley and the Idea of a National Church', in R. Robson, ed., *Ideas and Institutions of Victorian Britain*, Bell, London, 1967; Brooke Foss Westcott, *The National Church as the Spiritual Organ of the Nation*, London, 1893. At the Society's finance meeting in 1920, Sir Charles Lucas told a gathering chaired by the Lord Mayor at the Mansion House that the SPCK reflected 'the characteristics that made the Empire great overseas.' *CT*, 26 Feb. 1920.
2. H. E. Egerton, *A Short History of British Colonial Policy*, London, 1887. Quoted in Luke Trainor, 'Historians as Imperialists: Some Roots of British Imperial History, 1880–1900', *The New Zealand Journal of History*, 15, 1, Apr. 1981.
3. There is a general account of the range of missionary political ideologies, from 'Whiggish liberal to conservative,' in John C. B. Webster, 'British Missions in India', in Torben Christensen and William R. Hutchison, eds., *Missionary Ideologies in the Imperialist Era: 1880–1920*, Aros, Denmark, 1982.
4. Clive Dewey, 'The Education of a Ruling Caste: the Indian Civil Service in the Era of Competitive Examinations', *English Historical Review*, 88, 1973.
5. Tissington Tatlow, *The Story of the Student Christian Movement of Great Britain and Ireland*, SCM, London, 1933, ch. 6, 'A New Relationship to India' and ch. 35, 'Post-War Activities'. Paul was in demand as a speaker during the Round Table Conference, preaching for instance at All Hallows, Lombard St. in November 1930. *CT*, 14 Nov. 1930.
6. Paul spoke at a missionary conference at Norwood in 1919 about India's baptism in nationalism, her discovery of the clay feet of western civilization through the Russo-Japanese war and the Great War, the recovery of better elements in her own culture, but also of less healthy Indian antipathies to civilizing elements coming from the West and Britain. *Methodist Recorder*, 8 September 1919. S. K. Datta's book *Asiatic India*, 1932, was read by Lindsay before publication, when Datta was in London for the Conference. He found it 'thrillingly interesting'. L. Curtis to M. MacDonald, *Lothian Papers*, GD40/117/255.
7. Jawaharlal Nehru, *A Bunch of Old Letters*, Bombay, 1958. Thompson was close to Nehru in the mid-1930s, when he was at his most disillusioned with the British. He had resigned from the Methodist ministry in 1924, thereafter teaching Bengali to ICS probationers till 1933 and doing research into Indian history till his death in 1964, mostly as a Fellow of Oriel College, Oxford. He sought to 'reconcile' mainly through an extensive correspondence, and reviewers of the books seem to me uncertain how to handle a distinctive combination of radical perceptions and liberal preferences. See review of *The Other side of the Medal*, G, 18 Dec. 1925, and 'Castor' on *Rise and Fulfilment of British Rule in India* (with G. T. Garratt), G, 3 Aug. 1934. Thompson himself wrote to Lothian about the reviews of the latter book: 'What an extraordinary fate. To be cut dead or else found depressing by your own set and greeted by the conservatives.' E. Thompson to Lothian, 7 July 1934, *Lothian Papers*, GD40/17/288. So, despite his distinction, he is a marginal figure in the context of this study. His response to Gandhi was complex, critical and fluctuating. In

Farewell to India, 1931, p. 143, he writes that 'the spirit of God has used this man,' though he also felt at this time that 'God had nearly done with him.' Thompson has been placed in the context of a tradition of Protestant missionary writing by K. A. Ballhatchett. 'Some Aspects of Historical Writing on India by Protestant Christian Missionaries During the Nineteenth and Twentieth Centuries', in C. A. Philips, ed., *Historians of India, Pakistan and Ceylon*, OUP, 1961. I am grateful to Harish Trivedi, who has been working on the Thompson papers, for stimulating my interest in him.

8. Allen J. Greenberger, *The British Image of India*, London, 1969.

9. M. M. Thomas, op. cit., p. 239.

10. T. G. P. Spear, 'The State and the Individual', *YMI*, Aug. 1930; 'Nazi Rule in Germany', May 1934; 'Christianity and Nationalism', Sept. 1934.

11. Melvin Richter, op. cit. On Green's importance to Anglican social theology in the 1920s see Studdert-Kennedy, *Dog-Collar Democracy*, op. cit., ch. 4, 'Anglican Social Gospels'.

12. See, for example, J. N. C. Ganguly, 'Idealism in Hindu Politics', *YMI*, Sept. 1924. He is identifying an idealist vision of the State in the epics and later Sanskrit literature: '...the state is the machinery for the collective attainment of salvation (*moksha*) by the people under its care, through the fulfilment of their legitimate desires.' T. H. Green, like the Vedic philosophers in their conception of *viraj*, saw the ultimate reality through the insitutions of the state. Ganguly quotes:

> There's on earth a yet auguster thing,
> Veiled though it be, than Parliament and King.

(Green's *Political Obligation*, p. 82.) Ganguly was the author of *Raja Ram Mohun Roy*, YMCA, Calcutta.

13. K. T. Paul, 'Citizenship in Modern India', *YMI*, Jan. 1921.

14. K. T. Paul, 'What of the Night', (editorial as 'Watchman'), *YMI*, May 1922.

15. K. T. Paul, *The British Connection*, op. cit., p. 175.

16. K. T. Paul, 'The Dynamic of Public Opinion', *YMI*, Apr. 1930, p. 253. 'Experts like him were employed (in the European post-war recovery), drawn from various nations and they worked out what was really international co-operation in high finance.' Sir Basil Blackett, Finance Member 1922–8, also employed a corporatist rhetoric about imperial economics. 'The British Empire as an Economic Family', 4 Apr. 1930, *Lothian Papers*, GD40/17/447. Hirtzel noted Blackett's contribution to the debate on demands for grants in the Legislative Assembly in 1927, 'in a speech remarkable for its reference to the spiritual basis of government.' Hirtzel, *East India, Progress and Conditions: Statement Exhibiting the Moral and Material Progress and Condition of India During the Year*, 1926–7, Government of India, Calcutta, 1927. A. Hirtzel was Under Secretary of State for India. Blackett contributed to one of the Wesley Guild International Evenings at Teddington Church, with Datta, where he looked on the British connection 'with pride'. *MR*, 22 Oct. 1931.

17. Sir George Schuster, *Christianity and Human Relations in Industry*, Epworth Press, London, 1951.

18. Sir George Schuster and Guy Wint, *India and Democracy*, Macmillan, London, 1941.

19. K. T. Paul, *The British Connection*, op. cit., pp. 65–9.

20. K. T. Paul, *YMI*, May 1922.

21. 'The Situation Demands Reconciliation', by Paul as 'Watchman', *YMI*, Mar. 1922.

22. J. E. Neil (Wesley College, Madras), 'Non-cooperation and the Spirit of Christ', *YMI*, Aug. 1921. His themes are repeatedly worked over in general and with topical application over the next two decades. There are many examples in addition to articles in *YMI* already referred to: For example, G. B. Job, 'Christianity and Nationalism', Aug. 1931; Prof. N. C. Mukerjee, 'The Gandhian Christ', Mar. 1933 (reprinted from *The Holland Hall Magazine*, University of Allahabad, and reviewed in the *CT*, 21 Aug. 1931). P. N. F. Young wrote a neat summary of the fulfilment argument for his select flock in Simla in *Liddell's Simla Weekly*, reprinted *YMI*, Nov. 1933.

23. Geoffrey Ashe, *Gandhi: A Study in Revolution*, Heinemann, London, 1968, p. 205.

24. Stephen Koss, 'Wesleyanism and Empire', *Historical Journal*, 18, 1975; *Nonconformity in Modern British Politics*, Batsford, 1975.

25. Revd E. J. Thompson, MC, 'The Urgent Need of Indian Missions', *MR*, 27 Nov., 4 Dec. 1918.

26. *MR*, 29 Apr. 1920. Williams was Principal of St Andrew's (CMS) College, Gorakhpur from 1914–18, and Assistant Master at Rugby, 1920–1.

27. *G*, 26 Apr. 1929.

28. *G*, 25 May 1928; the editorial of 18 May applauded the Earl of Meath's Empire Day and the Archbishops' support for it. *MR*, 31 May 1923, 10 Apr., 29 May 1924. B Pollock, Bishop of Norwich, on the King's birthday, on 'The Throne and the Empire', asserted the corporate unity of the Empire and celebrated the public school boy, administering English law with sympathy and without fear in remote areas. *G*, 8 June 1923. The Bishop of Salisbury, at the fiftieth anniversary celebrations of the CMD: '...our thirst for God is as great as theirs; but because we are reserved, capable, efficient in commerce and government (all of which to a certain extent the Indian admires) we are judged to be materialists....' *G*, 10 June 1927.

29. As Edward Norman has pointed out, Headlam, like Henson, Bishop of Durham, and Dean Inge of St Paul's, were isolated figures in the Church of England. All three were hostile to the vaguely liberal moralism of COPEC and the ICF. E. R. Norman, *Church and Society in England*, 1770–1970, OUP, 1976, pp. 326 ff. Norman argues that they were much closer than the liberal establishment to lay sentiment among churchpeople. Inge had a substantial popular following well outside the church, based on his vigorous jounalism for the *Evening Standard*. His views on India align him with the Christian die-hards of the Tory Party. Dean Inge, *England*, Benn, 1927, pp. 143–4.

30. Review of John Mackenzie, *Hindu Ethics*, Milford, London, 1922 (in Farquhar's Religious Quest of India Series).

31. *G*, 2, 9, 16 Dec. 1927. The permeation of the kind of social anthropology referred to in these letters by fulfilment assumptions is illustrated by a quotation from a local ethnography, in the chapter on religions in O'Malley's volume for the Cambridge series of Provincial Geographies of India. The aboriginal Oraons of Chota Nagpur 'are taught that for the salvation of Christians one

great sacrifice is made, and they see that those who are baptised do not in fact reduce their live stock to propitiate the evil spirits. They grasp at this notion and, long afterwards, when they understand it better, the mystical washing away of sin by the blood of Christ is the doctrine on which their simple minds most dwell.' L. S. S. O'Malley, *Bengal, Bihar and Orissa Sikkim*, CUP, 1917, p. 219. The series was designed by and for ICS men.

32. *MR*, 28 July 1932.

33. Ibid.

34. Review of *Mahatma Gandhi at Work*, edited by C. F. Andrews, *G*, 8 Sept. 1931.

35. B. H. Streeter and A. J. Appasamy, *The Sadhu: A Study in Mysticism and Practical Religion*, Macmillan, 1922, p. 233. He is described at an overflowing meeting in London, summoned by Father Bull and the Secretaries of the SPG and the CMS, as a 'magnificent figure of masculine beauty...giving the impression of a man apart,' and as an implicit rebuke to the English clergy. *CT*, 12 Mar. 1920. Bishop King collected his characteristic sayings. *CT*, 1 Apr. 1920. Friedrich Heiler, *The Gospel of Sadhu Sundar Singh*, trans. Olive Wyon, Allen and Unwin, 1927; Mrs Arthur Parker, *Sadhu Sundar Singh: Called of God*, SCM, 1927, reviewed by J. G. Tasker in *MR*, 4 Aug. 1927. Younghusband's chapter on the Sadhu in *Dawn in India* represents him as embodying the form in which the spirit of Christ can reach India.

36. *CT*, 6 May 1921. The appeal of a Christian asceticism searching out an authentically eastern spirituality is reflected also in the favourable commentary on the Christa Seva Sangha, the ashram associated with Elwin and Winslow. Sir Francis Younghusband spoke at the third annual meeting, with the Bishop of Bombay presiding, on Elwin's joining the fellowship. *G*, 4 Oct. 1929. *The Christa Seva Sangha Review*, which started in the following year, initially at least made much of Gandhi as a Christian spirit, '...so much worthier to be called a follower of Christ than those of us who call ourselves by his name... perhaps it will be a Hindu who will lead us back to Jesus,' Apr. 1931.

37. *MR*, 1 May 1924.

38. 'Gandhi, the Man', *The Guardian Supplement*, 6 June 1924. At the time of Gandhi's arrest an Indian student put it to Holland that 'Calvary will always be repeated.'

39. P. N. F. Young, 'Englishmen in India', *G*, 14 Aug. 1925.

40. *G*, 13 June 1924.

41. Percival and Margaret Spear, *India Remembered*, Orient Longman, 1981.

42. W. Cunningham, Canon of Ely, is identified by E. R. Norman, op. cit., as the compelling voice of conservative reason in Anglican social theory, against which liberals like Temple shut their ears. It has been argued, on the contrary, that Temple and the ICF in the 1920s were much closer in their social thinking than their rhetoric suggests at times to conservative clerical intellectuals like Henson and Cunningham. Studdert-Kennedy, *Dog-Collar Democracy*, op. cit.

43. Ashe, *Gandhi*, op. cit., p. 82. '...inequalities of wealth, justly established, benefit the nation in the course of their establishment; and, nobly used, aid it yet more by their existence. That is to say, among every active and well-governed people, the various strength of individuals, tested by full exertion and specially applied to various need, issues in unequal, but harmonious results,

receiving reward or authority according to its class and service, while, in the inactive or ill-governed nation....' John Ruskin, *Unto This Last*, George Allen, edn. of 1909, p. 47.

44. *Bombay Diocesan Magazine*, Aug. 1930.

45. Joseph Butler, *The Analogy of Religion, Natural and Revealed, to the Constitution and Course of Nature*, 1736, new edition, Macmillan, 1900, p. 83. This replaced for theology students the Oxford edition of 1844 and Bishop FitzGerald's of 1880.

46. On natural and spiritual law Gandhi himself referred to H. Drummond's *Natural Law in the Spiritual World*, 1884, an explicitly Christian gloss on Bagehot and Spencer, which he had 'read with avid interest.' Margaret Chatterjee, *Gandhi's Religious Thought*, Macmillan, 1983, p. 63. Drummond argued that Spiritual and Natural Laws are not merely analogous, 'they are the same laws,' at different levels. He also observes, however, that Natural Laws may have no absolute existence, and are 'relative to man in his many limitations' (p. 4), a formulation closer to Kumarappa's than to Westcott's.

47. Westcott alluded to Romans 13 in a letter on Gandhi's objections to the Bengal Ordinances of 1925: 'I have been brought up on the Christian principle that rulers (and inferentially their laws) are not a terror to the good work but to the evil and therefore, if people agree to abandon revolutionary conspiracy and obtain their freedom on that condition, the ordinances will be to all intents and purposes dead as far as they are concerned.' In 1933 on Gandhi's fast: 'You will forgive me if I venture to say that there seems to me to be something in your fast of that spirit which actuates some of the Sadhus in India.' File marked 'Gandhiji etc., 1921–33,' 12 Feb. 1925, 4 May 1933, Bishop's College, Calcutta.

48. 'Editorial Notes', *CT*, 7 Jan. 1921. In fact Reading was to be preoccupied with the problem of drawing the Moslems closer to the Raj. Denis Judd, *Lord Reading*, Weidenfeld and Nicolson, 1982, ch. 14.

49. '...one voice persists in wailing, wild wailing (about Lord Irwin)... Lord Brentford.' Report on tributes to Irwin at Oxford Mission to Calcutta AGM. *CT*, 5 June 1931.

50. 'The Christian Viceroy', by 'Under Six Viceroys', *CT*, 3 Oct. 1930.

51. 'The Significance of Gandhi', editorial, *CT*, 3 Oct. 1930.

52. G, 1 May 1931. 'Lord Irwin has "seen beyond Empires", the *Manchester Guardian's* admirable comment' on Irwin's negotiations with Gandhi. *CT*, 6 Mar. 1931.

53. S. Gopal, *The Viceroyalty of Lord Irwin*, OUP, London, p. 21.

54. Max Warren, *Caesar, the Beloved Enemy*, SCM, 1955.

55. L. J. Trotter, *History of India*, revised by the Revd W. H. Hutton, SPCK, 1917. Hutton was Reader at Oxford from 1913–20. Though he had no immediate interest in India before his appointment, he argued for a comprehensive development of Oriental scholarship at Oxford in view of Britain's imperial responsibilities. Symonds notes that the First World War and his concurrent appointments, first as Archdeacon of Peterborough and then as Dean of Winchester, prevented him from initiating any significant development. Symonds, op. cit., p. 113.

56. Sir Bampfylde Fuller, *The Empire of India*, Pitman, 1913.

57. 'Indian Chapters', PHK, 2 June 1915, *Lothian Papers*, GD40/17/16.

58. J. R. M. Butler, *Lord Lothian*, Macmillan, 1960, p. 100.

59. Mansion House Speech, *Lothian Papers,* GD40/17/438.
60. Edwyn Bevan, *Christianity,* OUP, 1932, where he makes the conventional contrast between Christian and Hindu asceticism, p. 123; *Symbolism and Belief,* Gifford Lectures, Allen and Unwin, 1938. The Hindu religions took the right road, and Hinduism the 'disastrous aberration' of assuming the ultimate identity of God and man (pp. 70 ff). At least one of his India books was written simply as a potboiler to solve a personal financial difficulty. I am grateful to Erik Goldstein for this information. The books are of interest only because they run out standard formulae of the liberal Christian imperialist in summary and derivative form. On Bevan's contribution to the Peace Conference see Erik Goldstein, *Winning the Peace: British Diplomatic Strategy, Peace Planning and the Paris Peace Conference,* 1916–20, OUP, (forthcoming).
61. Bevan, *Indian Nationalism,* op. cit., p. 19.
62. Ibid., p. 47.
63. Ibid., 'The Seamy Side'.
64. Ibid., pp. 86, 33.
65. George Seaver, *Francis Younghusband: Explorer and Mystic,* Murray, 1952. Seaver points out that he 'captured the imagination of his countrymen,' by his pioneering explorations through the Himalayas and his mission to Tibet. His contribution on India to Sir Charles Lucas's volumes *The Empire at War,* complied for the Royal Colonial Institute, 'was regarded as the most important and the most comprehensive,' p. 292.
66. Seaver, op. cit., p. 332.
67. Younghusband, *Dawn in India,* op. cit., p. 219.
68. Ibid., p. 42.
69. Ibid., p. 149.
70. Ibid., ch. 8, 'Hindu-Moslem Tensions'.
71. Sir Sarvepalli Radhakrishnan was an influential exponent of Advaita Vedanta, with an international reputation as a philosopher. His encounter with Christian belief was unusually rigorous, as A.G. Hogg's outstanding MA student at Madras Christian College. He became India's Ambassador to Russia and ultimately President of India. Sarvepalli Gopal, *Radhakrishnan: A Biography,* OUP, 1989. A reprint of *The Hindu View of Life,* is published by Unwin Hyman, 1987. Younghusband was drawn into the work of the Indian Conciliation Group, with Andrews and others.
72. Ibid., p. 290.
73. Ibid., p. 80.
74. However, Dr W. R. Matthews, Inge's successor as Dean of St Paul's, joined the World Congress of Faiths, and Zetland, then Secretary of State for India, gave a government reception for the first assembly. Zetland, who was genuinely interested in this event, wrote an account of it to the Viceroy. Linlithgow's 'comment was brief and incisive; the function, he agreed, must have been of quite unusual interest—"but, a little confusing, surely, *pour le bon Dieu*".' Zetland, *Essayez,* Murray, London, 1956, p. 177.
75. G, 30 May 1924.
76. Ibid., 19 Feb. 1926.
77. Chirol, *Indian Unrest,* op. cit., p. 59.

78. Ibid., p. 161.
79. Ibid., ch. 14.
80. Ibid., p. 265.
81. Ibid., p. 167.
82. Zetland, *Great Britain and India*, Birmingham and Midland Institute, presidential address, 1930.
83. Zetland, *India, Retrospect and Prospect*, Cust Foundation Lecture, University of Nottingham, 1935.
84. Zetland, *India, Retrospect and Prospect*, op cit., p. 102.
85. Ibid.
86. The memoir of another Governor (United Provinces 1921–3), is closer in its emphases to Chirol: on Hinduism (of sexual abuses in the temples, 'there seems to be some connection between strong sunlight and sexual activity'), India's disinclination to connect words with facts and things, the profound importance of Christianity, Gandhi as reformer and as politician, and India's constant trembling on the brink of disorder. Sir Harourt Butler, *India Insistent*, Heinemann, 1931.
87. The term crops up repeatedly in his correspondence on behalf of the Indian Conciliation Group, but for one published example see 'The Psychology of India', *The Listener*, 30 Jan. 1935.
88. Lord Irwin, *Some Aspects of the Indian Problem*, Inaugural Massey Lecture, University of Toronto, OUP, Oxford, 1932.
89. Tinker, *Ordeal of Love*, op cit., p. 220.
90. C. F. Andrews, *The True India*, Allen and Unwin, London, 1930. *India and Britain: A Moral Challenge*, SCM, London, 1935, covers similar ground, and makes the same critique of British public opinion and political sluggishness, in the form of a series of dialogues.
91. Jack Winslow and Verrier Elwin, *The Dawn of Indian Freedom*, Allen and Unwin, 1931. Temple did not pretend to know much about India, but he does seem to have drawn on 'inside' knowledge from his brother who was an engineer there. Iremonger refers to their correspondence, but I have been unable to trace the letters. Datta was curt with Temple over his brother's ideas about the shortage of trained Indian administrators. *S. K. Datta Papers*, at IOL, F178/9, 23 Oct. 1931.
92. Ibid., p. 27.
93. Marjorie Sykes, *Quakers in India: A Forgotten Century*, Allen and Unwin, 1980, p. 91.
94. John S. Hoyland, *Indian Crisis: The Background*, London, 1943.
95. L. S. S. O'Malley, *Modern India and the West: A Study of the Interactions of their Civilisations*, foreword by the Lord Meston, OUP, 1941, published under the auspices of the Royal Institute of International Affairs.
96. Arthur Mayhew, *Christianity and the Government of India*, Faber and Gwyer, London, 1929. As a schoolmaster he is most unlikely to have suppressed his Indian experience. I am grateful to Mrs P. Hatfield, Eton College Archivist, for information on Mayhew, and for a search for information on Gandhi's visit to Eton in 1931. This is described in *Young India*, 12 Nov. 1931, with a disparaging contrast between the stilted questions of the young Empire builders

and those of the poor East End boys who had bombarded Gandhi with questions about 'his home, his dress, his sandals and his language.'

97. Mayhew, Ibid., p. 205.

98. Ibid., p. 238.

99. Ibid., p. 140.

100. Arthur Mayhew, 'The Religion of a Democrat', *The East and West Review*, SPCK, vol. 1, 1935.

101. *The Haileyburian*, 30 June 1930.

102. *The Cheltonian*, Aug./Sept. 1920, June 1921, June 1924.

103. *The Wykehamist*, 4 Nov. 1924. There is a submerged but inescapable literary allusion in the syntax of this final crescendo of conditionals and their resolution, to Kipling's poem 'If—'. 'If you can keep your head when all about you/Are losing theirs and blaming it on you,' etc. Kipling made a powerful contribution to the mythology of the service ideal but his ambiguities have been recognized more clearly by recent students of his work than during the terminal years of the Raj. See B. J. Moore-Gilbert, *Kipling and Orientalism*, Croom Helm, 1986, pp. 122 ff.

104. *The Wykehamist*, 19 May 1930. The obituary also praises his 'invaluable work' with the Working Men's College, founded by F. D. Maurice.

105. *The Wykehamist*, 17 Dec. 1930. In 1920 Monro had lectured to older boys on 'Mohammad and the Rise of Islam: Contradictions in the Hadith'. The following term Lord Chelmsford lectured on the inevitability of self-government in India, without enthusiasm but stressing the loyalty of the Service to the unavoidable if unattractive development of dyarchy, ibid., 2 Mar., 22 June 1921. Monro's obituary in the *Wykehamist*, of 14 Oct. 1958, stressed the intensity with which he prepared boys in his House for confirmation, his athleticism and scholarship, and his anxiety about the role of the public schools, following 'any future Plebeian advance.'

106. 'The preaching of Head Masters at public schools practically began with these two great pastors.' A. K. Cook, *About Winchester College*, Macmillan, 1917, p. 255.

107. Richard Brent, *Liberal Anglican Politics: Whiggery, Religion and Reform, 1830–1841*, OUP, 1987, p. 182; A. O. J. Cockshut, 'Arnold, Hook, Ward: A Wiccamical Sidelight on Nineteenth-Century Religion', in R. Custance, ed., *Winchester College: Sixth-Centenary Essays*, OUP, 1982.

108. Richard Gott recalls the strong impact of Anglicanism on many of his friends at Winchester as late as the mid-1950s, in 'Lessons of an Evil Empire', *Education Guardian*, 23 Aug. 1988. He is reflecting on his singularity in holding strongly radical political opinions, despite his education there. The letters of a Wykehamist of an earlier generation convey the Indian experience of a young ICS man, who was refreshed and sustained by his faith, and his contacts with the Cambridge Mission in Delhi. W. H. Saumarez-Smith, *A Young Man's Country: Letters of a Subdivisional Officer of the Indian Civil Service, 1936–1937*, Michael Russell, 1977.

109. Ruth Dudley Edwards, *Victor Gollancz: A Biography*, Gollancz, London, 1987, ch. 5, 'Serving a Teacher'.

110. Victor Gollancz and David Somervell, *Political Education at a Public School*, Collins, 1918, p. 30. Somervell also wrote *A Short History of our Religion*, 1922

and *A History of Tonbridge School*, Faber, 1947.

111. Gerald Studdert-Kennedy, 'Christian Imperialists and the Raj: Left, Right and Centre', in A. Mangan, ed., *Making Imperial Mentalities*, Manchester University Press, 1989. The *Cheltonian's* obituary in 1928 of Sir Lawrence Jenkins, Chief Justice of Calcutta, is a critical appreciation in miniature of the administration of justice under the Raj. The *Times* obituary of Commissioner Booth-Tucker is reprinted in *The Cheltonian* in 1929. Son of an ICS judge, he abandoned an ICS career to establish the Salvation Army in India, living as a fakir and marrying the second daughter of General Booth.

112. Numbers recruited into the ICS were very small and most schools produced ICS men in ones and twos in any given decade. Potter's figures show the dominance of the major public schools. More than half of those recruited before the First World War came from only fifteen Public Schools'. His Table 5, reproduced here with his kind permission, shows the thirty most popular schools for those recruited between 1915 and 1941. All are public schools and all but eight are among the 'Great Public Schools'. The list accounts for more than half of all ICS recruits in the period.

ICS Europeans: Most Popular Schools

Rugby	20	Bradfield	6
Winchester	15	Radley	6
Wellington	13	St Olave's	6
Charterhouse	10	Epsom	5
Cheltenham	10	Malvern	5
Haileybury	10	Merchant Taylor's	5
Marlborough	10	Rossall	5
Christ's Hospital	9	Shrewsbury	5
Dulwich	9	Westminster	5
Clifton	8	City of London	4
Uppingham	8	Kingswood (Bath)	4
Bradford Grammar	7	Manchester Grammar	4
Eton	7	Oundle	4
St Paul's	7	Sedburgh	4
Bedford	6	Tonbridge	4

Dr Potter's data are based on his classification of individual biographical entries for each of 1037 ICS Europeans listed in *The India Office and Burma Office List*, 1940 (excluding those listed who retired before 1930) together with the 1940 and 1941 ICS Europeans data in NAI Home Dept. File 35/38/41 Ests., 1941 'Appointments to the ICS on Probation in 1940', and Home Dept. File 32/41 Ests., 1941 'Results of the ICS Selection in England in 1941'. David Potter, *India's Political Administrators*, op cit., pp. 68–9.

CHAPTER 7

God's Providence and the Die-hards

1. Gerald Studdert-Kennedy, 'George Lansbury', in Keith Robbins, ed., *The Blackwell Biographical Dictionary of British Political Life in the Twentieth Century*, Blackwell, 1988.
2. *The Haileyburian*, 1926, p. 343. Furze, like Allenby powerfully built and vigorous, had been church commissioner for Bombay and Bishop of Pretoria. He was a member of the ICF Council.
3. *Morning Post*, 27 Mar. 1933.
4. My own copy was a birthday present from the author to the Revd A. V. Baillie in 1897. Baillie, a godson to Queen Victoria, was later responsible for maintaining symbolic links between imperial State and national church, as Dean of Windsor and Chaplain to the King.
5. It is not possible to make a complete and systematic analysis of this membership. Enrolment fell just short of 1000 in the period from February 1932 to August 1935. Approximately a quarter held commissioned rank in the services. As many were women. Around half were Mr or Dr, and nineteen or twenty were clergymen. The lists are spattered with decorations. Many of the names appear on the *India List* or in *Thacker's Directory*. Most of the male civilians were from the ICS, the Police or technical departments, for the most part senior or retired, with a number of businessmen, joining as individuals or in groups from particular companies. A handful were titled Indian landlords. Kipling's membership was widely publicized.
6. Ag Recter, *India: A Reflection, Suggestion and Appeal*, Lucas, Southend-on-Sea, 1934. *IER*, Feb. 1933; 'Religious Thought and Life in India; A Warning' by 'Senex', Ibid., June 1934. 'Senex' is deferentially respectful to Williams's formidable command of languages and the unique access this gave him on his visits to India.
7. Dorothy Crisp, *The Rebirth of Conservatism*, (introduction by Colonel John Buchan, MC, MP), Methuen, London, 1931.
8. Dorothy Crisp, *The Commonsense of Christianity*, London, 1938, 7, p. 68; *Christ is no Pacifist*, Boswell, London, 1938.
9. Dorothy Crisp, *England Mightier Yet*, National Review, London, 1938.
10. Captain J. E. Ellam, *Swaraj: The Problem of India*, Hutchinson, London, 1930, foreword by Lord Brentford; *The Religion of Tibet: A study of Lamaism*, Murray, 1927.
11. Patricia Kendal, *India and the British*, Scribners, 1931.
12. Robert Stokes, *New Imperial Ideals*, Murray, 1930.
13. R. Stokes, *The Moral Issue in India*, Murray, 1931; foreword by Lord Meston. In notes on Islam in India, contributed to M. Warburton, *The Mind and Ways of Islam*, Religions of the East, no. 2, 1947, he sees some hope for evolution towards Christianity among Moslems, of mass movements of conversion because of Islam's increasing 'rigidity'.
14. James Johnston, *The Political Future of India*, 1933; *Can the Hindus Rule India?*, King, London, 1935, p. 142.

15. Hugh Trevaskis, *The End of an Era*, Services Publications, n.d.
16. Hugh Trevaskis, *The Punjab of Today*, Lahore, 1931, p. 90.
17. Hugh Trevaskis, *Indian Babel*, London, 1935. This text is a fine Orientalist repository of sentences on Indian incompetence and sexuality.
18. He wrote on the White Paper to the *Morning Post*, 13 Aug. 1933, predicting the end of Christianity in India and the end of Islam. The Muslims, however, had sworn 'never to surrender' and therefore 'shame on us Christian brethren, that our religious zeal is less than that of the followers of the Arabian prophet.'
19. Other titles in the same general vein promoted by the *IER*: Lt.-Col. A. H. Lane, *The Alien Menace*, Boswell, 1932, foreword by Lord Sydenham; Sir John Marriott, *The English in India*, Clarendon, 1932; Harcourt Butler, *India Insistent*, op. cit.; Geoffrey Tyson (Editor of *Capital*, Calcutta), *Danger in India*, Murray, 1932; G. Cadogan, *The India We Saw*, op. cit.; Lt.-Col. F. W. P. Macdonald, *India's Financial Troubles*, Canterbury, n.d. (articles from the *Morning Post*).
20. Partly because it was not an exclusive sect and has declined sharply since the Second World War, British Israelism has not attracted much scholarly attention. The historical background is described by J. Wilson, 'British Israelism: the Ideological Restraints on Sect Organisation', in B. R. Wilson, ed., *Patterns of Sectarianism*, Heinemann, 1961. See also his general essay, 'British Israelism', *Sociological Review*, 16 Mar., 1968, and his *The History and Organisation of British Israelism: Some Aspects of the Religious and Political Correlates of Changing Status*, Ph.D. Thesis, Oxford University, 1966.
21. Other titles were *British Israel Star and Circle*, and *British Israel Herald*.
22. There is a copy in *Hume Collection*, Cambridge.
23. Prebendary A. W. Gough, FRSL, Exhibitioner of St John's College, Oxford, Vicar of Brompton, London, (a particularly well endowed middle-class parish): *Service and Sacrament*, 1909, *God's Strong People*, 1915, etc. Revd W. M. H. Milner (Scholar of Queen's College, Oxford, 1st Class Mods): *The Royal House of Britain*, 1903.
24. Another grand personage, who was involved with the popular speaker Herbert Garrison in establishing the British Israelite World Federation, was Helen, Countess-Dowager of Radnor, who had musical interests, recording tea with Lady Elgar, and Kipling's kind acknowledgment of her own setting of his 'Recessional'. She enjoyed a wide acquaintance among sympathetic clerics. The first annual meeting of the BIWF took place in Kensington Town Hall in 1920. Princess Alice and Lord Athlone were received in state by the Mayor. Also present was Lady Radnor's son-in-law, General Sir Henry Lawson, (Cheltenham College and Royal Engineers, former ADC to the King, with distinguished service in South Africa). Her husband, as Viscount Folkestone, was first President of the Anglo-Israel Association. Family membership of British-Israelism was common. *From a Great-Grandmother's Armchair*, Marshall Press, 1928.
25. The most important attack came from the Regius Professor of Divinity at Oxford, Canon H. L. Goudge, *The British-Israel Theory*, Mowbrays, Oxford, 1932. Canon R. J. Campbell wrote and preached about it in the cathedral at Chichester, whose diocese seems to have been particularly afflicted. 'The British Israel Cult', *The Chichester Diocesan Gazette*, Dec. 1930. Members were deeply hurt by an attack from the pulpit of Salisbury Cathedral by the scholar Canon

C. T. Dimont. Letter from Major W. Ord-Statter, Secretary of the Bournemouth Branch, *NM*, 15 Oct. 1932.

26. F. K. Tucker (Invercargill, New Zealand), 'A B-I Commentary on the Expansion of England (Professor J. R. Seeley)', *NM*, 28 Apr., 5 May 1934.

27. Sir Charles Marston, 'A Candid Examination of "the Crisis",' *Church Assembly*, 1930.

28. Norman, op. cit., p. 333.

29. Sir Charles Marston, *The Bible is True: The Lessons of the* 1925–1934 *Excavations in Bible lands Summerised and Explained*, The Religious Book Club, 1938; 'The Truth in Bible Narrative', *Morning Post*, 15 June 1933.

30. Sir Charles Marston, 'The Mystery of our Empire: What Archaeological Discovery is Likely to Establish in the Near Future', *Commonwealth and Empire Review*, Sept.-Nov., 1944.

31. R. G. F. Waddington, Trinity College, Dublin; Downes Divinity Prize; Organizing Secretary to Church Pastoral Aid Society; Vicar of Christ Church, Bradford, from 1921.

32. *NM*, 12 Dec. 1931. The Bishop in question was the elderly A. W. T. Perowne, from 1931 Bishop of Worcester. His succession by Blunt illustrates the latitudinarianism of the day. Blunt's biographer describes Perowne as distinctly evangelical in churchmanship and 'not well versed in either Theology or Bible knowledge.' Blunt thought fundamentalists a menace and was a biblical scholar with no time for British-Israelism. 'It is but the eccentric ingenuity of misdirected learning which has at times propounded and sought to maintain theories about the ultimate destination of the lost ten tribes.... Such speculations have nothing to do with serious history.' Blunt, *Israel in World History*, OUP, 1927, p. 59. The ICF enjoyed Blunt's support and Temple his admiration. John S. Peart-Binns, *Blunt*, Martin's Press, Bradford, 1969.

33. John M. MacKenzie mentions that Garrison was an evangelical, op. cit., p. 168. He was in fact the star, with Pascoe Goard, of the British-Israelite circuit, though he was not allowed to get onto the list of acceptable visiting speakers to the public schools. His published lecture *The British Empire or the Commonwealth of Nations*, Covenant, 1925, is a crude celebration, studded with imperialist quotations, from Amery and the Earl of Meath to Milner and Archbishop Davidson.

34. H. Pelling, *Social Geography of British Elections*, 1988.

35. The Revd W. D. Morrison, Rector of St Marylebone, and author of *The Jews under the Roman Empire*, 1908, accepted an invitation to sit on the IDL Council. Two clerics, including an archdeacon were on the committee of the Bath Group, and there were two on the committee of the Plymouth Group, neither of them Anglicans.

36. *NM*, 8 Aug., 18 Nov., 9 Dec. 1933.

37. Lady Radnor's memoir dwells on the arrival of Allenby at Dover after the War. Op. cit., p. 327.

38. Bishop Barne of Lahore, at Cheltenham with General Hazlet, officiated at the wedding service. Hume admired his down-to-earth vigour and the good sense of a sermon, whilst doubting if 'he comprehended the very British-Israelite lesson he read.' *Hume Papers*, 12 May, 19 Sept. 1936.

39. Colonel Hume successfully encouraged the British-Israelite leanings of a new

vicar at Terrington, though the Revd Boxley made enemies in the parish as a result. Col. Hume to A. Hume, 5 Nov. 1930, *Hume Collection*, Cambridge.

40. List in box 9, *Hume Collection*, Cambridge.

41. He had spent a year at the Ecole Normale, Lausanne, and visited Germany where he had upper class family connections. He, and British-Israelism generally, admired the efficiency, sense of purpose and discipline of Hitler's fascism, but regarded it as a parody of the truth about the chosen people.

42. See, for example, *Hume Papers*, IOL, 23 Feb. 1930.

43. Potter, op. cit., p. 38.

44. 'The police were splendid, in fact it was a task to restrain them,' *Hume Papers*, 1 Oct. 1930.

45. Ibid., 26 Nov. 1930.

46. Hume wrote an exciting account of controlling a Mohurram disturbance, 'A Night in the Life of an Assistant Commissioner', for the magazine of his old school, University College, Hastings, in June 1930. The editor commented that 'his contribution to the *Cinque Port* is particularly interesting at a time when sentimental faddists make light of the insuperable obstacles which separate the Hindu from the Muslim in differences racial and religious...the usual exciting incident—one man amidst a crowd of natives, and the white man triumphant....'

47. '...an absolutely *unmistakable, undeniable* witness to the fact of the practice by these people of the Phallic cult (not an edifying subject),' *Hume Papers*, 20 June 1928. He thought Mayo's material should have been published 'if it was really considered necessary...as a treatise for medical experts or officials coping with the problems.' Ibid., 9 Sept. 1928.

48. For example, '...the mind of the people on the whole is slovenly and untidy in the extreme, though I admit that this is no grounds for drawing the inference that it must therefore be depraved as well. I often feel quite nauseated and revolted by the filth and the disgusting habits of these people.' Ibid., 9 Sept. 1928. 'We all know that dealings with Indians are bound to be tainted as they are by nature corrupt.' Ibid., 22 Nov. 1934.

49. Ibid., '24 May, Empire Day', 1930.

50. Ibid., 15 Feb. 1931.

51. Col. Hume, *Hume Collection*, Cambridge, 10 Sept. 1930.

52. *Hume Papers*, 15 Feb. 1931.

53. Ibid., 8 Aug. 1932.

54. Ibid., 17 Sept. 1933.

55. Ibid., 3 Sept. 1936.

56. S. G. Millin, *Rhodes*, Chatto, 1933, p. 64.

57. *IER*, Nov. 1931.

58. *Hume Papers*, 7 June 1932.

59. Col. A. H. B. Hume to Archbishop Lang, *Hume Collection*, Cambridge, box 9.

60. Carl Bridge, *Holding Britain to the Empire*, op. cit., ch. 5 and 6.

61. *Hampshire Chronicle*, 24 June 1933. '...it is all very well to sneer at "vociferous politicians" and "local self-seekers."...' Leigh was provoked by Lord Lymington's remarks at a fete in Hurstbourne Park.

62. He had been its MP effectively since 1910, initially for Christchurch and for the new constituency of Bournemouth from 1918.

63. There is a full account of the objectives, perceptions and tactics of those involved in Bridge, op. cit.

64. Correspondence with Zetland, between 8 and 26 Feb. 1940, in the *Croft Papers*, CRFT 1/20, Churchill College, Cambridge.

65. Martin Gilbert, *Winston S. Churchill, vol. 5, 1922–1939*, Heinemann, 1976, p. 243. 'He regarded the Hindu-Muslim feud as the bulwark of British rule in India.' Zetland, Cabinet Memorandum, 1940, R. J. Moore, *Churchill, Cripps and India*: 1939–1945, Clarendon, 1979, p. 27. 'He has become—or perhaps it is more true to say—has always been, a much more vigorous Imperialist in the 1890–1900 sense of the word than you and me.' Irwin to Baldwin, quoted by Gilbert, ibid., p. 321.

66. Church leaders were well informed about the strength of grass roots feeling. The *Church Times* published a strong letter, in the vein of Colonel Hume's protest, on manipulation, in order to draw off opposition to the White Paper, of the Council meeting of 28 June, from E. P. Newton of Chard in Somerset, a reader of long standing who was also a member of the Central Council of the National Union of Conservative Associations. *CT*, 7 July 1933.

67. Lang's chaplain commented on Lloyd's visit to luncheon at Lambeth: '...Lloyd despairs of the Church of England, in its attempts to apply the principle of Christianity to secular affairs. He may yet seek refuge in the arms of Rome. An interesting, eager, forceful and utterly sincere man, who seemed destined to spend the remainder of his life protesting loudly....' *Diary of A. C. Don*, 9 Jan. 1932, MSS, Lambeth Palace Library.

68. Judith M. Brown, *Gandhi and Civil Disobedience: The Mahatma in Indian Politics*, 1928–34, CUP, 1977, pp. 260 ff.

69. 'The bishops may yet find that the course which they are so warmly approving is leading to the abandonment of India to anti-Christ.' Sir Reginald Craddock, 'The Tragedy of India: Quo Vadis?', *Nineteenth Century and After*, June 1931.

The church press deplored Lord Sydenham's swing to extreme reaction, particularly over India. 'Death of Lord Sydenham', *G*, 10 Feb. 1933. But his anxieties for Christianity centred more on Russian Bolshevism and the socialism emerging in Britain. In India he saw the rebellious elements in a morbid Brahmanism and among the western educated as the basis for an illusory nationalism which reversed earlier progress. He had little to add to the psychologism of Chirol's early work *Indian Unrest*. Lord Sydenham, *My Working Life*, Murray, 1927, pp. 222, 268, 444; *Studies of an Imperialist*, Chapman and Hall, London, 1928, ch. 21; *Times* articles of 21, 22, Dec. 1913.

Lloyd, writing with an eye on European fascism a few years later, makes a lucid statement of the general argument that the British conception of freedom derives directly from Christianity, slowly permeating society from above in a way denied to ethnically complex societies under autocracies, such as Russia and China, which 'have stood outside the course of progress throughout modern history.' Lord Lloyd, *The British Case*, Eyre and Spottiswood, 1939; introduction by Lord Halifax (Irwin).

70. *Yorkshire Post*, 14 May 1934. There are many cuttings of letters and articles by Page Croft covering his argument on India in the *Croft Papers*, Churchill College, Cambridge: for example, 'Conservatives and India; Where is the Mandate for

Abdication?', *Morning Post*, 21 Feb. 1933; 'Menace of an Independent India', *Financial Times*, 14 Mar. 1933; 'The Salvation of India', 1 and 2, *Yorkshire Herald*, 4–5 Oct. 1933; *Times*, 5 Oct. 1933; *Birmingham Post*, 9 Jan. 1934; *Times*, 14 May 1934; *News Chronicle*, 16 May 1934; *Times*, 6 Oct. 1934, 6 Feb. 1935: *Bournemouth Times and Directory*, 12 Apr. 1935. There are also numerous and often lengthy reports of speeches, in the Commons and on the stump, ranging from *Bournemouth Daily Echo*, 29 Jan. 1935 ('Henceforth India will be dominated by the Hindu religion and divorced from all Christian guidance....') to the *Christian Herald*, 13 June 1935 ('This India question has transfigured him and he has delivered some singularly effective and even moving speeches').

71. *CT*, 1 May 1934.
72. *Bournemouth Times and Directory*, 3 Feb. 1933.
73. *Waltham Abbey Weekly Telegraph*, 24 Mar. 1933.
74. There is quantitative data on the intensity and the geographical distribution of British-Israelism activity in Gerald Studdert-Kennedy, 'The Christian Imperialism of the Die-Hard Defenders of the Raj: 1926–1935', *Journal of Imperial and Commonwealth History*, Oct. 1990.
75. Bell to Schuster, 16 Oct. 1931, *Bell Papers*, Lambeth Palace Library. Indeed, 'events showed that (Gandhi's) political leadership was neither static nor assured,' J. Brown, op. cit.
76. *Don Diary*, 21 Oct. 1931.
77. Temple to Bishop Bell, 4 Dec. 1932, *Bell Papers*. He quotes as conclusive his brother's interpretation of the event, which was basically Ambedkar's (but not of all untouchable leaders), that it was a ploy by the exploitative caste Hindus.
78. Bell to Schuster, 12 Oct. 1931, *Bell Papers*.
79. There is a brief MSS account of this visit, presumably written by Mrs Bell, in the *Bell Papers*.
80. Ashe, op. cit., p. 309.
81. Bell to Lang, 17 May 1932, *Bell Papers*.
82. *Lang Papers*, Lambeth Palace, vol. 42, f. 168.
83. *Don Diary*, Lambeth Palace, 27 July, 2 Aug. 1933.
84. Ibid., 8 June 1937.
85. Lang to Willingdon, *Lang Papers*, 6 Dec. 1934.
86. But Lang grew very impatient with Westcott who seemed, in the Lambeth Palace view, to be losing touch with his responsibilities and going a bit off the rails in his new enthusiasm for the Oxford Group. *Don Diary*, 4, 25, 26 Oct. 1933.
87. After his first meeting, when Andrews brought Gandhi to Lambeth for tea, Lang gave Don his impression of Gandhi as a man of 'almost fanatical religious zeal combined with a somewhat unscrupulous political policy.' Ibid., 22 Oct. 1931.
88. Brown, op. cit., 304 ff. *Lang Papers*, vol. 42, Lang to Zetland, 20 July 1934, f. 387; Zetland to Lang, 22 Jan., f. 389; Lang to Zetland, 25 July 1935, f. 391.
89. Ibid., Willingdon to Lang, 10 Nov. 1935, f. 407; Lang to Willingdon, 2 Dec. 1935, pp. 432–4 ff. Willingdon boasted to Lang of the budget windfall distributed for rural development, which had floated Brayne into position as Commissioner for Rural Reconstruction in the Punjab.
90. *The Parliamentary Debates*, 95, 1934–1935, 309–21, Hansard, London.

CHAPTER 8

Conclusion

1. Bryan S. Turner, *Marx and the End of Orientalism*, Allen and Unwin, 1978, pp. 67 ff.
2. 'Memorandum on the Basis and Structure of Indian Government', 21 Jan. 1940, copy in the *Spear Collection*, Cambridge South Asia Archive. Memo Linlithgow to Zetland, Feb. 1940. MSS. Eur. D. 609/19, Cambridge South Asia Archive.
3. See Leo Kuper and M. G. Smith, eds., *Pluralism in Africa*, University of California, Los Angeles, 1969.
4. For example, 'The clarion call that summoned the Santhals to battle (in 1855) ...was to be heard in other parts of the country at the time of the Indigo Strike of 1860, the Pabna and Bogra Uprisings of 1872, the Maratha Peasant Rising in Poona and Ahmednagar in 1875–6. It was finally to merge in the massive demand of the peasantry all over the country for an end to zamindari and money lending oppression....' L. Natarajan, *Peasant Uprising in India*, 1953, quoted in Ranajit Guha 'The Prose of Counter-Insurgency', *Subaltern Studies 2*, OUP, 1983, p. 32.
5. Rosalind O'Hanlon, 'Recovering the Subject: Subaltern Studies and Histories of Resistance in Colonial South Asia', *Modern Asian Studies*, 22, 1, 1988, p. 93.
6. 'The teaching of the concept, which is also history's inescapable lesson, is that it is only when actuality is mature that the ideal first appears over against the real and that the ideal apprehends this same real world in its substance and builds it up for itself into the shape of an intellectual realm.... The owl of Minerva spreads its wings only with the falling of the dusk.' *Hegel's Philosophy of Right*, trans. T. M. Knox, Oxford, 1952, preface, p. 13. Hegel's powerful introduction to his *Lectures on the Philosophy of History* broods remotely over the Christian imperialist historiography, projecting its shadow from the liberal examination of Gandhi's candidacy for the status of a 'World-Historical person' to the providentialism thinly echoed by Page Croft.
7. 'Negativism' is familiar to the subaltern perspective as one form of resistance. The evaporation of Brayne's 'uplift' after his departure from Gurgaon was referred to earlier.
8. Guha, 'the Prose of Counter-Insurgency', *op. cit.*, p. 33. Italics in original.
9. O'Hanlon, op. cit., p. 100.
10. Ronaldshay, *Essayez*, op. cit., p. 119, quoted in Mushirul Hasan, *Nationalism and Communal Politics in India*, op. cit., p. 310.
11. Ibid., p. 308.
12. D. N. Dhanagare, *Peasant Movements in India*, 1920–1950, OUP, Delhi, 1983, ch. 3, 'The Moplah Rebellions', p. 82; S. F. Dale, *Islamic Society on the South Asian Frontier: The Mappilas of Malabar*, 1498–1922, Oxford 1980.
13. Gyan Pandey, 'Rallying Round the Cow: Sectarian Strife in the Bhojpuri Region, c. 1888–1917', Ranajit Guha, ed., *Subaltern Studies 2*, OUP, 1983.
14. Lescek Kolakowski, *Religion*, Fontana, 1982, p. 16.

Select Bibliography

Unpublished Records

India Office Library, London
    F. L. Brayne Paper
    S. K. Datta Papers
    A. Hirtzel *Diary*
    A. Hume Papers
    Irwin Papers
    Meston Papers
    A. Storrs Fox Papers
    Templewood Papers
    Willingdon Papers
    Zetland Papers
Lambeth Palace, London
    G. K. Bell Papers
    Diary of A. C. Don
    C. G. Lang Papers
    E. J. Palmer Papers
Friends' Meeting House, London
    Indian Affairs Committee Correspondence
    Indian Conciliation Group Papers
School of Oriental and African Studies, London
    London Methodist Missionary Society Papers
Church Missionary Society, London
    Letter Books
Society for the Propagation of the Gospel, London
    Series E
Churchill College, Cambridge
    Croft Papers
South Asia Archive, Cambridge
    Hume Collection
    P. Spear Collection
Bodleian Library, Oxford
    Curtis Papers
Rhodes House, Oxford

Coupland Papers
Fraser Papers
BBC Archive, Caversham
    Files on India E 1/883–97
Scottish Record Office, Edinburgh
    Lothian Papers
Bishop's College, Calcutta
    Westcott Papers (uncatalogued)

Journals

Those listed were used as primary sources.
Bombay Diocesan Magazine, Bombay
Calcutta Diocesan Record, Calcutta
Cheltonian, London
Christa Seva Sangha Review, Bombay
Church Missionary Society, Annual Reports, London
Church Times, London
Contemporary Review, London
Delhi, Delhi
Guardian, London
Haileyburian, London
Harrovian, London
Harvest Field, London
Indian Empire Review, London
Lahore Diocesan Magazine, Lahore
Lucknow Diocesan Chronicle, Lucknow
Madras Christian College Magazine, Madras
Methodist Recorder, London
Morning Post, London
National Message, London
Nineteenth Century and After, London
Reptonian, London
St John's College Magazine, Agra
St Stephens College Magazine, Delhi
Wykehamist, Winchester
Young India
Young Men of India, Calcutta

Books

Anderson, Sir G., and the Rt. Revd Henry Whitehead, *Christian Education in India*, Macmillan, London, 1932.

Andrews, C. F., ed., *Mahatma Gandhi at Work*, Allen and Unwin, London, 1931.

———, *The Renaissance in India*, United Council for Missionary Education, London, 1912.

———, *The True India*, Allen and Unwin, London, 1930.

———, *India and Britain: A Moral Challenge*, SCM, London, 1935.

Appasamy, A. J., *Christianity as Bhaktimarga*, Madras, 1926.

———, *What is Moksha?* Madras, 1931.

Bevan, E., *Indian Nationalism*, Macmillan, London, 1914.

———, *Thoughts on India's Discontents*, Allen and Unwin, London, 1929.

———, *Christianity*, OUP, London, 1932.

Brayne, F. L., *Socrates in an Indian Village*, Lahore, 1929.

———, *Socrates at School*, Bombay, 1933.

———, *Socrates Persists in India*, London, 1933.

———, *In Him was Light*, OUP, London, 1933.

———, *The Indian and the English Village*, OUP, London, 1933.

Brent, Richard, *Liberal Anglican Politics: Whiggery, Religion and Reform*, 1830–1841, OUP, London, 1987.

Bridge, C. *Holding India to the Empire*, Oriental, Delhi, 1986.

Brown, J., *Gandhi and Civil Disobedience: The Mahatma and Indian Politics*, 1830–1841, OUP, London, 1987.

———, *Modern India: The Origins of an Asian Democracy*, OUP, London, 1985.

Burrow, J. W., *A Liberal Descent: Victorian Historians and the English Past*, Cambridge University Press, 1981.

Butterfield, H., *The Whig Interpretation of History*, Bell, London, 1931.

———, *The Englishman and His History*, Cambridge University Press, 1944.

———, *Christianity and History*, Bell, London, 1949.

Chandra, B., *Nationalism and Colonialism in Modern India*, Orient Longman, Delhi, 1979.

Charmley, J., *Lord Lloyd and the Decline of the British Empire*, Weidenfeld, London, 1989.

Chattopadhyaya, D., *Lokayata: A Study in Ancient Indian Materialism*, People's Publishing House, Delhi, 1959.

Chaturvedi, B. and Marjorie Sykes, *Charles Freer Andrews*, Allen and Unwin, London, 1949.

Chaudhuri, N. C., *The Autobiography of an Unknown Indian*, Macmillan, London, 1951.

Chirol, Sir V., *Indian Unrest*, Macmillan, London, 1910.

———, *Indian Old and New*, Macmillan, London, 1921.

Copley, A., *Gandhi*, Blackwell, London, 1987.

Coupland, R., *The India Problem, 1833–1935*, OUP, London, 1942.

———, *India: A Restatement*, OUP, London, 1945.

Crisp, D., *The Rebirth of Conservatism*, Methuen, London, 1931.

———, *The Commonsense of Christianity*, London, 1938.

———, *Christ is no Pacifist*, Boswell, London, 1938.

Croft, Sir H.P., *The Path of Empire*, Murray, London, 1912.

———, *My Life of Strife*, Hutchinson, London, 1948.

Cross, J. A., *Sir Samuel Hoare: A Political Biography*, Cape, London, 1977.

Curtis, L. *The Problem of the Commonwealth*, London, 1915.

———, *The Commonwealth of Nations*, London, 1918.

———, *Dyarchy*, OUP, London, 1920.

———, *Civitas Dei*, vols. 1–3, Macmillan, London, 1934–7.

Darling, Sir M., *Apprentice to Power, India, 1904–1908*, Hogarth Press, London, 1966.

Dale, S. F., *Islamic Society on the South Asian Frontier: The Mappilas of Malabar, 1498–1922*, OUP, London, 1980.

Dhanagare, D. N., *Peasant Movements in India, 1920–50*, OUP, Delhi, 1983.

Dumont, L., *Homo Hierarchicus*, Weidenfeld and Nicolson, London, 1966.

Dunn, J., *Western Political Theory in the Face of the Future*, Cambridge University Press, 1979.

Egerton, H. E., *A Short History of British Colonial Policy*, London, 1887.

Ellam, E., *Swaraj: The Problem of India*, Hutchinson, London, 1930.

Elwin, see Winslow,

Farquhar, J. N., *Modern Religious Movements in India*, New York and London, 1915.

———, *The Crown of Hinduism*, OUP, London, 1913.

Forrester, D., *Caste and Christianity: Missions and Caste in India*, Curzon Press, London, 1984.

Gibbs, M. E., *The Anglican Church in India, 1600–1970*, SPCK, London, 1972.

Gilbert, M., *Winston Churchill, 1922–1939*, vol. 5, Heinemann, London, 1977.

Girouard, M., *The Return to Camelot: Chivalry and the English Gentleman*, Yale, 1981.

Gopal, S., *The Viceroyalty of Lord Irwin*, OUP, London, 1957.

———, *Jawaharlal Nehru, vol. 1, 1889–1947*, OUP, Delhi, 1975.

———, *Radhakrishnan*, OUP, Delhi, 1989.

Goudge, Canon H. L., *The British-Israel Theory*, Mowbray, Oxford, 1932.

Greenberger, A. J., *The British Image of India*, London, 1969.

Guha, R., *Subaltern Studies*, vols. 1–6, OUP, Delhi, 1982–9.

Gupta, P. S., *Imperialism and the British Labour Movement, 1914–1964*, OUP, London, 1968.

Hambye SJ, E. R., *A Bibliography on Christianity in India*, Church History Association of India, 1976, (mimeo, India Office Library.)

Harriss, J., *Capitalism and Peasant Farming: Agrarian Structure and Ideology in Northern Tamil Nadu*, OUP, Delhi, 1982.

Hasan, M., ed., *Communal and Pan-Islamic Trends in Colonial India*, Manohar, Delhi, 1981.

Heimsath, C. H., *Indian Nationalism and Hindu Social Reform*, Princeton, 1964.

Hick, J., *Problems of Religious Pluralism*, Macmillan, London, 1985.

Hirtzel, A., *The Church, the Empire and the World: Addresses on the Work of the Church Abroad*, SPCK, London, 1919.

———, *East India, Progress and Conditions: Statement Exhibiting the Moral and Material Progress and Condition of India During the Year* 1926–7, Government of India, Calcutta, 1927.

Hoare, S. (Lord Templewood), *Nine Troubled Years*, Collins, London, 1954.

Hogg, A. G., *Karma and Redemption*, Madras, 1910.

Holland, W. E. S., *The Goal of India*, CMS, London, 1917.

———, *The Indian Outlook*, London, 1927.

Hutchins, F. G., *The Illusion of Permanence: British Imperialism in India*, Princeton, 1967.

Irwin, Lord, *Some Aspects of the Indian Problem*, OUP, Oxford, 1932.

Kolakowski, L., *Religion*, Fontana, London, 1982.

Kumar, R., ed., *Essays on Gandhian Politics: The Rowlatt Satyagraha of* 1919, OUP, London, 1971.

———, *Essays in the Social History of Modern India*, OUP, Delhi, 1984.

Low, D. A., *Soundings in Modern South Asian History*, Weidenfeld and Nicolson, London, 1968.

———, *Lion Rampant*, Cass, London, 1973.

Lucas, B. *The Empire of Christ*, Macmillan, London, 1907.

———, *Christ in India*, Macmillan, London, 1910.

———, *Our Task in India: Shall we Proselytise Hinduism or Evangelise India?*, Macmillan, London, 1914.

MacKenzie, J. M., *Propaganda and Empire: The Manipulation of British Public Opinion*, 1880–1960, Manchester University Press, 1984.

Mangan, J. A., *The Games Ethic and Imperialism*, Viking, London, 1985.

Marris, Sir W., *India: The Political Problem*, University of Nottingham, 1930.

Mayhew, A., *Christianity and the Government of India*, Faber and Gwyer, London, 1929.

Mayo, K., *Mother India*, Cape, 1927.

Montagu, E. S., *An Indian Diary*, Heinemann, London, 1930.

Moore, J. R., *Churchill, Cripps and India:* 1939–1945, OUP, London, 1979.

Norman, E. R., *Church and Society in England*, 1770–1970, OUP, London, 1976.

Oddie, G. A., *Social Protest in India: British Protestant Missionaries and Social Reform*, 1850–1900, Manohar, Delhi, 1979.

Panikkar, *The Unknown Christ of Hinduism*, London, 1964.

Parekh, B., *Colonialism, Tradition and Reform: An Analysis of Gandhi's Political Discourse*, Sage, Delhi, 1989.

Paul, K. T., *The British Connection with India*, SCM, London, 1927, and Delhi, 1986.

Potter, D., *India's Political Administrators, 1919–1983*, OUP, London, 1986.

Richter, M., *The Politics of Conscience: T. H. Green and his Age*, Weidenfeld and Nicolson, London, 1964.

Ronaldshay, Earl of (Lord Zetland), *The Heart of Aryavarta: A Study of the Psychology of Indian Unrest*, Constable, London, 1925.

———, *India: Retrospect and Prospect*, Nottingham University, 1935.

———, *Essayez*, Murray, London, 1956.

Saberwal, S., *India: The Roots of Crisis*, OUP, Delhi, 1986.

Said, E. W., *Orientalism*, Routledge and Kegan Paul, London, 1978.

Schuster, Sir G., *Christianity and Human Relations in Industry*, London, 1951.

Schuster, Sir G. and G. Wint, *India and Democracy*, Macmillan, London, 1941.

Schwab, R., *The Oriental Renaissance: Europe's Rediscovery of India, 1660–1880*, New York, 1984.

Seal, A., *The Emergence of Indian Nationalism*, Cambridge University Press, 1968.

Sharpe, E., *Not to Destroy, But to Fulfill: The Contribution of J. N. Farquhar to Protestant Missionary Thought in India Before 1914*, Lund, 1965.

———, *The Theology of A. G. Hogg*, Christian Literature Society, Madras, 1971.

———, *Faith Meets Faith*, SCM, London, 1977.

Somervell, D. C., *The British Empire*, Christophers, London, 1930.

———, *A Short History of our Religion from Moses to the Present Day*, Bell, London, 1922.

Spear, P. and M. Spear, *India Remembered*, Orient Longman, Delhi, 1981.

Stewart, D. A., *The Place of Christianity Among the Great Religions of the World*, SPCK, London, 1920.

Stokes, E., *The English Utilitarians and India*, OUP, London, 1959.

Studdert-Kennedy, G., *Dog-Collar Democracy: The Industrial Christian Fellowship, 1919–1929*, Macmillan, London, 1982.

Sydenham, Lord, *Studies of an Imperialist*, Chapman and Hall, London, 1928.

Symonds, R., *Oxford and Empire*, Macmillan, London, 1986.

Thomas, M. M., *The Acknowledged Christ of the Indian Renaissance*, SCM, London, 1969.

Thompson, E. and E. Garratt, *Rise and Fulfilment of British Rule in India*, Macmillan, London, 1934.

Tinker, H., *Ordeal of Love: C. F. Andrews and India*, OUP, London, 1979.

Tomlinson, B. R., *The Political Economy of the Raj, 1914–1947*, Macmillan, London, 1979.

Toynbee, A., *Acquaintances*, OUP, London, 1967.

Trevaskis, Revd H., *The Punjab of Today*, Lahore, 1931.

———, *Indian Babel*, London, 1935.

Tyndale-Biscoe, C. E., *Kashmir in Sunlight and Shade*, Seely, London, 1925.

———, *Tyndale-Biscoe of Kashmir: An Autobiography*, Seely, London, 1951.

Tyndale-Biscoe, E. D., *Fifty Years Against the Stream: The Story of a School in Kashmir*, 1880–1930, Wesleyan Mission Press, Mysore, 1930.

Ward, W. E. F., *Fraser of Trinity and Achimota*, OUP, Oxford, 1965.

Warren, M., *Caesar, the Beloved Enemy*, SCM, London, 1955.

Westcott, Bishop Brooke Foss, *The National Church as the Spiritual Organ of the Nation*, London, 1893.

Whitehead, Rt. Revd H., *National Christianity in India*, Christian Literature Society for India, London, 1911.

Winslow, J. and V. Elwin, *The Dawn of Indian Freedom*, Allen and Unwin, London, 1931.

Wolpert, S. *Morley and India*, 1906–1910, California, 1961.

———, *Tilak and Gokhale: Revolution and Reform in the Making of Modern India*, University of California Press, California, 1961.

Younghusband, Sir F., *Dawn in India: British Purpose and Indian Aspiration*, Murray, London, 1930.

———, *Modern Mystics*, London, Murray, 1935.

Zetland, see Ronaldshay.

Unpublished Theses

C. Bridge, 'The British Conservative Party and All-India Federation, 1927–1940', (Ph.D. Thesis, Flinders University), 1977.

Vincent Kumarados, 'Protestant Missionary Impact and the Quest for National Identity: Tamil Nadu Experience, 1900–1921', (D. Phil. Thesis, University of Madras), 1983.

J. F. C. Watts, 'The Viceroyalty of Lord Irwin, 1926–31, With Special Reference to the Political and Constitutional Developments', (D. Phil. Thesis, Oxford University), 1973.

J. Wilson, 'The History and Organisation of British-Israelism: Some Aspects of the Religious and Political Correlates of Changing Status', (D. Phil thesis, Oxford University), 1966.

NAMES INDEX

SUBJECT INDEX